拯救

我的GRE+TOEFL写作
论据素材库

社会篇

GRE+TOEFL
Saving My GRE+TOEFL Writing┃Society

姜伟生◎编著

科学出版社

北京

图书在版编目（CIP）数据

拯救我的 GRE+TOEFL 写作论据素材库. 社会篇 / 姜伟生编著.
—北京：科学出版社，2014.5
（拯救我的北美留学写作）
ISBN 978-7-03-040596-8

Ⅰ. ①拯…　Ⅱ. ①姜…　Ⅲ. ① GRE-写作-自学参考资料
② TOEFL-写作-自学参考资料　Ⅳ. ① H315

中国版本图书馆 CIP 数据核字（2014）第 096849 号

责任编辑：张　培 / 责任校对：桂伟利
责任印制：赵德静 / 封面设计：无极书装

联系电话：010-6403 3862 / 电子邮箱：zhangpei@mail.sciencep.com

科 学 出 版 社 出版
北京东黄城根北街 16 号
邮政编码：100717
http://www.sciencep.com

北京佳信达欣艺术印刷有限公司 印刷
科学出版社发行　各地新华书店经销
*
2014 年 5 月第 一 版　　开本：B5（720×1000）
2014 年 5 月第一次印刷　印张：12 1/2
字数：290 000

定价：**35.00元**
（如有印装质量问题，我社负责调换）

社会面面观
A Multifaced Society

不只是
英文写作素材

谨以此书献给我的父亲母亲

To My Parents

参加各种英语考试，特别是出国留学考试（如 TOEFL、IELTS、SAT、GMAT 及 GRE）的中国考生，在写作部分都会遇到一个共同的问题，就是缺乏英文语料。经过基础教育锤炼的中国考生需要的就是，把自己以汉语为载体的知识和思想转换成对应的英文表达。

而笔者编写的这套丛书试图帮助中国考生解决这个问题。丛书从历史、科技、社会、艺术和哲学几个方面，为读者提供丰富的英文语料，试图打破以往人文类英语参考书"全篇英文""生涩难懂""卷帙浩繁"等让人畏而却步的印象，并采用"中英混排""逐句讲解""内容选材浅显实用"等编排方式，力求保证读者在短时间内能够收获大量实用语料。

外语学习重在模仿，比如，学习口语要模仿母语人士的语音、语调、节奏等，学习写作要模仿原版报纸、书刊文章的遣词造句、谋篇布局等。本书选取的英文语料难度高于日常英语水平，但低于英文原版学科专著水平，适合英语学习者口头和书面表达模仿使用。

本书中选取的优美隽永词句带给我们的不仅仅是知识，还有美的享受和深刻的思想。笔者希望通过重新整理和科学编排把更多语料介绍给读者。此外，有些语料的观点并不见得正确，仅供考生参考。笔者水平有限，且编写仓促，不足之处在所难免，恳请广大读者和专家不吝赐教。

最后，感谢爸爸妈妈的爱和支持。儿子爱你们。

姜伟生

2014 年 3 月

丛书编写特点

本书适合初级以上英语学习者，也适用于英语四、六级考生，北美地区英语考试（TOEFL、SAT、GMAT、GRE），IELTS 写作及口语部分备考。丛书特点：

- ○ 中英文混排，帮助读者短时间内掌握核心表达
- ○ 内容浅显易懂，阅读压力低
- ○ 英文语料地道生动，适合口语和书面交流

内容提要

丛书旨在帮助读者学习科技发展、社会学、文化交流、艺术、历史、哲学等方面常用的英语表达。本系列目前有五本书：

- ○ 《拯救我的 GRE+TOEFL 写作论据素材库·科技篇》
- ○ 《拯救我的 GRE+TOEFL 写作论据素材库·艺术篇》
- ○ 《拯救我的 GRE+TOEFL 写作论据素材库·社会篇》
- ○ 《拯救我的 GRE+TOEFL 写作论据素材库·历史篇》
- ○ 《拯救我的 GRE+TOEFL 写作论据素材库·哲学篇》

其中，《拯救我的 GRE+TOEFL 写作论据素材库·科技篇》以人类科学技术发展为主线，介绍影响人类发展的重大科技进步和人物故事。《拯救我的 GRE+TOEFL 写作论据素材库·社会篇》主要以社会学的视角介绍当今世界面临的各种挑战及解决办法。《拯救我的 GRE+TOEFL 写作论据素材库·艺术篇》从美术、音乐、建筑、影视等方面介绍具有影响力的艺术家和他们的主要作品。《拯救我的 GRE+TOEFL 写作论据素材库·历史篇》主要介绍对人类历史发展有重大影响的政治家、军事家及社会改革人士等。《拯救我的 GRE+TOEFL 写作论据素材库·哲学篇》介绍著名思想家和他们的主要观点。

TOEFL、IELTS、SAT、GMAT、GRE 介绍及写作备考

下面介绍一下这几门考试的主要特点。

TOEFL（Test of English as a Foreign Language，中文音译为"托福"）和 IELTS（International English Language Testing System，中文音译为"雅思"）具有极强的相似性，两者都考查语言应用能力，即听说读写能力。这两个考试在写作层面上主要考查考生的遣词造句及文章组织等语言基础能力；而在思想深度方面，雅思似乎比托福更加注重。不用说托福阅读和听力中的人文及科学等学术类考题，托福综合写作中更是涉及大量人文及科学类学科知识。目前，北美地区很多大专院校也接受雅思成绩；

同样，英国等欧洲国家也接受托福成绩。

另外，值得注意的是，托福听力、阅读和综合写作部分包括大量的学术类话题。这些话题取材广泛，涉及生命科学（life science）、生物学（biology）、人类学（anthropology）、生态学（ecology）、社会学（sociology）、心理学（psychology）、经济学（economics）、政治科学（political science）、历史学（history）、物理学（physics）、化学（chemistry）、天文学（astronomy）、地质学（geology）、文化（culture）、语言与文学（languages and literature）、艺术与音乐（art and music）及哲学（philosophy）等。为了取得理想的成绩，同时拓宽自己的知识视野，考生们了解科技人文方面的知识显得尤为重要。

SAT（Scholastic Aptitude Test）类似中国的高考，可以说难度远高于托福等语言考试，当然也不会设置听力和口语单项考试。SAT 考试写作部分明确指出要考查考生的"critical thinking skills"，即所谓的"批判性思维能力"。可以看出，除了语言表达以外，SAT 更看重考生的思想深度，需要读者有丰富的史实例证方面语料积累。

GMAT（Graduate Management Admissions Test）和 GRE（Graduate Record Examination）则类似于中国的硕士研究生考试。GRE 甚至被用于博士生入学考试中。现在很多北美顶尖商学院也接受 GRE 成绩以作为入学凭证。其中的写作单项考试更是要求考生有"complex and critical thinking skills"，即"复杂性和批判性思维能力"。对比托福阅读、听力和综合写作，GRE 阅读话题材料取材更广、难度更高。

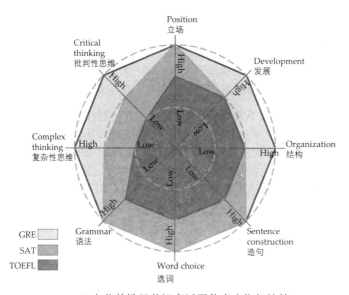

三大北美地区英语考试写作考查指标比较

仅以留学北美国家为例，出国攻读大学本科的中国考生需要完成"SAT + TOEFL"，申请国外大学研究生院出国攻读硕士和博士学位的中国考生需要完成"GRE / GMAT + TOEFL"。第一类考生写作水平要向 SAT 写作单项要求看齐；而第二类考生要满足 GRE 写作单项要求。而 SAT 和 GRE 考试都需要考生在文章中体现出"批判性和复杂性思维能力"，因此，积累科学人文类素材便成为考生必须要完成的工作。

使用方法

对于一般学习者：

○ 可以按章节顺序学习，迅速浏览汉语，了解每节的主要内容
○ 对于下划线部分，请试着翻译一下，而后参考脚注译文
○ 对于生词，请查阅英文词典，并将汉语释义和音标标注在书中译文处
○ 可以试着大声朗读英文释义部分
○ 阅读下划线部分回忆相应译文
○ 附录中的"历史事件列表"和"人名列表"可以帮助读者回忆所学内容

对于寻找写作素材的读者：

○ 建议先翻阅本书附录中的"历史事件列表"和"人名列表"
○ 然后对于感兴趣的人物或事件，查阅相关正文内容

其他资源

为了配合读者在阅读本书过程中查找参考资料学习，这里给大家介绍一些常用的英文类学习资源。

词典类推荐灵格斯（Lingoes），这个软件使用方便，受到众多英语学习者的欢迎。另外，Merriam-Webster、Oxford 和 Cambridge 都有网络在线版英文词典，而且能够保证音标和发音准确无误。

关于综合类知识网站，本书向读者推荐"在线百科全书"（www.encyclopedia.com），和 Wikipedia 不同的是，该网站的内容来自各种学科专著和各种纸质版的大百科全书，可以被列为参考文献。此外就是《大英百科全书》网络版（www.britannica.com），遗憾的是，如果不付费订购，就只能阅读其中部分内容；值得注意的是，《大英百科全书》也有软件版。此外，《微软百科全书》软件版也是很好的参考资料，可惜该软件目前已经停止发售，最新版本为《Encarta 2009》。

关于科技类网站，读者可以参考 HowStuffWorks 网站（www.howstuffworks.com）和探索频道官方网站（dsc.discovery.com）等。HowStuffWorks 的内容类似于科学技术百科，网站中有大量动画和视频可供读者学习使用。

对于哲学百科类，读者可以参考斯坦福大学哲学数据库（plato.stanford.edu）。

对于艺术类资源，这里要特别推荐的是 Google Art Project（www.googleartproject.com）。Google Art Project 和全球众多艺术博物馆都有合作关系，读者可以足不出户便欣赏到世界优秀艺术作品。另外，纽约大都会博物馆（Metropolitan Museum of Art）官网也有丰富的艺术方面的资源（www.metmuseum.org）。

对于对历史感兴趣的读者，本书首先推荐微软公司赞助、加利福尼亚大学伯克利分校（UC Berkeley）和莫斯科国立大学（Moscow State University）共同开发的 ChronoZoom（www.chronozoomproject.org），通过可放大缩小的时间轴，让宇宙从诞生发展到当今世界的这段漫长历史尽收眼底。另外，Big History Project（www.bighistoryproject.com）提供的讲述"大历史观"的课程，也适合普通英语学习者学习。

除了大家常用的 CNN、BBC、VOA、NYT 等可以获得咨询外，本书另外推荐两个网站，它们分别是 www.pbs.org（美国公共电视网，简称 PBS）和 www.npr.org（美国国家公共广播电台，简称 NPR）。此外，CNN 旗下的 CNN Student News（www.cnn.com/studentnews）也非常适合英语学习者学习。

对于网络公开课，这里主要向读者推荐全英文的网站。

○ 麻省理工学院可以说是最早一批将课程免费上线的大学之一，公开课官网（ocw.mit.edu/index.htm）上面列出该校几乎所有课程的讲义和作业，包括一些课程的课堂录像。其他北美地区的大学，如斯坦福大学（Stanford University）等名校也上传了大量免费网络课程。

○ Coursera（www.coursera.org）近年来深受追捧，该公开课平台和众多世界一流大学合作，大家可以注册学习该平台发布的名校课程。另外两个同类型的公开课网站是 Udacity（www.udacity.com）和 edX（www.edx.org）。

○ TED 论坛（www.ted.com）几乎每天都会发布各行各业优秀人士的演讲。

○ 可汗学院（www.khanacademy.org）网站免费发布大量该网站创始人自己录制的美国小学、初高中知识水平的课程。目前，该网站增加了很多有趣的互动课程。

○ Udemy（www.udemy.com）有大量有趣的课程，但是其中很多课程需要付费学习。

目录
Contents

The soul takes nothing with her to the next world but her education and her culture. At the beginning of the journey to the next world, one's education and culture can either provide the greatest assistance, or else act as the greatest burden, to the person who has just died.

Plato

文化是价值、信仰、行为和实物共同构建的一类人的生活方式。文化包括，我们所思考的，我们行事的方法，以及我们所拥有的。文化联系过去，并且引领未来。大多数人沉浸在文化中成长。他们通过家庭、仪式传统、语言、艺术、社会习惯和共同的历史来吸收文化。人们也可以通过学校、朋友和书籍学习文化。

非物质文化是某个社会的成员所创造的观念。物质文化，与之相反，是某个社会的

中国境内联合国教科文组织世界非物质文化遗产（部分）
UNESCO World Intangible Cultural Heritage in China

昆曲	Kunqu opera
雕版印刷	China engraved block printing technique
书法	Chinese calligraphy
剪纸	Chinese paper-cut
皮影戏	Chinese shadow puppetry
木活字印刷	Chinese printing with wooden movable type
京剧	Beijing opera
针灸	Acupuncture and moxibustion
宣纸工艺	The traditional handicrafts of making Xuan paper
篆刻	The art of Chinese seal engraving
端午节	The Dragon Boat Festival
丝绸工艺	Sericulture and silk craftsmanship of China

表达库
Bank of expressions

► 【The soul takes nothing with her to the next world but her education and her culture】除了教育和文化之外，灵魂不会把其他东西带到另外一个世界。

► 【文化是价值、信仰、行为和实物共同构建一类人的生活方式】Culture is the values, beliefs, behaviors, and material objects that together form a people's way of life.

► 【文化包括，我们所思考的，我们行事的方法，以及我们所拥有的】Culture includes what we think, how we act, and what we own.

► 【文化联系过去，并且引领未来】Culture is both our link to the past and our guide to the future.

► 【大多数人沉浸在文化中成长】Most people grow up immersed in their culture.

► 【他们通过家庭、仪式传统、语言、艺术、社会习惯和共同的历史来吸收文化】They absorb it from their family, through rituals and customs, through language, through the arts, through social habits, and through a shared history.

► 【人们也可以通过学校、朋友和书籍学习文化】People also learn about culture through school, friends, and books.

► 【非物质文化是某个社会的成员所创造的观念】Nonmaterial culture is the ideas created by members of a society.

► 【物质文化，与之相反，是某个社会的成员所创造的实物】Material culture, by contrast, is the physical things created by members of a society.

成员所创造的实物。最重要的文化元素包括历史、宗教、价值、社会组织和语言。传统反映出一个群体的共同身份，这通常来自根深蒂固的信念。历史是一张为社会成员指明未来的地图，并且世代传承。宗教影响商业活动、政治、个人举止等一切活动。

世界上每一种文化都是独特的。放在一起，他们构成了浩瀚的全球文化。对世界文化的更深层理解意味着人们可以受到很多不同生活方式的影响。

No man ever steps in the same river twice.

正如古希腊哲学家赫拉克利特[1]所说："人不能两次走进同一条河流。"文化是动态的。没有人可以否认，现代社会的文化体验已经极大地被大众传媒所影响。

加拿大魁北克古堡酒店前世界遗产标志
This is a 3D depiction of the UNESCO World Heritage Site logo in Quebec City.
A UNESCO World Heritage Site is a place (such as a forest, mountain, lake, island, desert, monument, building, complex, or city) that is listed by the UNESCO as of special cultural or physical significance.

社会的飞速变革导致文化的变化。文化随着人口增长、技术革新、环境危机、外来入侵、文化内部行为和价值的修正而变化。

我们生活在这样一个时代，世界上的所有人，不管他们是什么背景和文化，都相互交融。在过去的25年里，从波音747到万维网，现代科技让地球成为村落。通信卫星、先进的电视传输设备，以及光纤或无线连接系统让全世界的人们分享信息，并通过声音和画面去体验发生在千里之外的事件。

中国境内联合国教科文组织世界遗产目录（部分）
UNESCO World Heritage Sites in China (Part)

布达拉宫	Historic Ensemble of the Potala Palace
苏州园林	Classical Gardens of Suzhou
福建土楼	Fujian Tulou
大足石刻	Dazu Rock Carvings
云冈石窟	Yungang Grottoes
杭州西湖景区	West Lake Cultural Landscape of Hangzhou
长城	The Great Wall
天坛	Temple of Heaven
曲阜孔庙	Temple of Confucius
颐和园	Summer Palace
泰山	Mount Taishan
秦始皇皇陵及兵马俑	Mausoleum of the First Qin Emperor and Terracotta Army
莫高窟	Mogao Caves
周口店北京人遗址	Peking Man Site at Zhoukoudian

文化冲击通常指一种情况，即一个人由于移民或者游览一个新的国家而接触到不熟

表达库
Bank of expressions

► 【社会的飞速变革导致文化的变化】Rapid social change and revolution can cause changes in culture.

► 【文化随着人口增长、技术革新、环境危机、外来入侵、文化内部行为和价值的修正而变化】Cultural changes take place in response to such events as population growth, technological innovations, environmental crisis, the intrusion of outsiders, or modifications of behaviors and values within the culture.

► 【我们生活在这样一个时代，世界上的所有人，不管他们是什么背景和文化，都相互交融】We are living in an age when all of the people on earth, regardless of their background or culture, are interconnected.

► 【在过去的25年里，从波音747到万维网，现代科技让地球成为村落】Modern technology in the last 25 years—from Boeing 747 to the World Wide Web—has made our globe seem a small village.

► 【通信卫星、先进的电视传输设备，以及光纤或无线连接系统让全世界的人们分享信息，并通过声音和画面去体验发生在千里之外的事件】Communications satellites, sophisticated television transmission equipment, and fiber-optic or wireless connection systems permit people throughout the world to share information and to experience the sights and sounds of events taking place thousands of miles away.

► 【文化冲击通常指一种情况，即一个人由于移民或者游览一个新的国家而接触到不熟悉的生活习惯这种情况】Culture shock commonly refers to a situation when a person is experiencing an unfamiliar way of life due to immigration or a visit to a new country.

悉的生活习惯这种情况。不足为奇的是，当旅行者接触到不熟悉的文化时，他们会感觉不自在。文化冲击是一个双向的过程。旅行者也可能以令人不适的行事方式给当地人造成文化冲击。

　　人类历史详细记录着正在发生的对异己人士的憎恨和敌对。控诉移民对社会经济问题有不可推卸的责任的情况并不少见。20世纪见证了可以摧毁人类的化学武器、生物武器和核武器的引入和使用，士兵死伤成千上万，数百万无辜的人被卷入战争。

第一次世界大战期间索姆河战役使用的化学武器
The Battle of Somme, fought by armies of the British, French and German empires and took place during the First World War, started on July 1, 1916. Poisoned gas was widely used.

Fashion is not something that exists in dresses only. Fashion is in the sky, in the street; fashion has to do with ideas, the way we live, what is happening.

Coco Chanel

流行文化不同于民俗文化[1]和高雅艺术[2]。与民俗文化不同，流行文化是大规模生产出来的。它与高雅文化也不同，因为它是被大规模消费的。流行文化通过各种大众传媒进行传播，其中包括报纸、杂志、广播、电视、电影、音乐、书籍和廉价的小说、连环画、卡通和广告。

科技在娱乐文化传播方面扮演了重要角色。你的发型、着装、言行举止、饮食习惯、家庭生活方式，以及对世界的认识都不断地被广播、电视和电影所反映，所影响。

洛杉矶街头涂鸦
Los Angeles Graffiti Art by Retna
Located in Hollywood Boulevard and North Western Avenue, Los Angeles
Retna is a Los Angeles-based graffiti artist. His work can be seen throughout Los Angeles and in cities from New York and Miami to Taipei and Barcelona.

表达库
Bank of expressions

► 【流行文化是大规模生产出来的】popular culture is mass-produced
► 【它是被大规模消费的】it is mass-consumed
► 【流行文化通过各种大众传媒进行传播】Popular culture is distributed across many forms of mass communication...
► 【其中包括报纸、杂志、广播、电视、电影、音乐、书籍和廉价的小说、连环画、卡通和广告】including newspapers, magazines, radio, television, movies, music, books and cheap novels, comics, cartoons, and advertisements
► 【科技在娱乐文化传播方面扮演了重要角色】New technologies have played a pivotal role in the diffusion of an entertainment culture.
► 【你的发型、着装、言行举止、饮食习惯、家庭生活方式，以及对世界的认识都不断地被广播、电视和电影所反映，所影响】Your hairstyle, dress code, speech behavior, eating habits, family life style and understanding of the world are constantly reflected and influenced by radio, television and the film industry.

核心词
Keywords

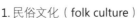

1. 民俗文化（folk culture）
2. 高雅艺术（high culture）

毫无疑问，看电视是世界上最受欢迎的休闲活动。电视传播文化价值或主流意识形态，它能满足不同观众的文化需求。电影可以提供娱乐，提供一种方法帮助理解人的内心深处。

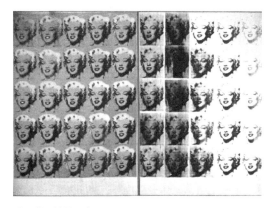

玛丽莲·梦露双连画
The Marilyn diptych
The work was completed during the weeks after Marilyn Monroe's death in August 1962 by Andy Warhol, an American artist who was a leading figure in the visual art movement known as pop art.

　　流行音乐无处不在，它已经成为生活不可或缺的一部分。我们在商场、街道，在工作场所、停车场、酒吧、俱乐部、餐馆、咖啡厅，在电视上、电影院里，都可能遇到流行音乐。我们对音乐的选择成为自我意识的一部分。时尚是个人身份的重要组成部分。

世界上现存最古老的牛仔裤
World's oldest jeans by Levi's

► 【毫无疑问，看电视是世界上最受欢迎的休闲活动】Watching TV is without doubt the world's most popular leisure activity.
► 【电视传播文化价值或主流意识形态】It transmits cultural values or dominant ideology.
► 【它能满足不同观众的文化需求】It is capable of satisfying the cultural needs of a diverse group of viewers.
► 【电影可以提供娱乐，提供一种方法帮助理解人的内心深处】Films can provide entertainment and a means to understand the depths of the human heart.
► 【流行音乐无处不在】Popular music is everywhere.
► 【它已经成为生活不可或缺的一部分】It has become more and more an unavoidable part of our lives.
► 【我们在商场、街道，在工作场所、停车场、酒吧、俱乐部、餐馆、咖啡厅，在电视上、电影院里，都可能遇到流行音乐】We encounter it in the shopping mall, on the streets, at work, in parks, in pubs, in clubs, in restaurants and cafes, on the television, at the cinema, and on the radio.
► 【我们对音乐的选择成为自我意识的一部分】Our musical choices contribute to partially our sense of self.
► 【时尚是个人身份的重要组成部分】Fashion is an important constituent of one's identity.

人们用"装扮"来表达自己。时尚通过社会阶层从上至下移动。富人通常是潮流领导者，因为他们吸引很多注意力，他们有钱花在奢侈品上。音乐人和其他文化偶像一直影响着我们的穿着。时尚包括炫耀性消费，人们买昂贵的产品，并不是他们需要去买这些东西，仅仅因为他们需要炫富。

从20世纪60年代起，一些受富人青睐的时尚来自社会地位较低的阶层。这种模式从蓝色牛仔裤开始，牛仔裤长期是从事体力劳动的人的着装。

三类时尚服饰
Types of Fashions

成衣 Ready-to-wear clothing or mass market clothing	Mass produced in factories Manufactured in standard sizes to fit the majority of people
名牌服饰 Designer clothing	Bears the name or logo of a specific popular designer Slightly more expensive
高级订制 Haute couture clothing or high fashion clothing	Created to custom fit one person, for instance, a fashion model or a movie star Often seen on red carpets and fashion runways Much more expensive

时尚趋势不断变化。在工业化之前的社会，衣着和外貌变化很小，反映传统的风格。男人女人，富人穷人，律师和木匠，穿完全不同的衣服，他们的衣着和发型反映了他们的职业和社会地位。

表达库
Bank of expressions

► 【他们衣着和发型反映了他们的职业和社会地位】their clothes and hairstyle reflected their occupations and social standing

表达库
Bank of expressions

► 【人们用"装扮"来表达自己】People use their "looks" to make a statement about themselves.

► 【时尚通过社会阶层从上至下移动】Fashion moves downward through the class structure.

► 【富人通常是潮流领导者，因为他们吸引很多注意力，他们有钱花在奢侈品上】Rich people are usually the trendsetters, because they attract lots of attention and they have the money to spend on luxuries.

► 【音乐人和其他文化偶像一直影响着我们的穿着】Musicians and other cultural icons have always influenced what we're wearing.

► 【时尚包括炫耀性消费，人们买昂贵的产品，并不是他们需要去买这些东西，仅仅因为他们需要炫富】Fashion involves conspicuous consumption as people buy expensive products not because they need such things but simply to show off their wealth.

► 【一些受富人青睐的时尚来自社会地位较低的阶层】many fashions favored by rich people are drawn from people from lower social position

► 【这种模式从蓝色牛仔裤开始】This pattern began with blue jeans...

► 【长期是从事体力劳动的人的着装】have long been worn by people doing manual labor

► 【时尚趋势不断变化】Fashion trends change constantly.

► 【在工业化之前的社会，衣着和外貌变化很小，反映传统的风格】In preindustrial societies, clothing and personal appearance change a little, reflecting traditional style.

► 【男人女人，富人穷人，律师和木匠，穿完全不同的衣服】Women and men, the rich and the poor, lawyers and carpenters wore distinctive clothes...

而在现代社会，人们不再关心传统，通常更热衷于尝试新风格。人们不断地被各种来自音乐、视频、书籍和电视的时尚理念轰炸着。

四大时装周
The "Big Four" Fashion Weeks

纽约时装周 New York Fashion Week	Held in February and September of each year biannually in New York
伦敦时装周 London Fashion Week	Held in London twice each year, in February and September
米兰时装周 Milan Fashion Week	Held semi-annually in Milan, Italy
巴黎时装周 Paris Fashion Week	Held semi-annually in Paris, France with Spring/Summer and Autumn/Winter events held each year; ending event of the Big Four
Some other facts	The Big Four always take place in this order: New York, London, Milan and Paris. The fall/winter collections from February and the spring/summer collections from September Fashion shows dictate clothing trends as they are about the latest in accessories: shoes, bags, jewelry, hats and make-up.

表达库
Bank of expressions

► 【人们不再关心传统，通常更热衷于尝试新风格】people care less about tradition and are often eager to try out new lifestyle
► 【人们不断地被各种来自音乐、视频、书籍和电视的时尚理念轰炸着】We are constantly being bombarded with new fashion ideas from music, videos, books, and television.

笔记
Notes

Religion has convinced people that there's an invisible man... living in the sky. Who watches everything you do every minute of every day. And the invisible man has a list of ten specific things he doesn't want you to do. And if you do any of these things, he will send you to a special place, of burning and fire and smoke and torture and anguish for you to live forever, and suffer, and burn, and scream, until the end of time. But he loves you. He loves you. He loves you and he needs money.

George Carlin

从古至今，宗教给世人提供建议、价值和指引。宗教长存，因为它满足生活各种基本需求，并且试图回答有关死亡和永生、受难、宇宙的起源等数不尽的问题。

自然界和宇宙的神秘自始至终激发着宗教情感。时至今日，科学不可能解释所有事情，人们依然使用宗教帮助他们解释世界上的各种问题。

I cannot conceive of a genuine scientist without that profound faith. The situation may be expressed by an image: science without religion is lame, religion without science is blind.

Religion and Science, Albert Einstein

科学不能给人类对于生命目的等基本问题提供答案。技术给人们力量改变、延长甚至创造生命，但是我们依然面对着越来越棘手的道德问题。

宗教通过提供对与错的概念、设定行为准则，广泛约束人们的行为。宗教塑造人与人之间的关系，影响家庭、社区、经济和政治生活。

不必大惊小怪的是，世界主要宗教有很多相似之处。大部分人，从出生到死亡，会问很多相同的问题，遇到很多相同的挑战。比如说，所有的宗教都试图回答三个相同的问题：我来自哪里？为什么我在这里？我死后会发生什么？这就需要仰赖宗教去回答这些普遍的问题。

世界主要的宗教包括：

- 基督教 [1]
- 伊斯兰教 [2]
- 印度教 [3]
- 佛教 [4]

梵蒂冈

The Vatican City, one of the most sacred places in Christendom, is the world's smallest fully independent nation-state. At its centre is St. Peter's Basilica, with its double colonnade and a circular piazza in front and bordered by palaces and gardens.

基督教是一套信仰、一种生活方式和一群人。基督教是北美地区主流世界观。世界范围内有三大主要的基督教派：

- 罗马天主教[1]
- 东正教[2]
- 新教[3]

基督教是一神论，集中在信仰基督耶稣作为人类的救世主。十字架象征着死亡和耶稣的复活。基督徒相信耶稣死在十字架上，而后复生。《圣经》将《新约圣经》和《旧约圣经》合并，包括耶稣及其信徒的教诲。

穆斯林在麦加大清真寺祈祷
Muslim pilgrims participating in the annual hajj pray at the Haram Mosque in the holy city of Mecca. Mecca, the holiest of Muslim cities, is located in the western Saudi Arabia. Muhammad, the founder of Islam, was born in Mecca. Because it is sacred, only Muslims are allowed to enter the city.

伊斯兰教信仰一个神，这个神就是真主安拉。对于穆斯林，穆罕默德是真主的使者。清真寺是穆斯林礼拜的主要场所。《古兰经》是伊斯兰教的圣书。

表达库
Bank of expressions

► 【基督教是一套信仰、一种生活方式和一群人】Christianity is a set of beliefs, a way of life, and a community of people.

► 【基督教是北美地区主流世界观】Christianity is the dominant worldview found in North America.

► 【基督教是一神论，集中在信仰基督耶稣作为人类的救世主】Christianity is a monotheistic tradition centered on faith in Jesus Christ as the savior humankind.

► 【十字架象征着死亡和耶稣的复活】The cross symbolizes the death and the resurrection of Christ.

► 【基督徒相信耶稣死在十字架上，而后复生】Christians believe that Jesus died on a cross and was resurrected.

► 【《圣经》将《新约圣经》和《旧约圣经》合并，包括耶稣及其信徒的教诲】The *Bible* combines *Old Testament* with *New Testament* that includes accounts of Jesus' teachings and those of his followers.

► 【伊斯兰教信仰一个神，这个神就是真主安拉】Islam believes in one god, and that god is Allah.

► 【对于穆斯林，穆罕默德是真主的使者】For Muslims, Muhammad was the messenger of God.

► 【清真寺是穆斯林礼拜的主要场所】Mosque serves as the main place of worship for Muslims.

► 【《古兰经》是伊斯兰教的圣书】*Quran* is the holy book of Islam.

核心词
Keywords

1. 罗马天主教（Roman Catholic Church）
2. 东正教（Eastern Orthodox Church）
3. 新教（Protestantism）

祈祷是核心的仪式，每天进行五次：日出（晨礼）、正午（晌礼）、午后（晡礼）、日落后（昏礼）和就寝前（宵礼）。祈祷者必须面朝麦加，背诵规定的经文，头朝地面拜倒。在经济允许的情况下，每个穆斯林一生都要完成一次到麦加的朝圣，以此证明自己对真主的虔诚。

印度科纳克太阳神庙
Konarak, popularly known as the Sun Temple. The name Konarak was dedicated to the Hindu sun god Surya.

印度教常被称为"现存最古老的宗教"。《吠陀经》[1]是其经典经文。绝大多数印度教的信徒居住在印度。佛教[2]和印度教有千丝万缕的联系。考虑到影响力，佛教远在印度教之上。

佛教诲人们他不是神，仅仅是个普通人。人们相信佛在菩提树下默念修炼达到涅槃。佛教诲，每个人都有潜能去独自探寻真理。佛教诲，苦难多是由欲望、妒忌、贪婪和无知导致的。

表达库
Bank of expressions

► 【祈祷是核心的仪式，每天进行五次：日出（晨礼）、正午（晌礼）、午后（晡礼）、日落后（昏礼）和就寝前（宵礼）】Prayer is a central ritual, performed five times a day: on rising, at noon, in the mid-afternoon, after sunset, and before retiring.

► 【祈祷者必须面朝麦加，背诵规定的经文，头朝地面拜倒】The prayer must face Mecca, recite a prescribed prayer, and be prostrate, with the head to the ground.

► 【在经济允许的情况下，每个穆斯林一生都要完成一次到麦加的朝圣，以此证明自己对真主的虔诚】Once in a lifetime every Muslim, if financially able, is to make a pilgrimage to Mecca, as the evidence of his or her devotion to Allah.

► 【印度教常被称为"现存最古老的宗教"】Hinduism is often called the "oldest living religion".

► 【佛教诲人们他不是神，仅仅是个普通人】Buddha taught that he was not a god but simply a man.

► 【人们相信佛在菩提树下默念修炼达到涅槃】The Buddha is believed to have found nirvana while meditating under a bodhi tree.

► 【佛教诲，每个人都有潜能去独自探寻真理】Buddha taught that each individual has the potential to seek the truth on their own.

► 【佛教诲，苦难多是由欲望、妒忌、贪婪和无知导致的】Buddha taught that much of the suffering is caused by craving, envy, greed, and ignorance.

核心词
Keywords

1.《吠陀经》（ Vedas ）
2. 佛教（Buddhism ）

卡尔·马克思[1]（以下简称"马克思"）认为，宗教通过维持现状合理化、从社会各种不平等处转移人们的注意力，来服务统治阶级。他曾有著名的论断，他把宗教看做是"精神鸦片[2]"。

Religion is the sigh of the oppressed creature, the heart of a heartless world, and the soul of soulless conditions. It is the opium of the people.

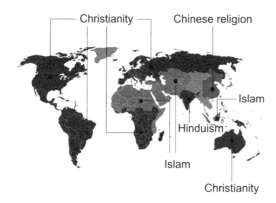

世界宗教信仰分布
Religions in the world map

卡尔·马克思
Karl Marx (1818-1883) German philosopher, economist, sociologist, historian, notable for *The Communist Manifesto and Capital*

表达库
Bank of expressions

▶【宗教通过维持现状合理化、从社会各种不平等处转移人们的注意力，来服务统治阶级】religion serves ruling elites by legitimizing the status quo and diverting people's attention from social inequalities

▶【Religion is the sigh of the oppressed creature, the heart of a heartless world, and the soul of soulless conditions. It is the opium of the people】宗教是被压迫生灵的叹息，是无情世界里的同情心，是没有灵魂的处境里的灵魂。它是人民的精神鸦片。

核心词
Keywords

1. 卡尔·马克思（Karl Marx）
2. 精神鸦片（opium of the people）

笔记
Notes

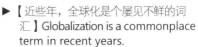

Where globalization means, as it so often does, that the rich and powerful now have new means to further enrich and empower themselves at the cost of the poorer and weaker, we have a responsibility to protest in the name of universal freedom.

Nelson Mandela

近些年，全球化是个屡见不鲜的词汇；但是，它描述的却是一个古老的过程。在古代，商人交换中国丝绸、非洲黄金、罗马玻璃制品和香料。区域服饰、烹饪、金属加工技术和装饰艺术从发祥地传到世界其他角落。全球化根植于移民主义。克里斯托弗·哥伦布[1]（以下简称"哥伦布"）在美洲的探险为世人所知，尽管他只注重从原住民处榨取尽量多的财富。更重要的是，他的航行开启了欧洲 450 年的殖民时代。

哥伦布登上"新大陆"
Columbus landing in the New World and receiving gifts from the cacique Guacanagari on 12 October 1492 by Theodore de Bry.

表达库
Bank of expressions

► 【近些年，全球化是个屡见不鲜的词汇】Globalization is a commonplace term in recent years.

► 【但是，它描述的却是一个古老的过程】It, however, describes an old process.

► 【在古代，商人交换中国丝绸、非洲黄金、罗马玻璃制品和香料】In ancient world, merchants exchanged Chinese silk, African gold, Roman glassware, and spices.

► 【区域服饰、烹饪、金属加工和装饰技术从发祥地传到世界其他角落】Regional clothing and cooking styles, and techniques of metalwork and decoration reached people on the other side of the globe from their points of origin.

► 【全球化根植于移民主义】Globalization is firmly rooted in the experience of colonialism.

► 【克里斯托弗·哥伦布在美洲的探险为世人所知】Christopher Columbus' adventure in the Americas was notable...

► 【尽管他只注重从原住民处榨取尽量多的财富】though his only focus was on extracting as much wealth as possible from the aboriginal land and the native people

► 【更重要的是，他的航行开启了欧洲 450 年的殖民时代】More importantly his voyages opened the door to 450 years of European colonialism.

核心词
Keywords

1. 克里斯托弗·哥伦布（Christopher Columbus）

廉价的原材料和奴隶从殖民地被贪婪地掠夺。在殖民时代，全球贸易迅速扩张。来自海外殖民地的财富涌入法国、英国、荷兰和西班牙。

铁路、公路、港口、水坝和城市在殖民地被建设。正是这长达几个世纪的帝国时代为今天的全球贸易奠定了基础。

信息通信技术蓬勃发展，运输技术进步，货物和资金壁垒瓦解，跨国公司对政治经济的影响力增强，在过去的三十年中，全球化的进程在加速。

三个塑造当今全球化时代的重要机构是：国际货币基金组织（简称 IMF），世界银行，和世界贸易组织（简称 WTO）。第二次世

谢赞泰（1872-1938）绘制的《时局图》（*The Situation in the Far East*），1898。图中鹰代表美国，熊代表俄国，蛙代表法国，太阳代表日本，虎代表英国，肠代表德国。Western powers were dividing China up like a melon. The eagle represents United States approaching from the Philippines; the bear represents Russia invading China from the north; the frog represents France coveting China in the Southeast Asia; the sun, the bulldog and its tail represent Japan, England and Germany placing their power on China in different areas.

界大战后，布雷顿森林体系[1]建立，确定以美元为中心的国际货币体系，美元成为储备货币，推动国际贸易发展。

全球化喜忧参半。全球化的积极方面包括分享知识、技术、投资、资源和道德价值。全球化的消极方面包括快速传播疾病、非法药品、犯罪、恐怖活动和非法移民。

In Globalization 1.0, which began around 1492, the world went from size large to size medium. In Globalization 2.0, the era that introduced us to multinational companies, it went from size medium to size small. And then around 2000 came Globalization 3.0, in which the world went from being small to tiny.

Thomas Friedman, author of *The World Is Flat*

► 【美元成为储备货币】US dollar became a reserve currency
► 【全球化喜忧参半】Globalization has both negative and positive aspects.
► 【全球化的积极方面包括分享知识、技术、投资、资源和道德价值】Among globalization's benefits are a sharing of basic knowledge, technology, investments, resources, and ethical values.
► 【全球化的消极方面包括快速传播疾病、非法药品、犯罪、恐怖活动和非法移民】Among the negative aspects are the rapid spread of diseases, illicit drugs, crime, terrorism, and uncontrolled migration.

核心词
Keywords

1. 布雷顿森林体系（Bretton Woods system）

克里斯托弗·哥伦布
Christopher Columbus
(1451-1506)
Master navigator and opened the way for European exploration, exploitation, and colonization of the Americas, and long been called the "discoverer" of the New World

笔记
Notes

The educated differ from the uneducated as much as the living differ from the dead.

Aristotle

有人称大学是"象牙塔[1]"，它代表着对未知的好奇、对知识的执著探索。在现代社会，大学是知识的源泉，是经济增长的推进器，一定程度上减少了人类的痛苦，改善了人们的生活。

在大学的发展过程中，下面几个名字值得了解：

- 学院[2]
- 学园[3]
- 亚历山大图书馆[4]
- 博洛尼亚大学[5]
- 柏林洪堡大学[6]

约公元前 387 年，柏拉图[7]在雅典创立的"学院"，代表着古希腊的高等教育。柏拉图在这里教授学生哲学、数学、天文、音乐等知识。

公元前 335 年，柏拉图的学生亚里士多德[8]创立"学园"。由于亚里士多德边在小树林散步边给学生上课，这所学校和他的学生获称"逍遥学派"。

亚历山大图书馆
Artistic rendering of
"The Great Library of Alexandria"

表达库
Bank of expressions

▶【对未知的好奇】the curiosity for the unknown
▶【对知识的执著探索】the persistent search for knowledge
▶【知识的源泉】powerhouse of knowledge
▶【经济增长的推进器】fundamental engine of economic growth
▶【一定程度上减少了人类的痛苦，改善了人们的生活】reduces mankind's suffering and improves lives to some extent
▶【古希腊的高等教育】higher education in ancient Greece
▶【由于亚里士多德边在小树林散步边给学生上课】Owing to his habit of walking about the grove while lecturing his students...
▶【这所学校和他的学生获称"逍遥学派"】the school and its students acquired the label of Peripatetic

核心词
Keywords

1. 象牙塔（ivory tower）
2. 学院（Academy）
3. 学园（Lyceum）
4. 亚历山大图书馆（Library of Alexandria）
5. 博洛尼亚大学（University of Bologna）
6. 柏林洪堡大学（Humboldt University of Berlin）
7. 柏拉图（Plato）
8. 亚里士多德（Aristotle）

始建于公元前 3 世纪左右埃及托勒密王朝[1]的亚历山大图书馆坐落在尼罗河入海口城市亚历山大市，是<u>古代最有名的图书馆</u>，据传<u>有当时世界上最多的藏书</u>。它是亚历山大博物馆[2]的一部分，<u>大批希腊和中东的学者慕名来到亚历山大博物馆和图书馆</u>。据传，<u>计算出地球周长</u>的埃拉托斯特尼[3]和阿基米德[4]曾在此工作。

博洛尼亚大学
The University of Bologna, founded in 1088, widely recognized as the oldest university in continuous operation

约创立于 11 世纪的博洛尼亚大学，是世界现存<u>最古老的大学</u>，被称作"欧洲大学之母"。著名校友包括尼古拉·哥白尼[5]。当时，意大利是文艺复兴[6]的发源地，也是近代科学的摇篮。

柏林洪堡大学皇家图书馆
The Royal Library of Humboldt University of Berlin, now seat of the Faculty of Law

表达库
Bank of expressions

▶【古代最有名的图书馆】the most famous library of classical antiquity
▶【有当时世界上最多的藏书】have the greatest collection of books in the ancient world
▶【大批希腊和中东的学者慕名来到亚历山大博物馆和图书馆】Alexandria attracted a flood of scholars from Greece and the Middle East to its museum and to the Library of Alexandria
▶【计算出地球周长】calculated the circumference of the earth
▶【最古老的大学】the oldest extant university in the world

核心词
Keywords

1. 埃及托勒密王朝（Ptolemaic Dynasty in Egypt）
2. 亚历山大博物馆（Alexandrian Museum）
3. 埃拉托斯特尼（Eratosthenes）
4. 阿基米德（Archimedes）
5. 尼古拉·哥白尼（Nicolaus Copernicus）
6. 文艺复兴（Renaissance）

不夸张地说，柏林洪堡大学是第二次世界大战之前的世界学术中心。它以其现代课程和重视研究的精神闻名于世，深刻影响了欧洲和北美洲的大学。曾在这里任职或学习过的著名人士包括阿尔伯特·爱因斯坦[1]（以下简称"爱因斯坦"）、马克斯·普朗克[2]、约翰·冯·诺依曼[3]、亚瑟·叔本华[4]、格奥尔格·威廉·弗里德里希·黑格尔[5]、马克思、奥托·冯·俾斯麦[6]等。

表达库
Bank of expressions

► 【以其现代课程和重视研究的精神闻名于世】attained world renown for its modern curriculum and research-intensive spirit

核心词
Keywords

1.阿尔伯特·爱因斯坦（Albert Einstein）
2.马克斯·普朗克（Max Planck）
3.约翰·冯·诺依曼（John von Neumann)
4.亚瑟·叔本华（Arthur Schopenhauer）
5.格奥尔格·威廉·弗里德里希·黑格尔（Georg Wilhelm Friedrich Hegel）
6.奥托·冯·俾斯麦（Otto von Bismarck）

柏拉图
Plato (428-348 BC)
Ancient Greek philosopher, student of Socrates, teacher of Aristotle, and founder of the Academy, best known as the author of philosophical works of unparalleled influence

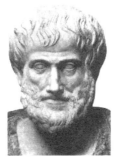

亚里士多德
Aristotle (384-322 BC)
Ancient Greek philosopher and scientist, one of the greatest intellectual figures of Western history

笔记
Notes

Education is the most powerful weapon which you can use to change the world.

Nelson Mandela

　　教育是当今时代关键词之一。没有接受教育的人是逆境下可悲的受害者，他们被剥夺了其中一次最好的机会。学校是让年轻人交往和融入当今社会的主要机构。教育是传播价值的重要途径，并可以创造平等机会。教育的任务之一是向年轻人传递社会文化价值和行为模式。

　　学校提供打开高收入和高社会地位职业大门的文凭。在学校里，学生学习基本的生活技能，比如，逻辑思维、分析和解决问题能力。学生通过参加多样活动而受益，这些

2013-2014《泰晤士高等教育》世界大学排名前10
World University Rankings, Top 10, *Times Higher Education*, 2013-2014

Rank	University	Country
1	California Institute of Technology (Caltech)	United States
2	University of Oxford	United Kingdom
2	Harvard University	United States
4	Stanford University	United States
5	Massachusetts Institute of Technology (MIT)	United States
6	Princeton University	United States
7	University of Cambridge	United Kingdom
8	University of California, Berkeley	United States
9	University of Chicago	United States
10	Imperial College London	United Kingdom

表达库
Bank of expressions

▶【教育是当今时代关键词之一】Education is one of the key words of our time.

▶【没有接受教育的人是逆境下可悲的受害者，他们被剥夺了其中一次最好的机会】A man without an education is an unfortunate victim of adverse circumstances deprived of one of the greatest opportunities.

▶【学校是让年轻人交往和融入当今社会的主要机构】Schools are expected to be primary institution for socializing the young and integrating them into the immediate society.

▶【教育是传播价值的重要途径，并可以创造平等机会】Education is a significant means of transmitting values, and creating equality of opportunity.

▶【教育的任务之一是向年轻人传递社会文化价值和行为模式】One of the tasks of education is to transmit the cultural values and behavior patterns of the society to its young members.

▶【学校提供打开高收入和高社会地位职业大门的文凭】Schools provide the credentials that open doors to high-income and high-status occupations.

▶【在学校里，学生学习基本的生活技能，比如，逻辑思维、分析和解决问题能力】In schools, students are taught extremely essential life skills, such as logical thinking, analysis and problem-solving abilities.

▶【学生通过参加多样活动而受益】Students benefit while being engaged in diverse activities...

活动可以培养诸如领导力、体育精神、组织和合作等能力。

教育是发展的核心。正是教育给社会以力量和目的来解决所面临的主要问题：国家间和国家内不断扩大的经济差距，堆积成山的债务负担，迅速增长的人口，普遍的环境退化，内乱和武装冲突。

但是，教育真的就是灵丹妙药吗？有人批评，学校似乎是最集权、最具破坏性和最危险的现代社会机构。他们认为，和其他社会机构相比，没有其他任何机构对人造成更持久的伤害，更能破坏人们的好奇心、独立性、信任、认同感和价值观。

教育批判者认为，学校教育是一种控制

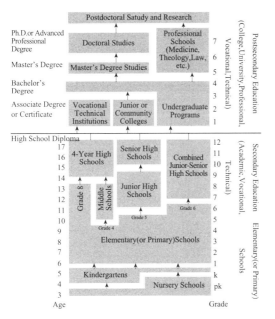

美国教育体系
US education system

表达库
Bank of expressions

▶【可以培养诸如领导力、体育精神、组织和合作等能力】are supposed to foster qualities, such as leadership, sportsmanship, the ability to organize, and the capability to cooperate with each other.

▶【教育是发展的核心】Education is at the heart of development.

▶【正是教育给社会以力量和目的来解决所面临的主要问题】It is education that gives societies the strength and sense of purpose to address the main problems confronting them today...

▶【国家间和国家内不断扩大的经济差距】widening economic disparities among and within countries

▶【堆积成山的债务负担】mounting debt burdens

▶【迅速增长的人口】rapid population growth

▶【普遍的环境退化】widespread environmental degradation

▶【内乱和武装冲突】civil strife and armed conflicts

▶【教育真的就是灵丹妙药吗】Is education thus the panacea?

▶【学校似乎是最集权、最具破坏性和最危险的现代社会机构】schools seem to be the most authoritarian, most destructive, and most dangerous institutions of modern society

▶【没有其他任何机构对人造成更持久的伤害，更能破坏人们的好奇心、独立性、信任、认同感和价值观】no other institution does more lasting harm to more people or destroys so much of their curiosity, independence, trust, and sense of identity and worth

▶【学校教育是一种控制人的方法】Schooling is a way of controlling people...

▶【强化人们接受现状】reinforcing acceptance of the status quo

人的方法，强化人们接受现状。很多学校在监控和其他控制技术方面投入巨资。正是在学校里，人们遇到、习惯于、学着相信完全受控的社会。

有人说，百年前，服务于无数当地社区的小而个性化的学校，已经演变成教育大工厂。官僚化的学校忽视当地文化特点和学生的个性化需求。高度官僚化的学校不让学生自学。人们没学到多少科学知识，反而学会崇拜科学家。马克·吐温[1]的下面这句名言正体现他对正规教育的抵制：

I have never let my schooling interfere with my education.

在《为什么教育是无用的》[2]这本书中，作者丹尼尔·科顿姆[3]认为，教育是无用的，因为它让人们远离实用性；教育是无用的，因为它把我们和其他人隔离开来；受过教育的人通常疏远普通人的情感；教育让我们脑袋像被填鸭，而且让我们的身体孱弱不堪。

Live as if you were to die tomorrow. Learn as if you were to live forever.

Mahatma Gandhi

核心词
Keywords

1. 马克·吐温（Mark Twain）
2.《为什么教育是无用的》（*Why Education Is Useless*）
3. 丹尼尔·科顿姆（Daniel Cottom）

All happy families are alike; each unhappy family is unhappy in its own way.

Leo Tolstoy

我们在某个家庭出生，在某个家庭成长，组建新的家庭，因死亡而离开家庭。有人说，当家庭不复存在，国家和我们生存的整个世界都将不复存在。一个国家的强大来自家庭的完整。

家庭是社会最基本的单位。作为个人归属的第一个社会群体，家庭构建了社会最基本的价值观。家庭在社会中和培育下一代上扮演着重要角色。血浓于水，这个词的意思是家庭关系比其他任何关系都要紧密。从传统到现代，家庭结构发生很多变化，其中重要的家庭组织形式包括：

国家家庭人口平均数量排名
Country ranking by average size of households

Country	国家	Household size
Burkina Faso	布基纳法索	5.9
India	印度	5.3
Ethiopia	埃塞俄比亚	4.7
Nepal	尼泊尔	4.7
Cambodia	柬埔寨	4.7
Swaziland	斯威士兰	4.7
Timor-Leste	东帝汶	4.7
Malaysia	马来西亚	4.6
Rwanda	卢旺达	4.5
Mexico	墨西哥	4.3
Ecuador	厄瓜多尔	4.2
Bolivia	玻利维亚	4.1
Peru	秘鲁	4
Colombia	哥伦比亚	3.9
Singapore	新加坡	3.6

表达库
Bank of expressions

► 【All happy families are alike; each unhappy family is unhappy in its own way】所有快乐的家庭是相似的；不幸的家庭各有各的不幸。

► 【我们在某个家庭出生，在某个家庭成长，组建新的家庭，因死亡而离开家庭】We are born into a family, mature in a family, form new families, and leave them at our death.

► 【当家庭不复存在，国家和我们生存的整个世界都将不复存在】As the family goes, so goes the nation and so goes the whole world in which we live.

► 【一个国家的强大来自家庭的完整】The strength of a nation derives from the integrity of the families.

► 【家庭是社会最基本的单位】The family is the most basic unit of society.

► 【作为个人归属的第一个社会群体】As the first community to which a person is attached...

► 【家庭构建了社会最基本的价值观】the family establishes society's most basic values

► 【家庭在社会中和培育下一代上扮演着重要角色】The family unit plays a critical role in our society and in the training of the generation to come.

► 【血浓于水】Blood is thicker than water...

► 【意思是家庭关系比其他任何关系都要紧密】means that your family ties are stronger than any other relationship

- 大家庭[1]
- 小家庭[2]
- 单亲家庭[3]
- 同性家庭[4]
- 没有孩子的家庭[5]

在大家庭里，父母和孩子的家庭生活在同一屋檐下。这种数代同堂的家庭通常包括一个家庭的几代人。大家庭坚持家庭成员要顺从长者。

一对已婚的夫妻是小家庭的核心。小家庭可以有一个或几个孩子，其中也包括领养家庭[6]。小家庭较少强调服从，而是鼓励探索和创造。离婚[7]的数量越来越多，这意味着单亲家庭越来越普遍。

世界上一些国家和地区允许同性婚姻，有些国家法律允许同性伴侣收养儿童。另外，人工授精[8]和代孕[9]的出现导致同性家庭已经不占少数。

丁克家庭[10]，来自英文 "Double Income with No Kids"，字面意思就是"双收入、没有孩子"，这类家庭的数量也在不断上升。

美国几种家庭构成演变，1940-2010
Percent distribution of US households by type 1940-2010

Household Type	1940	1960	1980	2000	2010
Family Households	90	85.1	73.7	68.1	66.4
Married couples with children	42.9	44.3	30.7	23.5	20.2
Married couples without children	33.4	30.5	30.2	28.1	28.2
Single parents with children	4.3	4.1	7.2	9.2	9.6
Other family	9.4	6.2	5.6	7.1	8.5
Nonfamily Households	10	15.1	26.4	31.9	33.6
One person	7.8	13.4	22.6	25.8	26.7
Other nonfamily	2.2	1.7	3.8	6.1	6

24 拯救我的GRE+TOEFL写作论据素材库·社会篇

表达库
Bank of expressions

► 【在大家庭里，父母和孩子的家庭生活在同一屋檐下】In an extended family, parents and their children's families may often live under a single roof.

► 【这种数代同堂的家庭通常包括一个家庭的几代人】This type of joint family often includes multiple generations in the family.

► 【一对已婚的夫妻是小家庭的核心】Nuclear families typically center on a married couple.

► 【小家庭可以有一个或几个孩子】The nuclear family may have any number of children...

► 【小家庭较少强调服从】Nuclear families have less emphasis on obedience...

► 【而是鼓励探索和创造】while exploration and creativity are encouraged

► 【意味着单亲家庭越来越普遍】means that single-parent families are becoming more common

► 【同性伴侣收养儿童】the adoption of children by lesbian and gay couples

核心词
Keywords

1. 大家庭（extended family）
2. 小家庭（nuclear family）
3. 单亲家庭（single-parent family）
4. 同性家庭（same-sex family）
5. 没有孩子的家庭（childless family）
6. 领养家庭（adoptive family）
7. 离婚（divorce）
8. 人工授精（artificial insemination）
9. 代孕（surrogacy）
10. 丁克家庭（DINK）

Cities force growth, and make men talkative and entertaining, but they make them artificial.

Ralph Waldo Emerson

城市是人类的一个发明，它们是为扩大社会生活的故意之举。城市是一个国家商业、工业、金融、政治和文化的中心。更长的寿命、更多的人口、扩展的知识和教育、健康改善、完善的福利、艺术和娱乐活动的扩散是城市生活的主要方面。

城市发展经历很多阶段，其中包括：

- 古典城市 [1]
- 中世纪城市 [2]
- 文艺复兴时期城市 [3]
- 工业革命时期城市 [4]

古典城市的两个代表位于古希腊 [5] 和古罗马 [6]。民主成为主流社会生活的新形式。

君士坦丁时期的罗马模型
Model of Constantine's Rome

表达库
Bank of expressions

- 【Cities force growth, and make men talkative and entertaining, but they make them artificial】城市推动成长，让人们变得健谈而有趣，但是也让他们变得更虚伪。
- 【城市是人类的一个发明】Cities are a human invention.
- 【它们是为扩大社会生活的故意之举】They are the result of a deliberate effort to expand social life.
- 【城市是一个国家商业、工业、金融、政治和文化的中心】Cities are the commercial, industrial, financial, political, and cultural centers of a nation.
- 【更长的寿命、更多的人口、扩展的知识和教育、健康改善、完善的福利、艺术和娱乐活动的扩散是城市生活的主要方面】Longer life spans, larger populations, expanded knowledge and education, improved health, improved welfare, and proliferation of the arts and of recreational activities are major aspects of the urban way of life.
- 【民主成为主流社会生活的新形式】Democracy had become a new and dominant form of social life.

核心词
Keywords

1. 古典城市（classic cities）
2. 中世纪城市（Middle Ages cities）
3. 文艺复兴时期城市（cities in the Renaissance era）
4. 工业革命时期城市（cities in the Industrial Revolution）
5. 古希腊（ancient Greek）
6. 古罗马（ancient Rome）

尽管奴隶制度依然存在，公民享有很多自由，包括言论和集会自由。理性、逻辑和科学是古典城市组织的基石。人们可以在雅典卫城这样的黄金地段瞻仰男神和女神。

城市困难地度过了黑暗时代。公元 11 世纪，小城市兴建，原有的城市恢复了生机。教堂和教堂广场居于中世纪城市统治的中心。中世纪城市被城墙包围。

随着西欧文艺复兴的到来，城市的增长和扩张加速。文艺复兴中的城市充满着创新和艺术的悸动。富商和神职人员成为艺术的赞助人。食物生产增长迅速，平均寿命加倍，

佛罗伦萨木版画，1493
A woodcut of Florence in 1493

芝加哥城市及高速路规划，1909
General diagram of exterior highways encircling and radiating from the City of Chicago; Taken from the 1909 Plan of Chicago, also known as the Burnham Plan, by Daniel Burnham and Edward Bennett

两者导致城市人口的增长。这时，城市文化的特点是人类最高的成就交织着瘟疫、饥饿、暴乱、犯罪、污染和其他社会问题。

工业革命提高生活水平、提供更好的医疗条件。人们从乡下蜂拥至城市，因为这里有更好的机会。但是，许多工厂的工作条件让人感觉恐怖，机器不安全，工作环境有害健康。住房不足，城市以贫民窟、卫生条件差和犯罪为标志。伴随着工业化，村庄变成城镇，城镇变成城市，最终，很多城市成为大都市。

现代城市有种种问题。城市面对的两个最严重的问题是住房和交通。合适住房的短

世界主要城市
Major cities in the world

City	Country
Bangkok	Thailand
Beijing	China
Berlin	Germany
Cairo	Egypt
Hong Kong	China
Istanbul	Turkey
London	UK
Los Angeles	USA
Miami	USA
Moscow	Russia
Mumbai	India
New Delhi	India
New York	USA
Paris	France
Rio de Janeiro	Brazil
Seattle	USA
Shanghai	China
Singapore City	Singapore
Sydney	Australia
Tokyo	Japan
Toronto	Canada
Vancouver	Canada

表达库
Bank of expressions

► 【导致城市人口的增长】resulted in the growth of city populations

► 【城市文化的特点是人类最高的成就交织着瘟疫、饥饿、暴乱、犯罪、污染和其他社会问题】Urban culture is characterized by the juxtaposing of man's highest achievements with plagues, famines, riots, crime, pollution, and other social problems.

► 【工业革命提高生活水平、提供更好的医疗条件】The Industrial Revolution produced a higher standard of living and better health conditions.

► 【人们从乡下蜂拥至城市，因为这里有更好的机会】People flocked from the countryside to the cities because of opportunities.

► 【许多工厂的工作条件让人感觉恐怖】Working conditions in many of the factories were appalling.

► 【机器不安全，工作环境有害健康】The machinery was dangerous and the working conditions were unhealthy.

► 【住房不足，城市以贫民窟、卫生条件差和犯罪为标志】Housing was inadequate, and cities became marked by slums, poor sanitation, and crime.

► 【伴随着工业化，村庄变成城镇，城镇变成城市，最终，很多城市成为大都市】With industrialism, villages became towns, towns became cities, and ultimately, many cities grew into metropolises.

► 【城市面对的两个最严重的问题是住房和交通】Two of the most crucial problems facing cities around the world are housing and transportation.

缺，特别是对于低收入的家庭和老年人，导致日益拥挤的公寓和贫民窟，这又导致其他问题，比如犯罪、青少年的不法行为和种族间关系紧张。大量增长的汽车阻塞每条街道，让停车场不堪负重，而且产生空气污染和噪声污染。城市意味着冷漠和隔绝，正如美国思想家亨利·戴维·梭罗[1]（以下简称"梭罗"）所说：

> *City life is millions of people being lonesome together.*

城市是上演人类悲喜剧的舞台。城市一直是一处可以参观的地方，一个有着无数可能、梦想、幻想和未来的地方。阶级的差异与不平等在城市发展之初被铭刻在每座城市的地貌上。

纽约城市中心天际线
New York City Midtown Skyline

表达库
Bank of expressions

► 【合适住房的短缺，特别是对于低收入的家庭和老年人，导致日益拥挤的公寓和贫民窟，这又导致其他问题，比如犯罪、青少年的不法行为和种族间关系紧张】A shortage of suitable housing, especially for low-income families and the elderly, has led to over-crowding apartments and slums, and has helped create the additional problems, such as crime, juvenile delinquency, and racial tensions.

► 【大量增长的汽车阻塞每条街道，让停车场不堪负重，而且产生空气污染和噪声污染】A tremendous increase in the number of automobiles has clogged streets, overburdened parking facilities, and tended to create air pollution and noise pollution.

► 【城市是上演人类悲喜剧的舞台】Cities are stages for the great triumphs and tragedies of humanity.

► 【城市一直是一处可以参观的地方，一个有着无数可能、梦想、幻想和未来的地方】The city is always a place to visit, a place of endless possibilities, dreams, fantasies, and a place of future.

► 【阶级的差异与不平等在城市发展之初被铭刻在每座城市的地貌上】Differences and inequalities of classes were inscribed on the landscapes of the cities from the early days of their development.

核心词
Keywords

1. 亨利·戴维·梭罗（Henry David Thoreau）

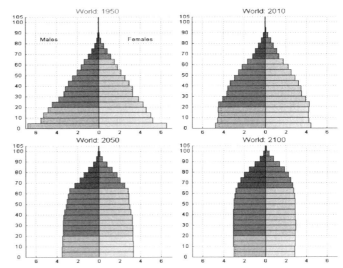

世界人口结构的过去
与未来
World population by
age groups

人体衰老的迹象包括：听力和视力下降，头发变白，皱纹加深，身高体重下降，肌肉力量减弱，皮肤和血管柔韧性变差，骨骼变脆，患慢性病，身体状况整体下降。

在高收入的国家，老年人所占比例迅速

表达库
Bank of expressions

▶ 【听力和视力下降】hearing and vision decline
▶ 【头发变白】hair turns gray
▶ 【皱纹加深】wrinkles grow deeper
▶ 【身高体重下降】height and weight lose
▶ 【肌肉力量减弱】muscle strength lessens
▶ 【皮肤和血管柔韧性变差】skin and blood vessels become less flexible
▶ 【骨骼变脆】bones become more brittle
▶ 【患慢性病】develop chronic illness
▶ 【身体状况整体下降】there is an overall decline in body tone
▶ 【在高收入的国家】in high-income nations

全球人口预期寿命排名
Top 10 countries or areas by life expectancy at birth

Rank	Country	Life expectancy at birth (years)
1	Monaco [摩纳哥]	89.68
2	Macau (China)	84.43
3	Japan	83.91
4	Singapore	83.75
5	San Marino[圣马力诺]	83.07
6	Andorra[安道尔]	82.5
7	Guernsey[格恩西岛]	82.24
8	Hong Kong (China)	82.12
9	Australia	81.9
10	Italy	81.86

上升，即所谓的社会老龄化[1]。产生这种情况有两点主要原因：低生育率和寿命延长。

随着节育技术的进步，越来越多的伴侣选择少生孩子。孩子不再改善家庭的经济状况，反而加重经济负担。特别是，越来越多的女性开始选择工作，而不是待在家里照看孩子。

寿命延长是工业革命的一大结果。更多的物质财富和医疗进步提高了生活水平，人们受益于更好的住房和营养。此外，医学进步几乎消除了主要的传染病，比如，天花[2]、白喉[3]和麻疹[4]等。社会老龄化的主要影响包括：

- 慢性病的专注治疗
- 医疗保健开支的大幅增长
- 老人收入和社会福利的安全性
- 劳动力短缺的风险

全球人口总数排名前十的国家, 2012
Ten Countries with the highest population in the world

Rank	Country	Population
1	China	1,343,239,923
2	India	1,205,073,612
3	United States	313,847,465
4	Indonesia	248,645,008
5	Brazil	199,321,413
6	Pakistan	190,291,129
7	Nigeria	170,123,740
8	Bangladesh	161,083,804
9	Russia	142,517,670
10	Japan	127,368,088

表达库
Bank of expressions

► 【老年人所占比例迅速上升】The share of elderly people is increasing rapidly...
► 【低生育率】low birth rates
► 【寿命延长】increasing longevity
► 【随着节育技术的进步】with advances in birth control technology
► 【越来越多的伴侣选择少生孩子】more and more couples choose to bear fewer children
► 【孩子不再改善家庭的经济状况，反而加重经济负担】Children no longer add to their family's financial well-being, but instead are a major expense burden.
► 【寿命延长是工业革命的一大结果】This longer life span is one result of the Industrial Revolution.
► 【更多的物质财富和医疗进步提高了生活水平】Greater material wealth and advances in medicine have raised living standards...
► 【人们受益于更好的住房和营养】people benefit from better housing and nutrition
► 【医学进步几乎消除了主要的传染病】medical advances have almost eliminated major infectious diseases
► 【慢性病的专注治疗】focusing on chronic diseases
► 【医疗保健开支的大幅增长】substantial in crease in health care costs
► 【老人收入和社会福利的安全性】security of the elderly persons' income and economic welfare
► 【劳动力短缺的风险】a risk of labor shortages

核心词
Keywords

1. 社会老龄化（aging society）
2. 天花（small pox）
3. 白喉（diphtheria）
4. 麻疹（measles）

隔绝是老年人最常见的问题。退休切断了一个重要的社会交际源头，身体问题限制了行动。产生与世隔绝的重要原因是一些生命中重要人物的离世，特别是配偶的去世。老年人需要他人的照料，特别是来自家人的照顾。如今的中年人被称为"夹层一代"，因为很多人在照料父母和子女上花差不多一样的时间。

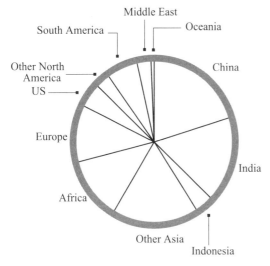

世界人口消费与收入，2008
Consumption level worldwide

表达库
Bank of expressions

► 【隔绝是老年人最常见的问题】Isolation is the most common problem among the elderly people.

► 【退休切断了一个重要的社会交际源头】Retirement closes off one major source of social interaction...

► 【身体问题限制了行动】physical problems may limit mobility

► 【产生与世隔绝的重要原因是一些生命中重要人物的离世，特别是配偶的去世】The greatest cause of social isolation is the death of significant others, especially the death of a spouse.

► 【老年人需要他人的照料，特别是来自家人的照顾】The elderly needs caring from people, especially from family members.

► 【如今的中年人被称为"夹层一代"】Today's middle-aged adults are called the "sandwich generation"...

► 【因为很多人在照料父母和子女上花差不多一样的时间】because many will spend as much time caring for their aging parents as for their own children

笔记
Notes

Poverty is the parent of revolution and crime.

Aristotle

　　贫困意味着缺乏生活必需品，比如，充足的营养、保暖的衣物、安全的住房、清洁用水和医疗服务。很多贫困人口经常遭受营养不良、流行性疾病的暴发、饥荒和战争等问题。

　　有史以来，贫困一直是各个社会关注的问题。有些人认为贫困源自缺乏资源。也有人认为，贫困是因为全球范围内的资源分布不均匀。导致贫困的常见原因包括：

- 人口过剩 [1]
- 资源分布不均匀
- 不能满足高水平生活标准
- 教育就业机会不公平
- 环境恶化 [2]
- 经济形势 [3] 不稳定

印度孟买的贫民窟
Mumbai Slums
The movie *Slumdog Millionaire* was filmed in the slums of Mumbai.

表达库
Bank of expressions

► 【Poverty is the parent of revolution and crime】贫困是革命和犯罪之母。
► 【贫困意味着缺乏生活必需品，比如，充足的营养、保暖的衣物、安全的住房、清洁用水和医疗服务】Poverty means a lack of basic human needs, such as adequate and nutritious food, warm clothing, safe housing, clean water, and health services.
► 【很多贫困人口经常遭受营养不良、流行性疾病的暴发、饥荒和战争等问题】Many people in poverty often suffer from severe malnutrition, epidemic disease outbreaks, famine, and war.
► 【有史以来，贫困一直是各个社会关注的问题】Poverty has been a concern in societies since the beginning of recorded history.
► 【有些人认为贫困源自缺乏资源】Some people believe that poverty results from a lack of adequate resources.
► 【也有人认为，贫困是因为全球范围内的资源分布不均匀】Others see poverty as an effect of the uneven distribution of resources around the world.
► 【资源分布不均匀】unequal distribution of resources
► 【不能满足高水平生活标准】inability to meet high standards of living and costs of living
► 【教育就业机会不公平】inadequate education and employment opportunities

核心词
Keywords

1. 人口过剩（overpopulation）
2. 环境恶化（environmental degradation）
3. 经济形势（economic trend）

过高的人口密度让有限的资源越发紧张。在发达国家，人口过剩通常不会成为贫困的主要原因，因为这些国家通过机械化耕作生产大量食物。

很多发展中国家缺乏重要原材料，以及缺乏通过教育和培训获得的知识技能。这些国家还缺乏基础设施，比如，交通运输系统和发电系统。

文盲和缺乏教育在贫困国家最平常不过。没有教育，多数人不能找到体面的工作。环境问题导致安全的食物、洁净的水、建筑材料和其他重要资源的短缺。发达国家的贫困和经济情况相联系。劳动力市场变化对贫困水平提高有影响。

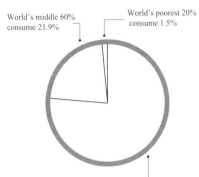

World's middle 60% consume 21.9%

World's poorest 20% consume 1.5%

World's riches 20% consume 76.6%

世界人口消费与收入，2008
Consumption level worldwide
The wealthiest 20% of the world accounted for 76.6% of total private consumption, while the poorest fifth just 1.5%.

世界各国生活在国家贫困线以下的居民百分比
Top 10 countries with population below poverty line

Rank	Country	Population below poverty line (%)
1	Chad[乍得]	80
2	Haiti[海地]	80
3	Liberia[利比里亚]	80
4	Congo[刚果]	71
5	Sierra Leone[塞拉利昂]	70.2
6	Nigeria[尼日利亚]	70
7	Suriname[苏里南]	70
8	Swaziland[斯威士兰]	69
9	Burundi[布隆迪]	68
10	Zimbabwe[津巴布韦]	68

贫困和人的行为也有千丝万缕的关系。中国古代春秋时期的管仲曾说："仓廪实则知礼节，衣食足则知荣辱"。《社会契约论》[1]的作者，法国哲学家让−雅克·卢梭[2]也有类似的说法：

It is too difficult to think nobly when one thinks only of earning a living.

贫困甚至和暴力、犯罪、动乱和革命紧密联系。《沉思录》[3]的作者罗马皇帝马可·奥勒留[4]曾说：

Poverty is the mother of crime.

特蕾莎修女[5]认为缺乏爱比遭受饥饿更可怕：

Being unwanted, unloved, uncared for, forgotten by everybody, I think that is a much greater hunger, a much greater poverty than the person who has nothing to eat.

核心词
Keywords

1.《社会契约论》（*Social Contract*）
2.让−雅克·卢梭（Jean-Jacques Rousseau）
3.《沉思录》（*Meditation*）
4.马可·奥勒留（Marcus Aurelius）
5.特蕾莎修女（Mother Teresa）

笔记
Notes

We live in a completely interdependent world, which simply means we cannot escape each other. How we respond to AIDS depends, in part, on whether we understand this interdependence. It is not someone else's problem. This is everybody's problem.

Bill Clinton

在 1981~1986 年的五年间，一种全新的、致命的、看似无法控制的疾病出现了——艾滋病[1]，全称为获得性免疫缺陷综合征[2]。

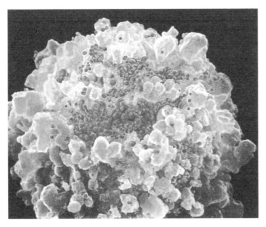

被攻击的 T 细胞
T cell infected with HIV, the agent that causes AIDS

艾滋病首先在旧金山男同性恋群体中发现，后在世界范围的易感人群内蔓延传播，如在经脉注射吸毒者中，而后进入普通人群。

艾滋病由人类免疫缺陷病毒[3]（HIV）导致，这种病毒可以攻击白细胞，削弱免疫系

表达库
Bank of expressions

▶ 【We live in a completely interdependent world, which simply means we cannot escape each other】我们生活在一个完全相互依存的世界，这意味着我们无法逃避彼此。

▶ 【在 1981~1986 年的五年间，一种全新的、致命的、看似无法控制的疾病出现了】In the five years between 1981 and 1986, a new, fatal and apparently uncontrollable disease appeared...

▶ 【首先在旧金山男同性恋群体中发现】First discovered among gay men in San Francisco...

▶ 【后在世界范围的易感人群内蔓延传播，如在经脉注射吸毒者中，而后进入普通人群】it spread across the world among vulnerable groups, such as intravenous drug users, finally into the population at large

▶ 【艾滋病由人类免疫缺陷病毒导致】AIDS is caused by the human immunodeficiency virus (HIV).

▶ 【攻击白细胞】attacks white blood cells

▶ 【削弱免疫系统】weaken the immune system

核心词
Keywords

1. 艾滋病（AIDS）
2. 获得性免疫缺陷综合征（acquired immune deficiency syndrome）
3. 人类免疫缺陷病毒（human immunodeficiency virus，缩写为 HIV）

统。艾滋病因此导致一个人容易受到各种病毒攻击而最终死亡。

常见的可能传染方式包括：

- 和感染者的性行为
- 输入受污染的血液
- 受感染的母亲通过生育或母乳传染给孩子

HIV 通过血液、无保护的性行为、精液或母乳在人际间传播，但是不会通过握手、拥抱、共用毛巾或器皿、一起游泳，甚至咳嗽和喷嚏等方式传播。经唾液传播病毒的风险很低。

通过使用避孕套，性行为传播 HIV 的概率可以大为降低。但是，节欲或与未感染者进行性行为是避免感染最保险的方法。

艾滋病病毒感染者面对着很多挑战，包

全球成人HIV感染率较高的10个国家
Top 10 HIV adult prevalence rate worldwide

Rank	Country	HIV adult prevalence rate (%)
1	Swaziland[斯威士兰]	25.9
2	Botswana[博茨瓦纳]	24.8
3	Lesotho[莱索托]	23.6
4	South Africa[南非]	17.8
5	Zimbabwe[津巴布韦]	14.3
6	Zambia[赞比亚]	13.5
7	Namibia[纳米比亚]	13.1
8	Mozambique[莫桑比克]	11.5
9	Malawi[马拉维]	11
10	Uganda[乌干达]	6.5

► 【艾滋病因此导致一个人容易受到各种病毒攻击而最终死亡】AIDS thus makes a person vulnerable to a wide range of diseases that eventually cause death.

► 【和感染者的性行为】sexual intercourse with an infected person

► 【输入受污染的血液】transfusion with contaminated blood

► 【受感染的母亲通过生育或母乳传染给孩子】transmission from an infected mother to her child because of birth or breast-feeding

► 【HIV 通过血液、无保护的性行为、精液或母乳在人际间传播，但是不会通过握手、拥抱、共用毛巾或器皿、一起游泳，甚至咳嗽和喷嚏等方式传播】HIV is transmitted from person to person through blood, unprotected sex, semen, or breast milk, but not through casual contact such as shaking hands, hugging, sharing towels or dishes, or swimming together or even coughing and sneezing.

► 【经唾液传播病毒的风险很低】The risk of transmitting the virus through saliva is extremely low.

► 【通过使用避孕套，性行为传播 HIV 的概率可以大为降低】The chance of transmitting HIV through sexual activity is greatly reduced by the use of condoms.

► 【节欲或与未感染者进行性行为是避免感染最保险的方法】However, abstinence or a relationship with an uninfected person is the only sure ways to avoid infection.

► 【艾滋病病毒感染者面对着很多挑战】A person diagnosed with HIV infection faces many challenges...

括选择合适的治疗方式、支付医疗费用，以及自己生病期间承担家庭负担。艾滋病感染者通常会感觉非常孤独，因为他们要独自应对灾难性的疾病。孤独、焦虑、恐惧、愤怒和其他情感通常需要更多关注。

象征抗击艾滋病的红丝带
The red AIDS ribbon, a symbol for the fight against AIDS

对于一些发展中国家困难的经济情况，艾滋病的流行导致其他负担。艾滋病通常会让正值壮年的年轻人毙命，这些人是养家糊口的主要支柱。在非洲，疾病严重影响那些有教育、懂技术的工人。熟练劳动力数量下降已经破坏非洲经济增长。

艾滋病被视为一系列新疾病的一种，暴露着人类在新型微生物面前脆弱的一面。

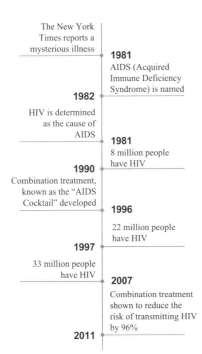

The New York Times reports a mysterious illness	**1981**
	AIDS (Acquired Immune Deficiency Syndrome) is named
1982	
HIV is determined as the cause of AIDS	**1981**
	8 million people have HIV
1990	
Combination treatment, known as the "AIDS Cocktail" developed	**1996**
	22 million people have HIV
1997	
33 million people have HIV	**2007**
	Combination treatment shown to reduce the risk of transmitting HIV by 96%
2011	

HIV 大事记
HIV/AIDS timeline

表达库
Bank of expressions

► 【包括选择合适的治疗方式、支付医疗费用，以及自己生病期间承担家庭负担】including choosing the best course of treatment, paying for health care, and providing for the needs of the family while ill

► 【艾滋病感染者通常会感觉非常孤独，因为他们要独自应对灾难性的疾病】People with AIDS often feel incredibly lonely as they try to cope with a devastating illness on their own.

► 【孤独、焦虑、恐惧、愤怒和其他情感通常需要更多关注】Loneliness, anxiety, fear, anger, and other emotions often require as much attention.

► 【对于一些发展中国家困难的经济情况】For the struggling economies of some developing nations...

► 【艾滋病的流行导致其他负担】the AIDS epidemic has brought yet another burden

► 【艾滋病通常会让正值壮年的年轻人毙命】AIDS tends to kill young adults in the prime of their lives...

► 【养家糊口的主要支柱】the primary breadwinners in families

► 【疾病严重影响那些有教育、懂技术的工人】the disease has had a heavy impact on educated and skilled workers

► 【熟练劳动力数量下降已经破坏非洲经济增长】The decline in the skilled workforce has already damaged economic growth in Africa.

► 【一系列新疾病】a series of emerging diseases

► 【暴露着人类在新型微生物面前脆弱一面】demonstrating how vulnerable humans are to newly encountered microbes

人类不断侵占热带雨林和其他原始森林，释放出未知的病原体。与此同时，全球旅行变得更快捷、更方便、更容易，这导致未知的病原体出现，并且在全世界迅速传播。尽管艾滋病的流行带来很多残酷的现实，但是，人类装备着实践证明行之有效的武器：知识、教育、预防和对病毒行为不断积累的认识。

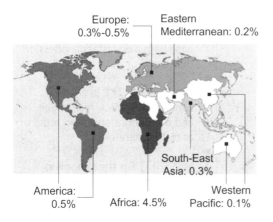

Europe: 0.3%-0.5%
Eastern Mediterranean: 0.2%
South-East Asia: 0.3%
America: 0.5%
Africa: 4.5%
Western Pacific: 0.1%

Global prevalence: 0.8%

世界范围 HIV 感染比率，2012
World adult HIV prevalence, 15-49 years, 2012
Since the beginning of the epidemic, almost 75 million people have been infected with the HIV virus and about 36 million people have died of HIV. An estimated 0.8% of adults aged 15–49 years worldwide are living with HIV. Sub-Saharan Africa remains most severely affected, with nearly 1 in every 20 adults living with HIV.

We must try to find ways to starve the terrorist and the hijacker of the oxygen of publicity on which they depend.

Margaret Thatcher

2001 年的 "9·11" 事件似乎注定要铭刻在每个人的记忆中。当他们听到恐怖分子[1]进攻并摧毁纽约世界贸易中心双子楼、严重损坏华盛顿五角大楼这个可怕消息时，几乎没有人会忘记他们身在何处。

"9·11" 恐怖袭击
Smoke and flames erupting from the twin towers of New York City's World Trade Center after the attacks on September 11, 2001; both towers subsequently collapsed.

"9·11" 事件打碎先前个人、国家及国际社会的主流安全感。事件最直接的产物就

表达库
Bank of expressions

▶【We must try to find ways to starve the terrorist and the hijacker of the oxygen of publicity on which they depend】我们必须设法切断恐怖分子和劫机者赖以生存的公众注意力。

▶【2001 年的 "9·11" 事件似乎注定要铭刻在每个人的记忆中】The events of 9/11 seem destined to remain permanently etched in the minds and memories of everyone.

▶【当他们听到恐怖分子进攻并摧毁纽约世界贸易中心双子楼、严重损坏华盛顿五角大楼这个可怕消息时，几乎没有人会忘记他们身在何处】Few, if any, will ever forget where they were when they first heard the horrendous news that terrorists had attacked and destroyed the twin towers of the World Trade Center in New York and severely damaged the Pentagon in Washington.

▶【"9·11" 事件打碎先前个人、国家及国际社会的主流安全感】The events of 9/11 shattered the preexisting, prevailing sense of personal, national, and international security.

▶【事件最直接的产物就是恐惧】The primary product of 9/11 was the generation of fear.

核心词
Keywords

1. 恐怖分子（terrorist）

是恐惧。热爱和平的人们如何能够摆脱危机四伏的困境？人们如何能够学会每日从容不迫地行走在死亡阴影之下？

恐怖主义是指故意制造和利用恐惧来实现政治目的。所有恐怖主义行为都涉及暴力或暴力威胁。恐怖主义目的在于破坏及削弱政府控制。恐怖活动基本的动机是获得承认或关注。暴力和流血总会引起人们的好奇心。

今天，在这个相互依存的世界，为获得国际承认的这种需要促使更多跨国恐怖行为的发生。宣传可能是一些组织的最高目标。当观众不断增多、更多样化，以及对恐怖活动更习以为常，恐怖分子必须竭尽所能制造震惊。恐怖主义的主要原因包括：

近年发生的恐怖袭击事件
List of recent terrorist attacks

Date	Est. death toll	Name	City
2009	155	Baghdad bombings	Baghdad
2008	175	Mumbai attacks	Mumbai
2007	198	Baghdad bombings	Baghdad
2006	209	Mumbai train bombings	Mumbai
2004	334	Beslan school hostage crisis	Beslan
2004	191	Madrid train bombings	Madrid
2002	202	Bali bombings	Bali
2002	170	Moscow theater hostage crisis	Moscow
2001	2977	September 11 attacks	World Trade Center, The Pentagon
1999	293	Russian apartment bombings	Moscow
1995	168	Oklahoma City bombing	Oklahoma City
1993	257	Bombay bombings	Mumbai
1988	270	Pan Am Flight 103	Lockerbie, Scotland

- 民族主义、分离主义和宗教
- 就业机会、社会地位或政治权利不平等
- 稀缺资源分配不平等
- 抵抗压迫者
- 对国内政治、社会和经济不公平的愤懑
- 抵制外来文化和物品的影响
- 跨国恐怖组织之间的联系

奥萨马·本·拉登[1]号召圣战[2]时说：

They violate our land and occupy it and steal the Muslims' possessions, and when faced by resistance they call it terrorism.

但是，也有人对"9·11"事件提出质疑，认为它是小布什政府自导自演的一场弥天大谎，其中包括迪伦·埃弗里[3]制作的纪录片《脆弱的变化》[4]。

近年发动多起恐怖袭击的组织
Selected terrorist groups

Al-Qaeda [基地组织]	Founded by Osama bin Laden September 11 attacks 1998 U.S. embassy bombings 2002 Bali bombings
Taliban [塔利班]	Originated in Afghanistan The spiritual leader is Mohammed Omar
Liberation Tiger of Tamil Eelam [猛虎组织]	Based in northern Sri Lanka
Hezbollah [真主党]	Based in Lebanon, but also exists in Iran and Syria
Hamas [哈马斯]	The organization was founded with the purpose of Jihad and to release Palestinians from Israeli occupation

表达库
Bank of expressions

▶ 【民族主义、分离主义和宗教】nationalism, separatism, and religion

▶ 【就业机会、社会地位或政治权利不平等】inequalities in employment opportunity, social status, or political rights

▶ 【稀缺资源分配不平等】inequalities in the distribution of scarce resources

▶ 【抵抗压迫者】resistance against an oppressor

▶ 【对国内政治、社会和经济不公平的愤懑】discontent emerging from perceived political, social, and economic inequities within states

▶ 【抵制外来文化和物品的影响】resentments to repel the foreign cultural and material influences

▶ 【跨国恐怖组织之间的联系】transnational links between terrorist groups

▶ 【They violate our land and occupy it and steal the Muslims' possessions】他们侵犯并占领我们的领土，偷窃穆斯林的财富。

核心词
Keywords

1. 奥萨马·本·拉登（Osama bin Laden）
2. 圣战（holy war）
3. 迪伦·埃弗里（Dylan Avery）
4. 《脆弱的变化》（*Loose Change 9/11: An American Coup*）

常见的和毒品相关的表达包括：罂粟[1]，鸦片[2]，吗啡[3]，海洛因[4]，大麻[5]，可卡因[6]，霹雳可卡因[7]，摇头丸[8]和美沙酮[9]。毒品对个人、家庭和社会造成了极大的伤害。

吸食毒品带来各种严重健康问题，影响生活质量，甚至可能威胁生命。长期滥用毒品对心脏、肺部和大脑都会造成伤害。毒品上瘾是一种脑部疾病，脑部的改变会影响个体的决策能力，导致对毒品强迫性渴求、寻找和使用。

家庭为每一个成员提供支持，也维系着社会文化的稳定。家庭以极大的影响力塑造孩子的态度、价值和行为。而毒品的介入，

罂粟流出的乳白汁液
The milky latex sap of opium poppies. Dried latex from the opium poppy is opium.

表达库
Bank of expressions

► 【影响生活质量】diminish the quality of life
► 【可能威胁生命】may threaten survival
► 【长期滥用毒品对心脏、肺部和大脑都会造成伤害】Long-term drug abuse may damage the heart, liver, and brain.
► 【毒品上瘾是一种脑部疾病】Drug addiction is a brain disease...
► 【脑部的改变会影响个体决策能力，导致对毒品强迫性渴求、寻找和使用】these brain changes interfere with an individual's ability to make decisions, leading to compulsive drug craving, seeking and use
► 【家庭为每一个成员提供支持】The family provides support for its individual members...
► 【也维系着社会文化的稳定】ensures the stability for the community and culture
► 【家庭以极大的影响力塑造孩子的态度、价值和行为】Families can have a powerful influence on shaping the attitudes, values and behavior of children.

核心词
Keywords

1. 罂粟（opium poppy）
2. 鸦片（opium）
3. 吗啡（morphine）
4. 海洛因（heroin）
5. 大麻（marijuana）
6. 可卡因（cocaine）
7. 霹雳可卡因（crack cocaine）
8. 摇头丸（ecstasy）
9. 美沙酮（methadone）

会削弱家庭观念，减少归属感。这样的家庭，可能充满各种不稳定[1]、暴力[2]、经济困难[3]、虐待儿童[4]、剥夺教育[5]等问题，以及传播性病的风险。

有组织贩毒[6]，产生大量非法获益，助长腐败，削弱国家权威和法制，严重影响公民的生计和生活质量。吸毒和卖淫有着内在的联系，特别是街头卖淫。此外，吸毒和无家可归有一定的联系。与毒品有关的犯罪也是重要的问题。跨国有组织犯罪和贩毒受到越来越多的关注。

常见毒品介绍
Some illegal drugs and their introductions

Heroin [海洛因]	Processed directly from the extracts of the opium poppy Converts into morphine when inserted into the body
Cocaine [可卡因]	Obtained from the leaves of the coca plant Using cocaine can rapidly lead to dependence and addiction
Marijuana [大麻]	Probably the most-used illicit drug in the world Also called pot, grass, weed, herb
Opium [鸦片]	Obtained from the opium poppy China was forced to legalize opium after the First Opium War (1840) and the Second Opium War (1858)
Crack Cocaine [霹雳可卡因]	One of the most addictive form of cocaine

现在人们越发认识到滥用毒品和贩毒带

表达库
Bank of expressions

► 【会削弱家庭观念】weaken the sense of family
► 【减少归属感】reduce the sense of belonging
► 【传播性病的风险】risk of sexually transmitted disease
► 【产生大量非法获益】generates vast illegal profits
► 【助长腐败】fuels corruption
► 【削弱国家权威和法制】undermines state authority and the rules of laws
► 【严重影响公民的生计和生活质量】has a significant impact on the livelihoods and quality of life of citizens
► 【吸毒和卖淫有着内在的联系，特别是街头卖淫】Drug use is intrinsically linked to prostitution, especially street prostitutes.
► 【吸毒和无家可归有一定的联系】a correlation exists between drug abuse and homelessness
► 【与毒品有关的犯罪也是重要的问题】Drug related crimes are also major concerns.
► 【跨国有组织犯罪和贩毒受到越来越多的关注】Transnational organized crime and drug trafficking is of growing concern.
► 【现在人们越发认识到滥用毒品和贩毒带来的问题】Today there is more awareness of the problems of illicit drug abuse and drug trafficking than ever before.

核心词
Keywords

1. 不稳定（instability）
2. 暴力（violence）
3. 经济困难（economic insecurity）
4. 虐待儿童（child abuse）
5. 剥夺教育（deprivation of schooling）
6. 有组织贩毒（drug trafficking and organized crime）

来的问题。随着经济全球化的影响，毒品从欠发达产地国运往通常较发达的消费国。贩毒问题给国家造成严重的状况，在这一问题上，<u>几乎没有任何国家能够脱离干系</u>。

表达库
Bank of expressions

► 【随着经济全球化的影响，毒品从欠发达产地国运往通常较发达的消费国】Illicit drugs move internationally from producer countries in less developed areas of the world to consumer countries that are usually more developed.
► 【几乎没有任何国家能够脱离干系】few, if any, countries are exempt

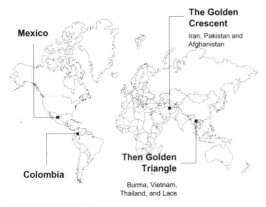

国际主要毒品输出地
World top producers of illicit drugs
The Golden Crescent overlaps three nations, Afghanistan, Iran, and Pakistan. The Golden Triangle overlaps Myanmar, Laos and Thailand.
Afghanistan produces more opium than any other country in the world. In addition, Afghanistan also supplies large amounts of marijuana to the world. Colombia produces more cocaine than any other country in the world. They grow huge amounts of the coca plant. They provide almost all of the cocaine consumed in the United States. Peru comes in second for cocaine production. Burma is the world's second largest producer of opium.

笔记
Notes

据历史记载，第一届古代奥林匹克运动会（以下简称"奥运会"）可以追溯到公元前776年。古代奥运会持续近12个世纪，直到罗马帝国狄奥多西皇帝在公元393年下令禁止举办奥运会。

奥林匹亚[1]，古代奥运会的举办场所，位于希腊南部的伯罗奔尼撒[2]。不论社会地位如何，所有自由的男性希腊公民都有权参加古代奥运会。

被称作"现代奥林匹克之父[3]"的法国人，皮埃尔·德·顾拜旦[4]，从古代奥运会获得灵感。1896年，在古代奥运会被禁止长达1500年后，第一届现代奥运会在雅典举行，旨在提醒人们奥运会起源于希腊。

以古希腊奥运会运动项目为题材的花瓶装饰图案
公元前5世纪，古希腊
Much of our knowledge about the ancient Olympics comes from engravings on ancient pottery, like the scene drawn on this 5th century BC vase.
The ancient Olympic Games were held in honor of Zeus, king of the gods, and were staged every four years at Olympia.

表达库
Bank of expressions

► 【据历史记载，第一届古代奥林匹克运动会可以追溯到公元前776年】 According to historical records, the first ancient Olympic Games can be traced back to 776 BC.

► 【古代奥运会持续近12个世纪，直到罗马帝国狄奥多西皇帝在公元393年下令禁止举办奥运会】 They continued for nearly 12 centuries, until Emperor Theodosius decreed in 393 AD that Olympics Games be banned.

► 【古代奥运会的举办场所】 the site of the ancient Olympic Games

► 【不论社会地位如何，所有自由的男性希腊公民都有权参加古代奥运会】 All free male Greek citizens were entitled to participate in the ancient Olympic Games, regardless of their social status.

► 【从古代奥运会获得灵感】 drew his inspiration from the ancient Olympic Games

► 【在古代奥运会被禁止长达1500年后，第一届现代奥运会在雅典举行，旨在提醒人们奥运会起源于希腊】 more than 1500 years after the ancient Games were banned, the first modern Olympic Games was held in Athens, as a reminder that the Olympic Games originated in Greece

核心词
Keywords

1. 奥林匹亚（Olympia）
2. 伯罗奔尼撒（Peloponnese）
3. 现代奥林匹克之父（the Father of the Modern Olympic Games）
4. 皮埃尔·德·顾拜旦（Pierre de Coubertin）

4年后的1900年法国巴黎奥运会，女性开始参加奥运会，但是只能参加网球和高尔夫两个体育项目。1912年斯德哥尔摩奥运会第一次迎来五大洲国家的代表团。

　　但是，服用兴奋剂[1]让"更高、更快、更强[2]"这一奥运口号[3]一再蒙羞。卷入兴奋剂丑闻的著名运动员包括：

- 本·约翰逊[4]
- 马里恩·琼斯[5]
- 兰斯·阿姆斯特朗[6]

　　本·约翰逊是加拿大田径运动员，在1988年汉城夏季奥运会，打破100米跑世界纪录，赢得金牌，赛后药检却发现他使用类固醇。随后他被剥夺金牌，并被禁赛两年。这在当时甚至现在都是奥林匹克精神的耻辱。1993年，他再次因使用类固醇被抓，被终身禁赛。

　　马里恩·琼斯是美国田径运动员。

第一届现代奥林匹克运动会会场，1896
The first modern Olympic Games in Athens, Greece, in 1896. Pierre de Coubertin is the founder of the International Olympic Committee and is considered the father of the modern Olympic Games.

表达库
Bank of expressions

▶【4年后的1900年法国巴黎奥运会，女性开始参加奥运会，但是只能参加网球和高尔夫两个体育项目】When women made their Olympic debut four years later at the 1900 Games in Paris (France), only two sports were open to them: tennis and golf.

▶【1912年斯德哥尔摩奥运会第一次迎来五大洲国家的代表团】The 1912 Games in Stockholm were the first to boast the presence of national delegations from the five continents.

▶【加拿大田径运动员】Canadian track athlete

▶【1988年汉城夏季奥运会】1988 Seoul Summer Games

▶【赢得金牌】won a gold medal

▶【赛后药检却发现他使用类固醇】a drug test taken after the race, however, revealed his use of steroids

▶【他被剥夺金牌】he was stripped of his Olympic gold medal

▶【这在当时甚至现在都是奥林匹克精神的耻辱】This was and still is a shame to the Olympic spirit.

▶【他再次因使用类固醇被抓，被终身禁赛】Johnson was caught using steroids again and was banned permanently from track competition.

▶【美国田径运动员】American track-and-field athlete

核心词
Keywords

1. 兴奋剂（doping）
2. 更高、更快、更强（Swifter, Higher, Stronger）
3. 奥运口号（Olympic motto）
4. 本·约翰逊（Ben Johnson）
5. 马里恩·琼斯（Marion Jones）
6. 兰斯·阿姆斯特朗（Lance Armstrong）

马里恩·琼斯曾获得悉尼奥运会"百米跑冠军"
Marion Jones sprinting to victory in the 100-metre race at the 2000 Olympic Games in Sydney, Australia

在数年大力否认后，她自己承认使用兴奋剂，最后职业生涯以耻辱告终。她曾在悉尼奥运会获得5枚奖牌，包括100米、200米短跑和4×100米接力金牌。而后，她被迫退回所有奖牌，并被禁赛。2008年，她因作伪证被判入狱6个月。

兰斯·阿姆斯特朗是美国自行车运动员，曾独得7次环法自行车赛冠军。2012年，美国反兴奋剂机构指控他曾使用兴奋剂，不久后便宣布对他终身禁赛，并剥夺所有荣誉。

表达库
Bank of expressions

► 【在数年大力否认后，她自己承认使用兴奋剂】She admitted using performance-enhancing drugs after vigorously denying it for years...
► 【最后职业生涯以耻辱告终】career ended in disgrace
► 【曾在悉尼奥运会获得五枚奖牌】won five medals at the 2000 Olympic Games in Sydney
► 【包括100米、200米短跑和4×100米接力金牌】including gold models in the 100-meter and 200-meter dashes and the 4 × 400-meter relay
► 【被迫退回所有奖牌】was forced to return all her medals
► 【被禁赛】was banned from the sport
► 【她因作伪证被判入狱6个月】she received a six-month prison sentence for committing perjury
► 【美国自行车运动员】American cyclist
► 【曾独得7次环法自行车赛冠军】was the only rider to have won seven Tour de France titles
► 【美国反兴奋剂机构指控他曾使用兴奋剂】the U.S. Anti-Doping Agency charged Armstrong with having used illicit performance enhancing drugs
► 【宣布对他终身禁赛，并剥夺所有荣誉】announced a lifetime ban from competition as well as the stripping of all titles

The mightier man, the mightier is the thing
That makes him honored or begets him hate;
For greatest scandal waits on greatest state.

William Shakespeare

政治丑闻[1]，通常是指政客或政府官员被指控从事犯罪、腐败或不道德的行为。谈到政治丑闻，就不得不介绍如下几个重要事件：

- 水门事件[2]
- 伊朗门事件[3]
- 拉链门事件[4]

1972年美国总统大选，时任总统的理查德·尼克松[5]（以下简称"尼克松"）为确保连任，利用权力指使他人，对民主党总部进行监听，最后导致首次在任美国总统辞职。水门事件严重动摇美国民众对总统的信心；但是另外一方面，水门事件展示着在法治国家没有人凌驾于法律之上，即便总统也不行。

在五个人因闯入位于水门大厦的民主党全国委员会办公室被抓后，尼克松要求手下

尼克松电视讲话，辞去美国总统，1974
Richard Nixon announces his resignation in 1974. Vice President Gerald R. Ford of Michigan takes the oath as the new President.

表达库
Bank of expressions

▶【The mightier man, the mightier is the thing】越强大的人，越会惹出更大的麻烦……
▶【That makes him honored, or begets him hate】给他带来荣誉的东西，也可能让他招恨……
▶【政客或政府官员被指控从事犯罪、腐败或不道德的行为】politicians or government officials are accused of engaging in various illegal, corrupt, or unethical practices
▶【对民主党总部进行监听】wiretap the Democratic Party's campaign headquarters
▶【导致首次在任美国总统辞职】culminating in the first resignation of a U.S. president
▶【水门事件严重动摇美国民众对总统的信心】The Watergate scandal severely shook the faith of the American people in the presidency.
▶【水门事件展示着在法治国家没有人凌驾于法律之上，即便总统也不行】watergate showed that in a nation of laws no one is above the law, not even the president
▶【在五个人因闯入位于水门大厦的民主党全国委员会办公室被抓后】Five men who were caught for breaking and entering into the offices of the Democratic National Committee at the Watergate apartment...

核心词
Keywords

1. 政治丑闻（political scandal）
2. 水门事件（Watergate Scandal）
3. 伊朗门事件（Iran-Contra Affair）
4. 拉链门事件（Lewinsky Scandal）
5. 理查德·尼克松（Richard Nixon）

用尽一切办法防止任何信息透露给媒体。《华盛顿邮报》两名记者通过不懈调查最终揭露出由白宫支持的对付政治对手的间谍计划。最终尼克松被裁定犯有滥用职权侵犯美国公民宪法权、在水门事件中阻碍司法公正等罪行。

　　1985~1986年，美国总统罗纳德·里根（以下简称"里根"）政府的高级官员安排秘密向伊朗出售武器。对伊朗秘密军售的目的，一方面是缓和与伊朗的关系，此外，从亲伊恐怖分子手中获得美国人质。1986年末，一本黎巴嫩杂志揭露美国政府和伊朗秘密军火生意谈判。事后调查结论为，没有证据显示里根违反法律，但是里根对于包庇行为可能参与或者知情。

莱温斯基和克林顿合照，1995
Monica Lewinsky and Bill Clinton photographed together in November 1995.

　　1998年，美国爆出时任美国总统比尔·克林顿[1]（以下简称"克林顿"）和22岁

表达库
Bank of expressions

▶【用尽一切办法防止任何信息透露给媒体】did whatever was necessary to stop leaks to the press
▶【《华盛顿邮报》两名记者通过不懈调查】Persistent investigation by two reporters for the *Washington Post*...
▶【最终揭露出由白宫支持的对政治对手的间谍计划】eventually helped uncover a White House-sponsored plan of espionage against political opponents
▶【滥用职权侵犯美国公民宪法权】misusing his power in order to violate the constitutional rights of U.S. citizens
▶【在水门事件中阻碍司法公正】obstructing justice in the Watergate affair
▶【美国总统罗纳德·里根政府的高级官员安排秘密向伊朗出售武器】high-ranking members in the administration of President Ronald Reagan arranged for the secret sales of arms to Iran
▶【缓和与伊朗的关系】better relations with Iran
▶【从亲伊恐怖分子手中获得美国人质】obtain the release of American hostages held in Lebanon by pro-Iranian terrorists
▶【一本黎巴嫩杂志揭露美国政府和伊朗秘密军火生意谈判】a Lebanese magazine disclosed that the United States government had negotiated an arms deal with Iran
▶【没有证据显示里根违反法律，但是里根对于包庇行为可能参与或者知情】there was no evidence that Reagan had broken the law, but he noted that Reagan may have participated in, or known about, a cover-up

核心词
Keywords

1. 比尔·克林顿（Bill Clinton）

白宫实习生莫尼卡·莱温斯基[1]（以下简称"莱温斯基"）的性丑闻[2]。1998 年，克林顿被弹劾，并被指控滥用权力。事后，克林顿向全国电视观众承认他和莱温斯基有不正当亲昵关系。但是民调显示，大部分美国人认为总统工作尽职，不应该被弹劾或免职。

表达库
Bank of expressions

- ▶ 【白宫实习生】White House intern
- ▶ 【被弹劾】was impeached
- ▶ 【被指控滥用权力】was accused of abuse of power
- ▶ 【克林顿向全国电视观众承认他和莱温斯基有不正当亲昵关系】Clinton acknowledged to a national television audience that he had "inappropriate intimate contact" with Lewinsky
- ▶ 【民调显示大部分美国人认为总统工作尽职，不应该被弹劾或免职】polls showed that a large majority of Americans thought the president was doing a good job and that he should not be impeached or removed from office

核心词
Keywords

1. 莫尼卡·莱温斯基（Monica Lewinsky）
2. 性丑闻（sex scandal）

理查德·尼克松
Richard Nixon (1913-1994)
37th president of the United States, who, faced with almost certain impeachment for his role in the Watergate Scandal, became the first American president to resign from office

罗纳德·威尔逊·里根
Ronald Wilson Reagan (1911-2004)
40th president of the United States, noted for his appealing personal style

比尔·克林顿
Bill Clinton (1946-)
42nd president of the United States, who oversaw the country's longest peacetime economic expansion

笔记
Notes

A business that makes nothing but money is a poor business.

Henry Ford

　有很多人说，公司只需要服从其所在国家的法律，为股东带来最大回报。作为社会的一部分，解决社会面临的迫切问题符合企业的利益。仅当在其运作的社会和生态环境健康时，企业才能蓬勃发展。对社会负责任的企业提供的产品或服务建立在3个基本元素之上：

- 整个社会的福祉
- 满足客户的需求
- 为公司获得利益

　常见的不符合企业社会责任的行为包括：雇佣童工[1]，投资欺诈[2]，污染环境[3]，就业歧视[4]，违反劳工权益[5]，强迫劳动[6]和工作环境恶劣[7]等。

　承担企业社会责任能带来一系列好处，其中包括：

企业社会责任构成
Corporate social responsibility triangle

表达库
Bank of expressions

- 【服从其所在国家的法律】to obey the laws of the countries within which they operate
- 【为股东带来最大回报】maximize returns to its shareholders
- 【作为社会的一部分，解决社会面临的迫切问题符合企业的利益】As a part of society, it is in business' interest to contribute to addressing pressing problem facing society.
- 【仅当在其运作的社会和生态环境健康时，企业才能蓬勃发展】Business can only flourish when the communities and ecosystems in which they operate are healthy.
- 【建立在3个基本元素】is founded on three basic elements
- 【整个社会的福祉】the well-being of the entire society
- 【满足客户的需求】satisfying consumers' needs
- 【为公司获得利益】achieving profit for the company

核心词
Keywords

1. 雇佣童工（employment of child labor）
2. 投资欺诈（investment fraud）
3. 污染环境（environmental pollution）
4. 就业歧视（employment discrimination）
5. 违反劳工权益（labor rights violation）
6. 强迫劳动（forced labor）
7. 工作环境恶劣（hostile work environment）

- 推动创新
- 对环境和社会负责任的产品吸引消费者
- 树立一个公司的品牌和声誉
- 增强招聘和留住员工的能力
- 实现可持续发展

表达库
Bank of expressions

▶ 【推动创新】drive innovation
▶ 【对环境和社会负责任的产品吸引消费者】environmentally or socially responsible products attract customers
▶ 【树立一个公司的品牌和声誉】build a company's brand and reputation
▶ 【增强招聘和留住员工的能力】enhance the ability to recruit and retain staff
▶ 【实现可持续发展】achieve sustainable development

笔记
Notes

20世纪初美国，女童工凝视工厂窗外
A moment's glimpse of the outer world.
Collection of Child Labor in America 1908-1912 by Lewis W. Hine. Said the girl in the photo was 11 years old, been working over a year.

《财富》世界500强前十名公司，2013
Fortune Global 500 Top 10, 2013

Rank	Company name	Operation
1	Royal Dutch Shell	Anglo–Dutch multinational oil and gas company
2	Wal-Mart Stores	American multinational retail corporation
3	Exxon Mobil	American multinational oil and gas corporation
4	Sinopec Group	Asia's largest oil refining and petrochemical enterprise
5	China National Petroleum	Chinese state-owned oil and gas corporation
6	British Petroleum	British multinational oil and gas company
7	State Grid	Chinese state-owned electric utilities company
8	Toyota Motor	Japanese automotive manufacturer
9	Volkswagen	German automobile manufacturer
10	Total	French multinational integrated oil and gas company

Equipped with his five senses, man explores the universe around him and calls the adventure Science.

Edwin Powell Hubble

科学不断质疑自己，理论不断被推翻。科学就是不断搜集新证据、检验想法和假设、完善和扩大我们对宇宙的认识，它还为未来的研究带来新问题。对于一个话题或理论人们可能有共识，但是新的发现可能推翻这个共识，推动科学进步。

伽利略·伽利雷（以下简称"伽利略"）象征着以自由质疑精神反对权威。他第一个将望远镜对准天空的人，他搜集充足数据、勇敢地下结论，最后导致亚里士多德理论的倒台。因此，伽利略被称作"现代科学之父[1]"。

影响科学进程的10位科学家
Ten greatest scientists of all time

Albert Einstein (1879-1955)	General theory of relativity $E=mc^2$ (e equals mc squared) The photoelectric effect
Charles Darwin (1809-1882)	Developed theory of evolution Natural selection
Galileo Galilei (1564-1642)	Father of Modern Science Improved the telescope
James Clerk Maxwell (1831-1879)	Contributed greatly to the understanding electro-magnetism
Leonardo da Vinci (1452-1519)	Contributed to anatomy, understanding of flying, and physics
Louis Pasteur (1822-1895)	Vaccination for rabies, anthrax and other infectious diseases Microbial fermentation
Marie Curie (1867-1934)	Discovered radiation Won Nobel Prize in both Chemistry and Physics
Michael Faraday (1791-1867)	Contributed to electromagnetism and electrochemistry
Nikola Tesla (1856-1943)	Contributed to the design of modern electrical system
Sir Isaac Newton (1642-1726)	Law of gravity Three laws of motion

表达库
Bank of expressions

▶ 【科学不断质疑自己】Science is an area that regularly questions and undermines itself...

▶ 【理论不断被推翻】theories are repeatedly overturned

▶ 【科学就是不断搜集新证据、检验想法和假设、完善和扩大我们对宇宙的认识】Science is continually gathering new evidence, testing ideas and hypotheses, refining and expanding our knowledge of the universe...

▶ 【为未来的研究带来新问题】leads to new questions for future investigation

▶ 【对于一个话题或理论人们可能有共识】There might be some consensus over one specific topic or theory.

▶ 【但是新的发现可能推翻这个共识，推动科学进步】However, new discoveries could overturn the consensus and result in progress in science.

▶ 【伽利略象征着以自由质疑精神反对权威】Galileo Galilei stands as a symbol of the battle against authority for freedom of inquiry.

▶ 【他第一个将望远镜对准天空的人】He has been the first to turn a telescope to the sky

▶ 【搜集充足数据】collected enough data

▶ 【勇敢地下结论】drew conclusions fearlessly

▶ 【最后导致亚里士多德理论的倒台】finally caused a downfall of Aristotle's theory

核心词
Keywords

1. 现代科学之父（the Father of Modern Science）

科学研究就是有逻辑地、系统地针对某个特定的话题寻找新的有用的信息。它是一个探寻知识、寻找隐藏真理的过程。只有通过研究，某个领域才可能取得进步。

科学研究通常由以下几个先后阶段构成：选定研究题目，定义研究问题，收集并阅读文献，分析选定题目目前研究情况，形成假设，设计研究，实际研究，分析数据，解释结论和作报告。

科学研究可以分为：

- 基础研究[1]
- 应用研究[2]

基础研究又称纯研究[3]，或者以好奇为导向的研究[4]。基础科学以研究者的好奇心或兴趣为驱动力，有助于扩展人类的知识，但是没有明显或直接的商业价值。

瑞士日内瓦欧洲粒子加速器设备内部
Large Hadron Collider
The Large Hadron Collider (LHC) is
the world's largest and most powerful particle
accelerator. It first started up on September 10, 2008.
Inside the accelerator, two high-energy particle beams
travel at close to the speed of light before they are
made to collide.

应用研究，又称为以目的为导向的研究[1]，指向一个可以实现的目标。它们的目的在于解决现代社会的实际问题，而不是"为知识而追求知识"。

现代科学各个分支的基础研究都为之后的应用科学打下了基础。基础研究的进步以知识创新和训练有素的科学人员推动应用研究，应用型研究最终创造有销路的产品，促进产生新工作，以及促进经济发展。

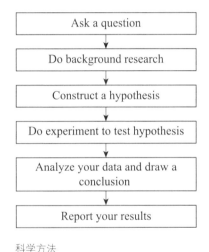

科学方法
Scientific method

不确定性是基础研究的固有特点。自然系统本质上是可变的。可变性让预测变得不确定。测量也伴随着不确定性。研究员使用的仪器，以及作测量的人都会引入不确定性。不完整的知识或观察会导致不确定性。

表达库
Bank of expressions

► 【指向一个可以实现的目标】is directed at a realizable aim

► 【它们的目的在于解决现代社会的实际问题】Applied research is designed to solve practical problems of the modern world...

► 【而不是"为知识而追求知识"】rather than to acquire knowledge for knowledge's sake

► 【现代科学各个分支的基础研究都为之后的应用科学打下了基础】Curiosity-driven researches of all branches of modern science lay down the foundation for the applied science that follows.

► 【基础研究的进步以知识创新和训练有素的科学人员推动应用研究】Fundamental advances in basic research fields fuel applied research with creative knowledge and well-trained workforce...

► 【应用型研究最终创造有销路的产品，促进产生新工作，以及促进经济发展】applied research ultimately creates new marketable products, fuels creation of new jobs, and stimulates economic expansion

► 【不确定性是基础研究的固有特点】Uncertainty is an inherent characteristic of basic research.

► 【自然系统本质上是可变的】Natural systems are inherently variable.

► 【可变性让预测变得不确定】Variability can make predictions uncertain.

► 【测量也伴随着不确定性】Measurement also comes with uncertainty.

► 【研究员使用的仪器，以及作测量的人都会引入不确定性】Instruments researchers use, and people who do the measurement will all introduce inaccuracies.

核心词
Keywords

1. 以目的为导向的研究（goal-oriented research）

科学家和研究者不能准确地预测从基础研究中会发展出怎样的结果。不确定性出现在基础研究的各个阶段。不确定性的价值不能被低估，因为它为研究者留下余地去推翻假设、得出新的结论和作出新的发现。不确定性常常点燃研究者的好奇和疑问。

一些意外的科学发明
Some accidental discoveries

Continental Drift	Alfred Wegener, 1912
Dynamite	Alfred Nobel, 1833
Gunpowder	One of Four Great Inventions
Microwave Oven	Percy Spencer, 1945
Nuclear Fission	Otto Hahn, 1938
Pacemaker	John Hopps, 1941
Penicillin	Alexander Fleming, 1928
Saccharin	Constantin Fahlberg, 1878
The Big Bang	Arno Penzias and Robert Woodrow Wilson, 1964
Viagra	Initially studied for use in high blood pressure, 1990s
Vulcanized Rubber	Charles Goodyear, 1839
X-ray	Wilhelm Röntgen, 1895

表达库
Bank of expressions

► 【不完整的知识或观察会导致不确定性】Incomplete knowledge or observation will result in uncertainty.

► 【科学家和研究者不能准确地预测从基础研究中会发展出怎样的结果】Scientists and researchers cannot well enough predict what's going to develop from basic research.

► 【不确定性出现在基础研究的各个阶段】Uncertainty goes hand in hand with basic research at all stages of the research process.

► 【不确定性的价值不能被低估，因为它为研究者留下余地去推翻假设、得出新的结论和作出新的发现】Uncertainty should not be devalued, because it leaves room for researchers to disprove hypotheses, arrive at new conclusions, and make new discoveries.

► 【不确定性常常点燃研究者的好奇和疑问】Uncertainty usually sparks researchers, curiosity and inquiry.

笔记
Notes

Science never solves a problem without creating ten more.

George Bernard Shaw

　　科技对社会产生巨大影响力，而且这种影响在不断加强。发明或采用新技术为社会带去阵阵变化的涟漪。科学技术成为创新、增加社会福利、提高生产力和创造财富的主要推动力。

　　科技以不同的方式直接或间接地影响人类，比如：

- 科学变化提高公众福祉
- 重大科技革命带来世界观的深刻变化
- 科学技术也带来无数的问题
- 人类改变自我形象

　　科学成就有助于提高公众福祉。通过装备着工业技术，人们使自然屈从于人类的意愿，穿山凿岭、堵塞河流、灌溉沙漠、开采石油。

历史上重要医学进步
Major medical advances of all time

Anesthetics	Crawford W. Long, 1849
Aspirin	Felix Hoffmann, 1897
Blood circulation	William Harvey, 1628
Contraceptives	Birth control pills, condoms and other forms of contraception, 20th century
DNA structure	James Watson and Francis Crick, 1953
Genetics	Gregor Mendel, 1863
Germ Theory	Louis Pasteur, 1864
Insulin	Frederick Banting, 1922
Penicillin	Alexander Fleming, 1928
Smallpox vaccination	Edward Jenner, 1798
Vitamins	Frederick Hopkins, 1901
X-ray	Wilhelm Röntgen, 1895

表达库
Bank of expressions

▶ 【科技对社会产生巨大影响力】Science and technology have had a major impact on society...

▶ 【这种影响在不断加强】their impact is growing

▶ 【发明或采用新技术为社会带去阵阵变化的涟漪】Inventing or adopting new technology sends ripples of change throughout a society.

▶ 【科学技术成为创新、增加社会福利、提高生产力和创造财富的主要推动力】Science and technology are regarded as primary drivers of innovation, social welfare, increased. productivity and wealth creation.

▶ 【科技以不同的方式直接或间接地影响人类】Science and technology affects people in several ways, both directly and indirectly...

▶ 【科学变化提高公众福祉】scientific achievements serve to enhance the public's welfare

▶ 【重大科技革命带来的世界观深刻变化】the profound changes in worldview that have accompanied major scientific revolutions

▶ 【科学技术也带来无数的问题】a myriad of problems which have been created

▶ 【人类改变自我形象】changes on humanity's self-image

▶ 【科学成就有助于提高公众福祉】Scientific achievements serve to enhance the public's welfare.

▶ 【通过装备着工业技术，人们使自然屈从于人类的意愿，穿山凿岭、堵塞河流、灌溉沙漠、开采石油】Armed with industrial technology, we are able to bend nature to our will, tunneling through mountains, damming rivers, irrigating deserts, and drilling for oil.

医学进步有助于提高体质和延长寿命。汽车使人们到处旅行。电话和手机帮助人们高效地进行相互交流。物理学和工程学进步让楼房、桥梁和其他建筑更安全。精彩世界尽在点击间。多亏互联网和电脑，人们可以从世界每一个角落获得信息。

改变世界的发明
Inventions that changed the world

Airplane	The Wright brothers, 1903
Compass	First invented in the Chinese Han Dynasty
Computer	The principle of the modern computer first described by Alan Turing, 1936
Internal combustion engine	Nikolaus Otto made it practical, 1861
Internet	Tim Berners-Lee develops HTML, 1990
Light bulb	Improved by Thomas Edison, 1879
Paper	Cai Lun, Han Dynasty
Printing press	Bi Sheng, 1041, Song Dynasty Johannes Gutenberg, 1450
Steam engine	Patented by James Watt, 1781
Telephone	Patented by Alexander Bell, 1876
Wheel	Enables efficient movement of an object

无可否认科技是一把双刃剑，既能造福又能为祸。技术造成各种环境问题，比如，全球变暖、核废料、物种灭绝和臭氧空洞。人力让步于燃烧化石燃料的发动机，先是煤炭，而后是石油。这样的机器对环境有两方面的影响，

表达库
Bank of expressions

► 【医学进步有助于提高体质和延长寿命】Advances in the medical treatment have facilitated to enhance our physical well-being and lengthen life span.

► 【汽车使人们到处旅行】Automobiles have enabled people to travel from place to place.

► 【电话和手机帮助人们高效地进行相互交流】Telephones and mobile phones help people to communicate with each other more efficiently.

► 【物理学和工程学进步让楼房、桥梁和其他建筑更安全】Advances in physics and engineering make buildings, bridges, and other architectures much safer.

► 【精彩世界尽在点击间】Wonders of the world is just a click away.

► 【多亏互联网和电脑，人们可以从世界每一个角落获得信息】Thanks to the internet and computers, people get access to information from every corner of the world.

► 【无可否认科技是一把双刃剑】No one can deny that technology is a two-edged weapon sword...

► 【既能造福又能为祸】which can be applied equally for good or evil

► 【技术造成各种环境问题，比如，全球变暖、核废料、物种灭绝和臭氧空洞】Technology has caused the environmental consequences such as, global warming, nuclear waste, extinction of species, and holes in the ozone.

► 【人力让步于燃烧化石燃料的发动机】Muscle power gave way to engines that burn fossil fuels...

► 【先是煤炭，而后是石油】coal at first and then oil

► 【这样的机器对环境有两方面的影响】Such machinery affects the environment in two ways...

人类消耗更多自然资源，向环境释放更多污染物。

人们见识到技术破坏性的一面，比如说开发潜艇、机关枪、战舰和化学武器。冷战[1]期间，人们深受核武器的威胁，害怕世界被核武器毁灭。

近代，科技成为人类信仰系统的维度。科学在人类社会享有巨大权威，占有丰富资源。有些人甚至认为，自然科学统治其他任何对生命的解释，比如，哲学的、宗教的、神话的、精神的、人文主义的解释。

科技发明与负面效应
List of inventions and their side effects

Animal testing	Animal suffering
Antibiotics	Abuse of antibiotics and development of antibiotic resistance, creation of multidrug-resistant bacteria
CFCs	Ozone depletion
Computer	Hackers, malicious software, spamming, phishing, and health problem
Fast food	Obesity, type 2 diabetes, heart disease, less of nutrients
Genetically modified food	Unknown genetic effects on humans
Gunpowder and TNT	Machine gun
Mass production of wood furniture	Deforestation
Nuclear fusion	Nuclear weapons Radioactive contamination
Offshore drilling	Oil spill Environmental impacts
Plastic products	Contamination and chemical side effects
Steam engine and automobile	Depleting fossil fuel, vehicle emission, and climate change

虽然科学很强大，但是其局限性也是明显的，比如：

- 科学不作道德判断
- 科学不作审美判断

表达库
Bank of expressions

▶【人类消耗更多自然资源】human consume more natural resources

▶【向环境释放更多污染物】release more pollutants into the environment

▶【人们见识到技术破坏性的一面，比如说开发潜艇、机关枪、战舰和化学武器】People have seen the destructive sides of the technology, such as the development of submarines, machine guns, battleships and chemical weapons.

▶【人们深受核武器的威胁】people were threatened by the nuclear weapons

▶【害怕世界被核武器毁灭】feared the world being destroyed by nuclear weapons

▶【近代，科技成为人类信仰系统的维度】Science and technology have taken on the dimensions of a belief system in recent times.

▶【科学在人类社会享有巨大权威】Science has an immense authority in our society...

▶【占有丰富资源】commandeer abundant resources

▶【自然科学统治其他任何对生命的解释，比如哲学的、宗教的、神话的、精神的、人文主义的解释】natural science has authority over all other interpretations of life, such as philosophical, religious, mythical, spiritual, or humanistic explanations

▶【科学不做道德判断】science doesn't make moral judgments

▶【科学不做审美判断】science doesn't make aesthetic judgments

核心词
Keywords

1. 冷战（the Cold War）

■ 科学不能为生活提供目标、价值和方向

科学不涉及道德判断。比如，科学不能有效地回答如下这些问题。安乐死是否应该立法？其他动物是否应该有权利？科学揭示未知，让我们认清世界；但是每个人作道德判断时，科学就难帮上忙了。科学不能告诉人们如何使用科学知识，这解释了为什么很多科技对环境、人类和社会有负面影响。

科学不能告诉我们一首沃尔夫冈·阿玛多伊斯·莫扎特的曲子是否优美。科学不能判断文森特·凡·高的《星夜》有怎样的价值。不同个体自己作判断时根据个人的审美标准和品位。正所谓"萝卜白菜各有所爱"。爱因斯坦认为：

Science without religion is lame; religion without science is blind.

小马丁·路德·金（以下简称"马丁·路德·金"）认为：

Science investigates; religion interprets. Science gives man knowledge, which is power; religion gives man wisdom, which is control. Science deals mainly with facts; religion deals mainly with values. The two are not rivals.

表达库
Bank of expressions

▶ 【科学不能为生活提供目标、价值和方向】scientific knowledge cannot provide life with goals, values or direction

▶ 【其他动物是否应该有权利】Should other animals have rights？

▶ 【科学不能告诉人们如何使用科学知识】Science doesn't tell you how to use scientific knowledge...

▶ 【不同个体自己作判断时根据个人的审美标准和品位】Individuals make those decisions for themselves based on their own aesthetic criteria and taste.

▶ 【科学离开宗教就好比瘸了腿；宗教离开科学就像瞎了眼】Science without religion is lame；religion without science is blind.

核心词
Keywords

1. 安乐死（euthanasia）
2. 沃尔夫冈·阿玛多伊斯·莫扎特（Wolfgang Amadeus Mozart）
3. 文森特·凡·高（Vincent van Gogh）
4.《星夜》（*Starry Night*）
5. 萝卜白菜各有所爱（One man's meat is another man's poison）
6. 小马丁·路德·金（Martin Luther King Jr.）

笔记
Notes

Chance favors the prepared mind.

Louis Pasteur

历史一次次地证明，<u>抓住运气可以产生更多科学发现</u>。"幸福的意外[1]"确实在科学进步上起了重要作用，其中包括：

- 艾萨克·牛顿[2]（以下简称"牛顿"）与掉落的苹果[3]
- 威廉·伦琴[4]（以下简称"伦琴"）与 X 射线[5]
- 亚历山大·弗莱明[6]（以下简称"弗莱明"）发现青霉素[7]

1665 年，牛顿从剑桥回到乡下躲避肆虐的黑死病。据说，一次他坐在树下，看到一颗苹果从树上掉落，这促发他得出了万有引力定律[8]。

1895 年，伦琴在研究阴极射线[9]时，

牛顿受掉落苹果启发的故事
There is a popular story that Newton was sitting under an apple tree, an apple fell on his head, and he suddenly thought of the universal law of gravitation.

表达库
Bank of expressions

► 【抓住运气可以产生更多科学发现】
luck can be harnessed to make more scientific discoveries
► 【幸福的意外确实在科学进步上起了重要作用】Happy accidents have indeed played an important role in scientific progress...
► 【从剑桥回到乡下躲避肆虐的黑死病】escaped the worst ravages of the Black Plague
► 【看到一颗苹果从树上掉落】saw an apple falling from a tree

核心词
Keywords

1. 幸福的意外（happy accident 或 serendipity）
2. 艾萨克·牛顿（Isaac Newton）
3. 掉落的苹果（falling apple）
4. 威廉·伦琴（Wilhelm Röntgen）
5. X 射线（X-rays）
6. 亚历山大·弗莱明（Alexander Fleming）
7. 青霉素（penicillin）
8. 万有引力定律（universal law of gravitation）
9. 阴极射线（cathode ray）

笔记
Notes

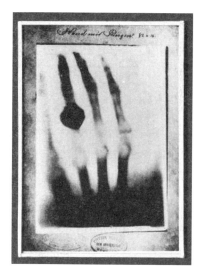

伦琴妻子右手的 X 射线片
The hand belonged to Anna Bertha, wife of German physicist Wilhelm Röntgen, the discover of X-rays. The black glob on the fourth finger is a ring made of gold, which absorbs X-rays. Röntgen stumbled across X-rays on November 8, 1895 and the photo was taken on December 22 1895.

意外地把手放到真空管前，结果发现自己骨头的轮廓被投射到荧光屏上去。伦琴发现 X 射线以不同的程度通过不同的物质，不久，X 射线在医疗诊断方面的应用很快便展开了。

　　1928 年，弗莱明没有清理试验台就去度假。度假回来他发现培养皿里长着霉菌，而霉菌的周围没有细菌生长。经过进一步实验，弗莱明认定这种霉菌产生抑制大量致病细菌生长的物质。弗莱明因发现世界上第一种抗生素而根本改变人类医学。

弗莱明在自己的实验室
Alexander Fleming discovered penicillin

放射性现象[1]、苯环结构[2]、微波炉[3]、糖精[4]、聚四氟乙烯[5]、心脏起搏器[6]、安全玻璃[7]等发明或发现都有一定运气成分。但是，机遇总是垂青时刻做好准备的人。托马斯·阿尔瓦·爱迪生[8]（以下简称"爱迪生"）曾经说过："<u>天才就是百分之九十九的汗水加百分之一的灵感</u>。"

表达库
Bank of expressions

► 【天才就是百分之九十九的汗水加百分之一的灵感】Genius is one percent inspiration and ninety-nine percent perspiration.

核心词
Keywords

1. 放射性现象（radioactivity）
2. 苯环结构（structure of benzene）
3. 微波炉（microwave oven）
4. 糖精（saccharin）
5. 聚四氟乙烯（teflon）
6. 心脏起搏器（pacemaker）
7. 安全玻璃（safety glass）
8. 托马斯·阿尔瓦·爱迪生（Thomas Alva Edison）

笔记
Notes

牛顿
Sir Isaac Newton
(1643-1727)
English physicist and mathematician, the culminating figure of the scientific revolution of the 17th century

威廉·伦琴
Wilhelm Röntgen
(1845-1923)
Physicist who was a recipient of the first Nobel Prize for Physics, in 1901, for his discovery of X-rays, which heralded the age of modern physics and revolutionized diagnostic medicine

克隆
Cloning

从格雷戈尔·孟德尔的豌豆实验奠定现代遗传理论，到詹姆斯·沃森和弗朗西斯·克里克确定脱氧核糖核酸分子结构，再到人类基因组计划，遗传学进步很大。但是，这些科学进步同样也伴随着严峻的伦理道德问题。

克隆人，一旦成为现实，将会是最近几十年生殖技术的重大突破。之前几次重大的生殖技术进步，包括人工受孕、试管授精及试管婴儿、代孕妈妈和将精子直接注入卵子。

克隆在自然界很常见，比如，细菌一

遗传学发展里程碑
Timeline of milestones in the history of genetics

1866	Austrian botanist Gregor Mendel laid foundation of the science of genetics
1869	Swiss biochemist Johann Friedrich Miescher became the first to isolate nuclein—now known as DNA
1900	Mendel's experiments were rediscovered
1931	Chromosomes was founded to form the basis of genetics
1944	DNA was prove to be the genetic material of the cel
1953	James Watson and Francis Crick determined the molecular structure of DNA
1970s	The techniques for DNA sequencing were proposed
1990	The Human Genome Project (HGP) began

分为二自我克隆，产生两个相同的细菌。现在科学家开始研究人工克隆哺乳动物技术。1997 年，克隆的多利羊[1]出生。原则上讲，和多利羊一样，人类也可以被克隆。

但是克隆人技术却遇到巨大的争议。赞成这项技术的人持的观点包括：

- 对抗众多遗传疾病
- 为需要器官移植的病人提供可替换的器官和组织
- 为不孕不育夫妇提供解决办法

一种可以预见的可能是，使用克隆技术治疗糖尿病、帕金森综合征或某些其他血癌。造血干细胞研究使用干细胞修复受损或病变组织。例如，人体无法修复或替换因疾病或损伤而破损的神经细胞。干细胞移植可以发育成神经细胞来治愈帕金森综合征。

反对克隆技术的人所持观点包括：

孟德尔修道院的豌豆园，今在捷克共和国境内
Gregor Mendel's garden at the Augustine monastery
in the Czech Republic

表达库
Bank of expressions

▶ 【产生两个相同的细菌】produce two identical bacteria
▶ 【现在科学家开始研究人工克隆哺乳动物技术】Now scientists have developed artificial cloning techniques that work with mammals.
▶ 【原则上讲，和多利羊一样，人类也可以被克隆】In principle, humans could be cloned in the same way as Dolly.
▶ 【对抗众多遗传疾病】combat a wide range of genetic diseases
▶ 【为需要器官移植的病人提供可替换的器官和组织】provide replacement of internal organs and tissues for patients in need of transplants
▶ 【为不孕不育夫妇提供解决办法】provide a solution to the infertility issue among couples
▶ 【一种可以预见的可能是，使用克隆技术治疗糖尿病、帕金森综合征或某些血癌】One possibility envisioned would be to use cloning techniques to treat diseases like diabetes, Parkinson's disease or perhaps certain cancers of the blood.
▶ 【造血干细胞研究使用干细胞修复受损或病变组织】Stem cell research is investigating the use of stem cells to repair damaged or diseased tissue.
▶ 【人体无法修复或替换因疾病或损伤而破损的神经细胞】the body cannot repair or replace nerve cells damaged by disease or injury
▶ 【干细胞移植可以发育成神经细胞来治愈帕金森综合征】Transplanted stem cells could be grown to develop into new nerve cells to treat Parkinson's disease.

核心词
Keywords

1. 多利羊（Dolly the Sheep）

- 遗传多样性之美可能失去
- 故意在人体里产生令人讨厌的特征
- 严重贬低生命价值
- 提出严重的道德问题

克隆人研究在一些国家被禁止。人类可能复制克隆人用来做仆人或打仗。我们可能克隆某些影星或体育明星。克隆人不是一个独一无二的个体。在这些情况下，克隆人不会因自身价值而受到重视，也不会作为一个独特的人而被尊重。更不用说克隆人技术对传统家庭价值和伦理道德的冲击。

克隆可能只是少数富人的特权。富裕的家庭可以利用克隆技术给他们的后代可以想象到的最好的特征。这样，贫富之间的差距会比想象中还要大。

詹姆斯·杜威·沃森
James Dewey Watson (1928-)
American geneticist and biophysicist who played a crucial role in the discovery of the molecular structure of deoxyribonucleic acid (DNA)

弗朗西斯·克里克
Francis Crick (1916-2004)
British biophysicist, who, with James Watson and Maurice Wilkins, received the 1962 Nobel Prize for Physiology or Medicine for their determination of the molecular structure of deoxyribonucleic acid (DNA)

表达库
Bank of expressions

▶ 【遗传多样性之美可能失去】the beauty of genetic diversity could be lost

▶ 【故意在人体里产生令人讨厌的特征】deliberately produce undesirable traits in human beings

▶ 【严重贬低生命价值】seriously devalues and undermines the value of human life

▶ 【提出严重的道德问题】raises several serious moral questions

▶ 【克隆人研究在一些国家被禁止】Human cloning research has already been banned in many countries.

▶ 【人类可能复制克隆人用来做仆人或打仗】We might make clones that could be used for doing menial work or fighting wars.

▶ 【我们可能克隆某些影星或体育明星】We might want to clone certain stars of the screen or athletic arena.

▶ 【克隆人不是一个独一无二的个体】The person cloned would not be a unique individual.

▶ 【这些情况下，克隆人不会因自身价值而受到重视，也不会作为一个独特的人被尊重】In all of these cases, the clone would neither be valued for his or her own self nor respected as a unique person.

▶ 【富裕的家庭可以利用克隆技术给他们的后代可以想象到的最好的特征】Wealthy families might use cloning technology to give their offspring the best characteristics imaginable.

▶ 【贫富之间的差距会比想象中还要大】the divide between the wealthy and the poor could widen farther than ever imagined

Coal, oil and gas are called fossil fuels, because they are mostly made of <u>the fossil remains of beings</u> from long ago. The chemical energy within them is a kind of <u>stored sunlight originally accumulated by ancient plants</u>. <u>Our civilization runs by burning the remains of humble creatures</u> who inhabited the Earth hundreds of millions of years before the first humans came on the scene. Like some <u>ghastly cannibal cult</u>, we subsist on the dead bodies of our ancestors and distant relatives.

Carl Sagan

人类离不开能源,从古至今主要的能源包括:

- 使用火 [1]
- 化石燃料 [2]
- 水力发电 [3]
- 核能 [4]
- 地热能 [5]
- 风能 [6]
- 太阳能 [7]

<u>原始人主要以食物方式获取能量,他们通过食用采集或捕杀来的植物或动物消耗能量。随后,人类发现了火。</u>他们对能源的需求上升,因为他们开始使用木柴满足煮饭和

表达库
Bank of expressions

- ► 【fossil remains of beings】生物化石遗迹
- ► 【stored sunlight originally accumulated by ancient plants】最初由远古植被积累的太阳能
- ► 【Our civilization runs by burning the remains of humble creatures】燃烧这些卑微生物遗骸推动人类文明……
- ► 【ghastly cannibal cult】恐怖的食人部落
- ► 【原始人主要以食物方式获取能量】Primitive men required energy primarily in the form of food.
- ► 【他们通过食用采集或捕杀来的植物或动物消耗能量】They consumed energy by eating plants or animals which they gathered or hunted.
- ► 【随后人类发现了火】Subsequently they discovered fire.
- ► 【他们对能源的需求上升,因为他们开始使用木柴满足煮饭和取暖的需求】Their energy needs increased as they started to make use of wood to supply the energy needs for cooking as well as for keeping himself warm.

核心词
Keywords

1. 使用火(control of fire)
2. 化石燃料(fossil fuel)
3. 水力发电(hydropower)
4. 核能(nuclear energy)
5. 地热能(geothermal energy)
6. 风能(wind power)
7. 太阳能(solar energy)

取暖的需求。掌握生火技能让人类的在夜晚活动，使人类免受捕食者的伤害。随着时间的推移，人类开始开垦土地种植作物。通过驯养动物为其服务，人类在使用能源方面又进一步。随着对能源的进一步需求，人类开始利用风能驱动船只和风车，以及利用水能驱动水轮。

在依靠人力很久之后，人类终于找到汲取深埋在地下的能量的方法。石油、煤炭，这部分被储存起来的太阳能量把人类从辛苦的耕作中解脱出来。石油让人类挣脱时间的枷锁。

工业革命开始于蒸汽机的发明和改进。人类第一次开始大规模使用煤炭。不久后，

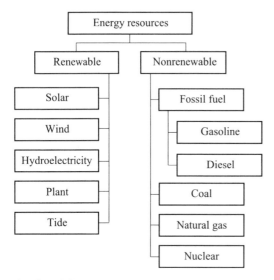

常见能源分类
Types of energy resources. Renewable energy is generally defined as energy that comes from resources which are naturally replenished on a human timescale such as sunlight, wind, rain, tides, waves and geothermal heat. Fossil fuels, such as coal, petroleum, and natural gas, are nonrenewable energy.

表达库
Bank of expressions

▶【掌握生火技能让人类的在夜晚活动】Making fire also allowed the expansion of human activity into the colder hours of the night...

▶【使人类免受捕食者的伤害】provided protection from predators

▶【随着时间的推移，人类开始开垦土地种植作物】With the passage of time, men started to cultivate land for agriculture.

▶【通过驯养动物为其服务，人类在使用能源方面又进一步】They added a new dimension to the use of energy by domesticating and training animals to work for them.

▶【随着对能源的进一步需求，人类开始利用风能驱动船只和风车】With further demand for energy, men began to harness the wind for sailing ships and for driving windmills...

▶【利用水能驱动水轮】used the force of falling water to turn water wheels

▶【在依靠人力很久之后，人类终于找到汲取深埋在地下的能量的方法】After relying on muscle-power for so long, humankind found a way to tap into the energy buried deep in the earth.

▶【这部分被储存起来的太阳能量把人类从辛苦的耕作中解脱出来】this pocket of sunlight freed humans from their toil on the land

▶【石油让人类挣脱时间的枷锁】Fossil oil began the era of humans who break free of the shackles of time.

▶【工业革命开始于蒸汽机的发明和改进】The Industrial Revolution began with the invention and improvement of the steam engine.

▶【人类第一次开始大规模使用煤炭】For the first time, men began to use coal in large quantities.

内燃机被发明，石油和天然气被广泛使用。由于化石燃料，人类获得前所未有的舒适。化石燃料，如煤炭和石油，是非可再生能源。现在，化石能源迅速地消耗殆尽，化石燃料的时代逐渐走向终结。此外，化石燃料燃烧时排放有害废气。

　　水能是一种自然资源。从古代，水能一直被用来灌溉和驱动各种机械，如水车等。等进入 20 世纪，发电机改进、水轮机进一步改良，以及对电力的需求不断增长，水力重获新生。水电是一种无污染的可再生能源。在水力发电站，水能被转化成电能，然

世界著名水坝
List of amazing dams in the world

Three Gorges Dam	Yangtze River, China The world's largest power station in terms of installed capacity
Aswan Dam	Nile River in Aswan, Egypt Control floods, provide water for irrigation, and generate hydroelectricity
Jinping-I Hydropower Station	Yalong River, China The tallest dam in the world
Hoover Dam	Black Canyon of the Colorado River

中国三峡水电站
Three Gorges Dam
Today it generates enough electricity to power nations the size of Switzerland and Pakistan.

表达库
Bank of expressions

► 【不久后，内燃机被发明】A little later, the internal combustion engine was invented...

► 【石油和天然气被广泛使用】oil and natural gas began to be used extensively

► 【由于化石燃料，人类获得前所未有的舒适】Thanks to fossil fuel, human acquired unprecedented comforts.

► 【化石燃料，如煤炭和石油，是非可再生能源】Fossil fuels such as coal and petroleum are nonrenewable energy sources.

► 【化石能源迅速地消耗殆尽】Fossil fuel resources are fast depleting...

► 【化石燃料的时代逐渐走向终结】fossil fuel era is gradually coming to an end

► 【化石燃料燃烧时排放有害废气】fossil fuels release harmful waste gases when burnt

► 【水能是一种自然资源】Water power is a natural resource.

► 【从古代，水能一直被用来灌溉和驱动各种机械，如水车等】Since ancient times, water power has been used for irrigation and the operation of various mechanical devices, such as watermills.

► 【等进入 20 世纪，发电机改进、水轮机进一步改良，以及对电力的需求不断增长，水力重获新生】The rebirth of hydropower had to await the development of the electric generator, further improvement of the hydraulic turbine, and the growing demand for electricity by the turn of the 20th century.

► 【水电是一种无污染的可再生能源】Hydroelectricity is a nonpolluting renewable energy source.

► 【在水力发电站，水能被转化成电能】In a hydroelectric power plant, water power is turned into electricity...

后通过输配电网送至用户。

第二次世界大战后，一种新能源——核能——横空出世。核能是在核反应期间，大量能量以热量形式被释放出来的。这部分热量可以用来发电。铀和其他核物质具有放射性，它们能释放有害生物的核辐射。在民用核能的历史上已经发生了三次重大的反应堆事故。

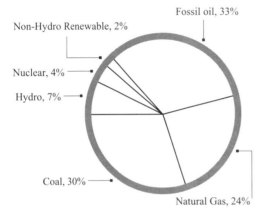

Non-Hydro Renewable, 2%

Fossil oil, 33%

Nuclear, 4%

Hydro, 7%

Coal, 30%

Natural Gas, 24%

世界能源消耗
World energy consumption by source, 2012

风能是一种可再生能源，可以替代化石燃料。几个世纪以来，农民一直用风车抽水和碾碎谷物。风能不会造成温室气体排放。大型风电场可以包括几百个独立的风力涡轮机组。地热能利用地球内部的热量，是一种可再生能源。

人们可以通过地热能发电。在冰岛，人们利用地热能发电，为房屋供暖。

太阳能，来自太阳的辐射光和热量，自古就被人类利用。太阳能产生风，能让植物生长，能产生降水。水电、风能、潮汐能都来自太阳。煤炭、石油和天然气是数以百万计捕捉阳光的植物，深埋地下数百万年形成的能源。只要太阳存在，太阳能就取之不尽用之不竭。在 20 世纪，爱迪生对于太阳能等可再生能源[1]表现出乐观态度，他说：

We are like tenant farmers chopping down the fence around our house for fuel when we should be using Nature's inexhaustible sources of energy—sun, wind and tide. ... I'd put my money on the sun and solar energy. What a source of power! I hope we don't have to wait until oil and coal run out before we tackle that.

伊万帕太阳能发电设施，美国加州
Ivanpah Solar Power Facility, one of the world's largest solar thermal plant, in the California Mojave Desert, 40 miles (64 km) southwest of Las Vegas

表达库
Bank of expressions

► 【人们可以通过地热能发电】 People now can produce electricity from geothermal energy.

► 【在冰岛，人们利用地热能发电，为房屋供暖】 In Iceland, people use geothermal power to make electricity and heat homes.

► 【太阳能，来自太阳的辐射光和热量，自古就被人类利用】 Solar energy, radiant light and heat from the sun, has been harnessed by humans since ancient times.

► 【太阳能产生风，能让植物生长，能产生降水】 The sun causes winds to blow, plants to grow, rain to fall.

► 【水电、风能、潮汐能都来自太阳】 Hydroelectric power, wind power and wave power are all derived from the sun.

► 【煤炭、石油和天然气是数以百万计捕捉阳光的植物，深埋地下数百万年形成的能源】 Coal, oil, and natural gas are millions of plants which captured the energy of sun light and buried deep in the earth for millions of years.

► 【只要太阳存在，太阳能就取之不尽用之不竭】 As long as the sun exists, the sun's energy will be inexhaustible.

► 【We are like tenant farmers chopping down the fence around our house for fuel】 人类就像是佃农，砍倒房子周围的篱笆用作燃料……

► 【inexhaustible sources of energy】 用之不竭的能量来源

核心词
Keywords

1. 可再生能源（renewable energy）

A nation that can't control its energy sources can't control its future.

Barack Obama

能源安全[1]可以被定义成：提供价格合理、可以依赖，并且有益于环境的能源。保障国家能源供给成为每个国家的实力政策。当今世界的游戏不仅仅是政治和经济影响范围的角力，更是有关制定能源市场的游戏规则。

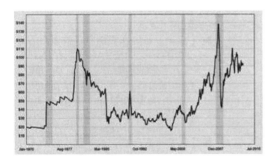

原油价格历史走势
Crude oil price history chart

世界上剩余的油气储备主要集中在波斯湾地区、中亚地区和俄罗斯。一些国家在不远的未来将面临依赖能源强国的危险。此外，大部分中东地区政治不稳定导致石油生产无法预测。让我们一起回顾一下几次主要的能源危机：

表达库
Bank of expressions

► 【可以被定义成】could be defined as
► 【提供价格合理、可以依赖，并且有益于环境的能源】the provision of reasonably priced, reliable and environmentally friendly energy
► 【保障国家能源供给成为每个国家的实力政策】Securing national energy supply has become the tough realpolitik for every country.
► 【当今世界的游戏不仅仅是政治和经济影响范围的角力】Today's game is not only about wrestling for political and economic influence zones...
► 【更是有关制定能源市场的游戏规则】it is more about defining the rules of the game for the energy markets
► 【世界上剩余的油气储备主要集中在波斯湾地区、中亚地区和俄罗斯】The remaining oil and gas reserves are concentrated in the Persian Gulf, in central Asia and Russia.
► 【在不远的未来将面临依赖能源强国的危险】face the risk of becoming dependent on the new great energy powers in the near future
► 【大部分中东地区政治不稳定导致石油生产无法预测】political instability in much of the Middle East has created a situation where oil production is unpredictable

核心词
Keywords

1. 能源安全（energy security）

- 第一次石油危机[1]
- 第二次石油危机[2]
- 第三次石油危机[3]

石油危机中排队等待买油的美国民众
Line-up at a Los Angeles gas station in anticipation of rationing, May 11, 1979

第一次石油危机开始于 1973 年，石油输出国组织[4]利用石油作为武器打击西方对以色列的支持。第二次石油危机发生在 1979 年，先是伊朗爆发伊斯兰革命[5]，而后伊朗和伊拉克爆发两伊战争[6]，导致原油产量锐减。第三次石油危机发生于 1990 年，主要原因是海湾战争[7]爆发。

石油和天然气的储量在不断减少，但是需求却不断增加。只有煤炭储备看上去在一定时间内是充足的。但是燃烧煤炭给环境带来巨大的负担，世界范围的温室气体排放会进一步增加。自然资源开采正在威胁北极圈、海洋、热带雨林、北欧森林的原始生态环境。有毒废物威胁本土动植物群落。虽然

表达库
Bank of expressions

► 【利用石油作为武器打击西方对以色列的支持】 used oil as a weapon to attack the West's support of Israel

► 【石油和天然气的储量在不断减少】 Reserves of oil and gas are diminishing...

► 【但是需求却不断增加】 while demand is increasing

► 【只有煤炭储备看上去在一定时间内是充足的】 Only coal reserve still appear to be sufficient for a while.

► 【但是燃烧煤炭给环境带来巨大的负担】 However, the combustion of coal reserves would place an enormous burden on the environment.

► 【世界范围的温室气体排放会进一步增加】 Worldwide emissions of the greenhouse gas would increase even further.

► 【自然资源开采正在威胁北极圈、海洋、热带雨林、北欧森林的原始生态环境】 Exploitation of natural resources is threatening the once pristine environment in the Arctic, in the oceans, and in tropical rain forests and Nordic forests.

► 【有毒废物威胁本土动植物群落】 Poisonous waste threaten the indigenous fauna and flora.

核心词
Keywords

1. 第一次石油危机（the 1973 Oil Crisis）
2. 第二次石油危机（the 1979 Oil Crisis）
3. 第三次石油危机（the 1990 Oil Price Spike）
4. 石油输出国组织（Organization of the Petroleum Exporting Countries，简称 OPEC）
5. 伊斯兰革命（Iranian Revolution）
6. 两伊战争（Iran-Iraq War）
7. 海湾战争（Gulf War）

一些国家发现储量丰富的油砂[1]，但是从油砂中提取石油消耗大量通过燃烧天然气加热的水。并且，大规模开采油砂对环境产生的影响目前只能大致估计。

加拿大开采油砂的矿场
The Athabasca Oil Sands, Alberta, Canada. These oil deposits make up the largest reservoir of crude bitumen in the world. However, collateral damage from the booming oil sands sector may be irreversible and pose a significant environmental risk to the local environment.

世界十大石油产地, 2013
List of top 10 largest oil producers in the world, 2013

Rank	Country	Production (bbl/day)	Share of World's output (%)
1	Russia	10,730,000	12.65
2	Saudi Arabia	9,570,000	11.28
3	United States	9,023,000	10.74
4	Iran	4,231,000	4.77
5	China	4,073,000	4.56
6	Canada	3,592,000	3.90
7	Iraq	3,400,000	3.75
8	United Arab Emirates	3,087,000	3.32
9	Mexico	2,934,000	3.56
10	Kuwait	2,682,000	2.96

Conversion from oil barrel to cubic meter:
1 bbl = 0.1589873 m^3

► 【从油砂中提取石油消耗大量通过燃烧天然气加热的水】the petroleum extracted from oil sands consumes large quantities of water heated by natural gas combustion
► 【大规模开采油砂对环境产生的影响目前只能大致估计】The environmental impact of large-scale exploitation of oil sand can only be estimated.

核心词
Keywords

1. 油砂（oil sand）

笔记
Notes

I would like nuclear fusion to become a practical power source. It would provide an inexhaustible supply of energy, without pollution or global warming.

Stephen Hawking

　　常见的核反应堆之一是沸水反应堆。沸水反应堆通过煮沸水产生电能。核燃料加热水，水沸腾后产生蒸汽，蒸汽驱动涡轮机组发电，冷却后的蒸汽凝结成水，然后这些水又继续被核燃料加热。常见的核燃料是氧化铀[1]。

　　1954 年，苏联建成第一座核反应堆。很多人曾经一度期望核能可以替代日益稀缺的化石燃料，降低空气污染，并且降低电价。但是，人们对核能有种种顾虑：

- 由泄漏导致的环境污染
- 核废料问题没有解决办法
- 掩埋核废料伴随着环境和健康风险
- 存在核辐射泄漏的危险

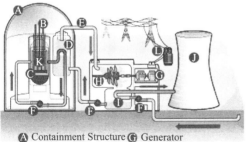

A Containment Structure　G Generator
B Control Rods　　　　 H Turbine
C Reactor　　　　　　　 I Cooling Water Condenser
D Steam Generator　　　 J Cooling Tower
E Steam Line　　　　　　K Fuel Rods
F Pump　　　　　　　　 L Transformer

核电站内部结构
Inside a nuclear power plant

表达库
Bank of expressions

▶ 【provide an inexhaustible supply of energy】提供取之不尽的能源
▶ 【沸水反应堆】boiling water reactor
▶ 【通过煮沸水产生电能】produce electricity by boiling water
▶ 【核燃料加热水】The nuclear fuel heats water...
▶ 【水沸腾后产生蒸汽】the water boils and creates steam
▶ 【蒸汽驱动涡轮机组发电】the steam then drives turbines that create the electricity
▶ 【冷却后的蒸汽凝结成水】the steam is then cooled and condensed back to water
▶ 【这些水又继续被核燃料加热】the water returns to be heated by the nuclear fuel
▶ 【核能可以替代日益稀缺的化石燃料，降低空气污染，并且降低电价】nuclear power would replace increasingly scarce fossil fuels, reduce air pollution, and lower the cost of electricity
▶ 【由泄漏导致的环境污染】environmental pollution caused by leakage
▶ 【核废料问题没有解决办法】nuclear wastes are an unresolved problem
▶ 【掩埋核废料伴随着环境和健康风险】burying nuclear waste is an environmental and health risk
▶ 【存在核辐射泄漏的危险】existence of radiation exposure hazards

核心词
Keywords

1. 氧化铀（uranium oxide）

- 铀矿开采产生大量的温室气体
- 发生重大事故的危险
- 核电厂需要大量的水将废热排到环境中
- 核电厂容易受到恐怖袭击

同时，不断发生的核事故让核能的未来变得扑朔。世界范围内发生的重大核事故包括：

- 三里岛事故[1]
- 切尔诺贝利核事故[2]
- 福岛第一核电站事故[3]

1979 年，美国宾夕法尼亚州三里岛[4]的核电站发生核电历史上最严重的事故之一。该次事故的原因是堆芯熔化，导致少量的核物质泄漏到环境中。

1986 年，发生在乌克兰[5]的切尔诺贝利核事故，被认为是人类历史上最严重的核电站事故。爆炸和大火导致大量的核污染物释放到大气当中。

切尔诺贝利核事故
In the early hours of April 26 1986, one of four nuclear reactors at the Chernobyl power station exploded

表达库
Bank of expressions

- 【铀矿开采产生大量的温室气体】uranium mining produces substantial amounts of greenhouse gas
- 【发生重大事故的危险】risk of a major disaster
- 【核电厂需要大量的水将废热排到环境中】nuclear plants require significant quantities of water to remove the waste heat into the environment
- 【核电厂容易受到恐怖袭击】nuclear power plants are vulnerable to terrorist attacks
- 【堆芯熔化】core meltdown
- 【导致少量的核物质泄漏到环境中】results in the release of small amounts of radioactive substances into the environment
- 【爆炸和大火导致大量的核污染物释放到大气当中】An explosion and fire released large quantities of radioactive contamination into the atmosphere.

核心词
Keywords

1. 三里岛事故（Three Mile Island accident）
2. 切尔诺贝利核事故（Chernobyl disaster）
3. 福岛第一核电站事故（Fukushima Daiichi nuclear disaster）
4. 三里岛（the Three Mile Island）
5. 乌克兰（Ukraine）

福岛第一核电站事故
Fukushima Daiichi nuclear disaster

2011 年，日本发生地震[1]和海啸[2]，随后导致<u>反应堆堆芯熔毁</u>，<u>大量辐射污染释放</u>。

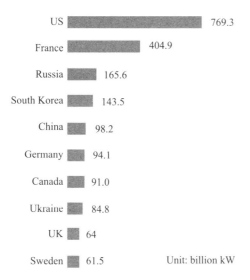

US 769.3
France 404.9
Russia 165.6
South Korea 143.5
China 98.2
Germany 94.1
Canada 91.0
Ukraine 84.8
UK 64
Sweden 61.5   Unit: billion kW

Top 10 nuclear generating countries, 2012
世界核能发电量排名前十国家

表达库
Bank of expressions

► 【反应堆堆芯熔毁】reactor core meltdown
► 【大量辐射污染释放】releases of high level of radioactive materials

核心词
Keywords

1. 地震（earthquake）
2. 海啸（tsunami）

笔记
Notes

The Internet is becoming the town square for the global village of tomorrow.

Bill Gates

我们处在一个新世纪和新千年的开始。同时，我们也正将离开工业时代，迈入人类历史的新时代——网络时代。今天，人类正在创造网络时代全新的经济、社会、文化和政治环境。

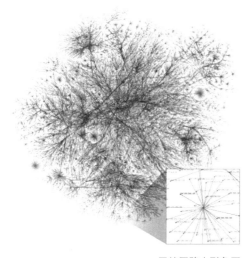

因特网路由形象图
An Opte Project, started by Barrett Lyon, an American Internet entrepreneur, visualization of routing paths through a portion of the Internet

在这个网络化的世界里，我们是网络社会的一部分，我们在信息经济环境里运作，在网络都市里工作，在地球村里生活，在无边界的世界里从事贸易。网络为与外界相对隔离封闭的社会提供开放的机会。

对于多数大众传媒，信息流动仅是单方向的，即从信息发布者到公众。而网络，却

表达库
Bank of expressions

► 【The Internet is becoming the town square for the global village of tomorrow】因特网正在成为未来地球村的城市广场。

► 【我们处在一个新世纪和新千年的开始】We stand at the start of a new century and a new millennium.

► 【同时，我们也正将离开工业时代，迈入人类历史的新时代——网络时代】At the same time, we are leaving the Industrial Age and crossing the threshold of a new age in human history, the Cyber Age.

► 【今天，人类正在创造网络时代全新的经济、社会、文化和政治环境】Today we are creating the new economic, social, cultural, and political environments of the Cyber Age.

► 【在这个网络化的世界里，我们是网络社会的一部分，我们在信息经济环境里运作，在网络都市里工作，在地球村里生活，在无边界的世界里从事贸易】In the new networked world we are now part of a network society, operate in an information economy, work in a cyber metropolis, live in a global village, and trade in a borderless world.

► 【网络为与外界相对隔离封闭的社会提供开放的机会】The internet affords dramatic possibilities for opening up societies that are relatively insular and closed to the outside world.

► 【对于多数大众传媒，信息流动仅是单方向的，即从信息发布者到公众】In most mass media, information flows in one direction only, from its creators to the public.

创造一个共享信息的虚拟社区，网站提供平等的、不拘形式的交流平台让更多人发表言论。视频分享网站让用户上传分享各种各样的电影剪辑、电视节目剪辑、音乐视频和原创短片等。网络聊天成为最常用的社交手段。视频聊天和语音聊天很受欢迎。

贝尔实验室研制的调制解调器，1958
Bell Labs invented modem, 1958
Bell Labs researchers invented the modem, which converts digital signals to electrical (analog) signals and back, enabling communication between computers

　　社交软件包括一系列让用户交换和分享数据的软件。即时消息应用程序让人们利用网络实时交流。网络论坛让用户发布主题与他人分享，其他用户可以查看话题并发表自己的意见。每天都有成千上万来自网络好友的更新信息，现在普通人的朋友圈子比以前大很多。人们现在可以很自由地和不同背景的人进行讨论。

网络极大地改变了人类世界。人们可以上网理财、购物、订机票，以及炒股。网上银行改变了人们的理财方式。人们可以通过网络支付、转账，并且比以往任何时候都能更加细节地了解他们的银行账户。

客户可以舒服地待在家里，在一天任何时候网购杂货。超市网站列出所有库存商品，客户可以浏览挑选自己需要的东西，然后安排时间送货。

ASCII Alphabet			
A	1000001	N	1001110
B	1000010	O	1001111
C	1000011	P	1010000
D	1000100	Q	1010001
E	1000101	R	1010010
F	1000110	S	1010011
G	1000111	T	1010100
H	1001000	U	1010101
I	1001001	V	1010110
J	1001010	W	1010111
K	1001011	X	1011000
L	1001100	Y	1011001
M	1001101	Z	1011010

1963 年提出的美国信息交换标准代码
ASCII developed, 1963
The first universal standard for computers, ASCII (American Standard Code for Information Exchange) is developed by a joint industry-government committee. ASCII permits machines from different manufacturers to exchange data.

信息技术给人们带来方便，但是这些便利却不乏代价，也带来数不尽的麻烦。

表达库
Bank of expressions

► 【现在普通人的朋友圈子比以前大很多】It turns out the size of the common people social circle is larger today than before.

► 【人们现在可以很自由地和不同背景的人进行讨论】People are now open to discuss with others from different backgrounds.

► 【网络极大地改变了人类世界】The internet has changed the world we live in dramatically.

► 【人们可以上网理财、购物、订机票，以及炒股】People can do their banking and shopping, book flights, and do stock trading on line.

► 【网上银行改变了人们的理财方式】Online banking has changed the way people handle their finances.

► 【人们可以通过网络支付、转账，并且比以往任何时候都能更加详细地了解他们的银行账户】They can pay bills online, transfer funds, and get a more detailed view of their bank accounts than ever before.

► 【客户可以舒服地待在家里，在一天任何时候网购杂货】Shoppers can order their groceries on line 24 hours a day from the comfort of their own homes.

► 【超市网站列出所有库存商品】Supermarket websites list all the goods available in the store.

► 【客户可以浏览挑选自己需要的东西，然后安排时间送货】Shoppers can browse and select what they want, then arrange a time for delivery.

► 【信息技术给人们带来方便】Information technology has brought us convenience.

► 【但是这些便利却不乏代价】However, these conveniences came at a price.

► 【带来数不尽的麻烦】caused incalculable problems

你的信用卡账号、身份证号码可能被窃。人们的隐私可能被侵犯。人们也看到各种网络犯罪，比如，电子邮件欺诈、色情、网络赌博。人们无视版权，从网络上下载音乐，打印文章。

万维网标志设计
World Wide Web logo designed by Robert Cailliau
The World Wide Web is made available to the public for the first time on the Internet in 1991. Robert Cailliau together with Tim Berners-Lee, developed the World Wide Web.

有人说，技术让人们与朋友和社会日益分离。人们花越来越多的时间盯着屏幕或喋喋不休地打着手机，而不是面对面地真诚地交流。网络和其他即时通信形式可能会影响生活质量。有了短信，只需发出信息，你就会很快得到回复。手机变成了生活的遥控器。与世隔绝在我们的生活中变得日益普遍。

网络可以用来逃避现实或填补空虚。网瘾患者没有时间概念，废寝忘食。网瘾患者认为网络比家庭、朋友和工作更为重要。他们宁愿牺牲最珍视的东西来继续上网。越来越多的青少年沉溺网络，上网过度会对学业和家庭生活产生严重负面影响。大学生是上网成瘾的高危人群。很多学生在电脑屏幕前虚度青春。很多城市青少年犯罪和网络有关。网络色情泛滥催生一种新形式的性瘾。网络色情和网络色情上瘾会影响社会关系，甚至毁掉人的一生。

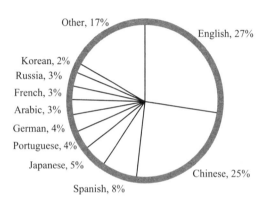

全球各国因特网用户，根据语言排名
Percentage of Internet users by language

► 【网络可以用来逃避现实或填补空虚】The internet serves as an escape or to fill a void.

► 【网瘾患者没有时间概念，废寝忘食】People who have internet addiction can lose all track of time or neglect eating and sleeping.

► 【网瘾患者认为网络比家庭、朋友和工作更为重要】Internet addicts make the internet a priority more important than family, friends, and work.

► 【他们宁愿牺牲最珍视的东西来继续上网】They are willing to sacrifice what they cherish most in order to continue their unhealthy behavior.

► 【越来越多的青少年沉溺网络】More and more teenagers are addicted to the internet.

► 【上网过度会对学业和家庭生活产生严重负面影响】Their devotion to the cyber world has created serious negative effects in their school and home lives.

► 【大学生是上网成瘾的高危人群】College students are the highest risk for internet addiction.

► 【很多学生在电脑屏幕前虚度青春】Students may waste too much of their youth in front of a computer screen.

► 【很多城市青少年犯罪和网络有关】Most juvenile crimes in the city are internet-related.

► 【网络色情泛滥催生一种新形式的性瘾】The widespread availability of sexual content online has given rise to a new form of sexual addiction.

► 【网络色情和网络色情上瘾会影响社会关系，甚至毁掉人的一生】Cyber-porn and cyber-sexual addictions destroy relationships and ruin one's life.

人体需要食物生长、繁殖及保持健康。均衡的饮食[1]包含碳水化合物[2]、蛋白质[3]、脂肪[4]、维生素[5]、矿物质[6]和纤维[7]。

缺乏蛋白质可能导致发育迟缓。过多的脂肪和糖分可能导致肥胖。血液中胆固醇含量过高和心脏病、中风及其他健康问题有联系。身体需要少量维生素和矿物质来触发体内大量化学反应，以保持健康。

常见的和食品有关的话题包括：

- 工业化农业生产[8]
- 食品安全[9]
- 有机农业[10]
- 方便食品[11]
- 素食主义[12]

工业化的农业方法产出廉价的肉制品：

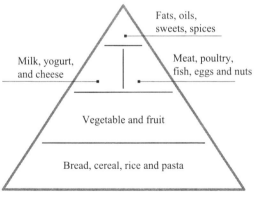

膳食金字塔
Food guide pyramid
Also called the healthy eating pyramid

表达库
Bank of expressions

► 【人体需要食物生长、繁殖及保持健康】Human beings require food to grow, reproduce, and maintain good health.
► 【缺乏蛋白质可能导致发育迟缓】Lack of protein can cause stunted growth.
► 【过多的脂肪和糖分可能导致肥胖】Too much fat and sugar can result in obesity.
► 【血液中胆固醇含量过高和心脏病、中风和其他健康问题有联系】High levels of cholesterol in the blood have been linked to the development of heart disease, strokes, and other health problems.
► 【身体需要少量维生素和矿物质来触发体内大量化学反应，以保持健康】Both vitamins and minerals are needed by the body in very small amounts to trigger the thousands of chemical reactions necessary to maintain good health.
► 【工业化的农业方法产出廉价的肉制品：牛肉、猪肉和鸡肉】Industrialized farming methods produce cheap meat product: beef, pork and chicken.

核心词
Keywords

1. 均衡的饮食（balanced diet）
2. 碳水化合物（carbohydrate）
3. 蛋白质（protein）
4. 脂肪（fat）
5. 维生素（vitamin）
6. 矿物质（mineral）
7. 纤维（fiber）
8. 工业化农业生产（industrial agriculture）
9. 食品安全（food safety）
10. 有机农业（organic farming）
11. 方便食品（convenience food）
12. 素食主义（vegetarianism）

牛肉、猪肉和鸡肉。使用杀虫剂和肥料产出廉价的谷物和蔬菜。大量廉价食物的出现也伴随着巨大的代价：砍伐森林[1]，土壤荒漠化，化肥和农药的滥用，化石燃料的减少，对全球生物多样化的威胁，疯牛病[2]，沙门氏菌[3]等。

人类的饮食从来没有像今天这样危险；但是其他人坚称由于科技创新，人类饮食达到了前所未有的安全。当今的食品种类几乎要超出政府的监管范围。全球化的食品运输，加上需要延长保质期，意味着需要使用化学品处理食物。基因工程可能引起进一步的危害。<u>每年有越来越多的食物中毒事件被报道</u>。

世界各国成年人肥胖比率
Obesity—adult prevalence rate 2014 Country/Area Ranks

Rank	Country/Area	Prevalence rate (%)
1	American Samoa [美属萨摩亚]	74.6
2	Tokelau [托克劳群岛]	63.4
3	Tonga [汤加]	56
4	Kiribati [基里巴斯]	50.6
5	Saudi Arabia	35.6
6	United States	33.9
7	United Arab Emirates	33.7
8	Egypt	30.3
9	Kuwait	28.8
10	New Zealand	26.5

有机农业不使用化学合成农药[4]、抗生素[5]、

表达库
Bank of expressions

► 【使用杀虫剂和肥料产出廉价的谷物和蔬菜】The use of pesticides and fertilizers produces cheap grain and vegetables.
► 【化肥和农药的滥用】fertilizers and pesticides abuse
► 【化石燃料减少】fossil fuel depletion
► 【对全球生物多样化的威胁】threats to global biodiversity
► 【人类的饮食从来没有像今天这样危险】Our consumption of food has never been such a hazardous activity as it is today.
► 【但是其他人坚称由于科技创新，人类饮食达到了前所未有的安全】while others insist that thanks to scientific innovations, it has never been safer.
► 【当今的食品种类几乎要超出政府的监管范围】The range of foods available today is nearly outstripping governmental efforts to inspect them.
► 【全球化的食品运输，加上需要延长保质期，这意味着需要使用化学品处理食物】The global transport of foods, coupled with the need to extend their shelf-life, means the use of chemical treatments.
► 【基因工程可能引起进一步的危害】Genetic engineering also may be giving rise to further hazard.
► 【每年有越来越多的食物中毒事件被报道】More and more food poisoning cases are reported each year.

核心词
Keywords

1. 砍伐森林（deforestation）
2. 疯牛病（mad cow disease）
3. 沙门氏菌（salmonella）
4. 化学合成农药（synthetic pesticides）
5. 抗生素（antibiotics）

转基因种子和动物品种、生长激素[1]等。有机农业使用从植物、动物粪便和矿物中提取的杀虫剂和农药，利用一种生物体去抑制其他生命体来控制害虫。这些方法可以增加土壤肥力，平衡昆虫数量，减少空气、土壤和水的污染。

方便食品通常是一些包装食品[2]，可以快速轻松地准备好，比如说，各种现成的菜、冷冻食品、加工好的肉制品、软饮料和各种垃圾食品等。方便食品中通常含盐分、糖分和脂肪过多，长期使用增加患肥胖[3]、糖尿病[4]和高血压[5]的风险。方便食品增加了对塑料的使用。

食素的原因各有不同，比如，有些人出于对生命的尊重拒绝吃肉，也有一些人是由于宗教信仰的原因食素，还有的人是出于保护动物权利[6]，而越来越多的人为了健康而食素。素食主义者有很多种，其中完全拒绝动物产品的称为"严格素食主义[7]"。

几种不同的素食主义
Levels of different vegetarianisms

素食主义	禁忌食物
Vegan [纯素食主义]	Meat, meat by-products, eggs, dairy, honey
Lacto vegetarianism [奶素食主义]	Meat, Meat by-products, eggs
Ovo vegetarian [蛋素食主义]	Meat, Dairy by-product (milk, cheese)
Locto-ovo vegetarian [奶蛋素食主义]	Meat
Pollotarian [禽肉素食主义]	Red meat (beef, lamb, pork), fish and seafood
Pescetarian [鱼素食主义]	Red meat (beef, lamb, pork), poultry and fowl

表达库
Bank of expressions

► 【转基因种子和动物品种】 genetically modified seeds and animal breeds
► 【使用从植物、动物粪便和矿物中提取的杀虫剂和农药】 uses pesticides and fertilizers derived from plants, animal wastes, and minerals
► 【利用一种生物体去抑制其他生命体】 uses one organism to suppress another
► 【控制害虫】 control pests
► 【增加土壤肥力】 increase soil fertility
► 【平衡昆虫数量】 balance insect populations
► 【减少空气、土壤和水的污染】 reduce air, soil, and water pollution
► 【可以快速轻松地准备好】 can be prepared quickly and easily
► 【现成的菜】 ready-to-eat dish
► 【冷冻食品】 frozen product
► 【加工好的肉制品】 processed meat
► 【软饮料】 soft drink
► 【垃圾食品】 junk food
► 【增加了对塑料的使用】 increases usage of plastics
► 【出于对生命的尊重拒绝吃肉】 object to eating meat out of respect for life
► 【宗教信仰】 religious belief

核心词
Keywords

1. 生长激素（growth hormones）
2. 包装食品（packaged food）
3. 肥胖（obesity）
4. 糖尿病（diabetes）
5. 高血压（high blood pressure）
6. 动物权利（animal right）
7. 严格素食主义（veganism）

经过近一个世纪，人类从马车跨越到一个充满成千上万辆汽车的世界。从 T 型车到最新的跑车，有一样东西保持不变——内燃发动机。

在这些发动机中，混合均匀的汽油和空气被喷入燃烧室。当引入火花，油气混合物爆炸，驱动活塞下行，并旋转曲轴。活塞上行时将燃烧残余排出燃烧室。这个往复的循环被称为奥托循环 [1]。

用尾气中未燃烧的燃料、二氧化碳和一氧化碳的量，乘以马路上汽车的数量，你就明白为什么传统汽车被看做是环境的重大威

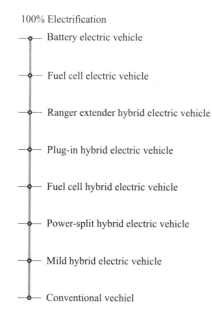

100% Electrification

— Battery electric vehicle

— Fuel cell electric vehicle

— Ranger extender hybrid electric vehicle

— Plug-in hybrid electric vehicle

— Fuel cell hybrid electric vehicle

— Power-split hybrid electric vehicle

— Mild hybrid electric vehicle

— Conventional vechiel

几种清洁能源汽车
Types of clean energy vehicles

表达库
Bank of expressions

▶【人类从马车跨越到一个充满成千上万辆汽车的世界】we have gone from the horse and buggy to a world teeming with hundreds of millions of automobiles

▶【从 T 型车到最新的跑车，有一样东西保持不变】From the Motel T to the latest race cars, one thing remains the same…

▶【内燃发动机】internal combustion engine

▶【混合均匀的汽油和空气被喷入燃烧室】a fine mixture of gasoline and air is sprayed into the combustion chamber

▶【当引入火花，油气混合物爆炸，驱动活塞下行，并旋转曲轴】When a spark is added, the mixture of air and fuel explodes, driving the piston down and spinning the crankshaft.

▶【活塞上行时将燃烧残余排出燃烧室】As the piston moves back up, it pushes the remnants of the combustion out of the chamber.

▶【用尾气中未燃烧的燃料、二氧化碳和一氧化碳的量，乘以马路上汽车的数量】Take the unburned fuel, carbon dioxide and carbon monoxide in that exhaust, multiply it by the number of cars on the roads…

▶【你就明白为什么传统汽车被看作是环境的重大威胁了】you can see why the conventional automobile is considered such a serious threat to the environment.

核心词
Keywords

1. 奥托循环（Alto Cycle）

胁了。化石燃料储量不断减少，油价不断飙升，环境问题越发紧迫，这些促使人类加快了发明和制造绿色环保汽车的步伐。

新推出的有益于环境的汽车包括：

- 混合动力汽车[1]
- 电动车[2]
- 燃料电池电动车[3]
- 太阳能汽车[4]

混合动力车以内燃发动机[5]和电动机[6]作为动力。换句话说，传导到车轮的能量可以来自由车载电池能量驱动的电动机，或者来自内燃机，或者来自两个动力的混合。

混合动力车在一些情况下可以减少燃油消耗。从全球角度来看，混合动力车有助

混合动力汽车
The Toyota Prius was the first mass-produced hybrid electric vehicle (HEV). HEVs are environmentally friendly, fuel efficient and operating smoothly

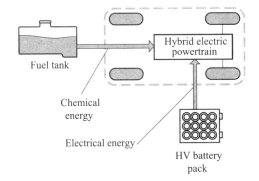

混合动力车动力系统
Hybrid electric vehicle powertrain

表达库
Bank of expressions

▶ 【化石燃料储量不断减少，油价不断飙升，环境问题越发紧迫，这些促使人类加快了发明和制造绿色环保汽车的步伐】Ever-decreasing fossil fuel reserves, soaring oil prices, pressing environmental concerns, pushes human to speed up steps to invent and produce environmentally friendly cars.

▶ 【传导到车轮的能量可以来自由车载电池能量驱动的电动机】power to the wheel can either come from an electric motor which is powered by energy stored in batteries on the vehicles

▶ 【或者来自内燃机】or from the internal combustion engine

▶ 【或者来自两个动力的混合】or from a combination of both propulsion sources

▶ 【混合动力车在一些情况下可以减少燃油消耗】HEVs could reduce petroleum consumption under certain circumstances.

▶ 【从全球角度来看，混合动力车有助于减少温室气体排放】At a global level, HEV can help to reduce the emissions of greenhouse gases.

核心词
Keywords

1. 混合动力汽车（hybrid electric vehicle，简称 HEV）
2. 电动车（electric vehicle）
3. 燃料电池电动车（fuel cell electric vehicle）
4. 太阳能汽车（solar vehicle）
5. 内燃发动机（internal combustion engine）
6. 电动机（electric motor 或 electric machine）

于减少温室气体排放。从地区角度来看，特别是城市，混合动力车能减少空气中氮氧化物。

1900 年左右，电动车是主要的运输方式，但是它没能克服自身缺点，从而失去早期竞争优势。蓄电池是它的致命弱点。插电式混合动力车[1]指的是通过外部电源，比如说墙上插座，进行充电的汽车。电动汽车可以改善空气质量，减少燃油消耗。

目前，制约电动汽车的主要因素有：当前电池技术的限制，基础设施的缺口，安全性能不确定，市场前景不明朗，售价过高。电动车项目任重道远。

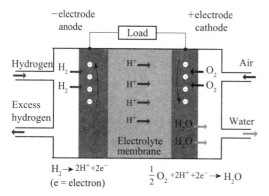

-electrode anode

Load

+electrode cathode

Hydrogen H_2 H_2

H^+ H^+ H^+ H^+

Air O_2 O_2

Excess hydrogen

Electrolyte membrane

H_2O H_2O

Water

$H_2 \rightarrow 2H^+ + 2e^-$
(e = electron)

$\frac{1}{2}O_2 + 2H^+ + 2e^- \rightarrow H_2O$

质子交换燃料电池
Schematic of proton exchange membrane (PEM) fuel cell. PEM fuel cells used in automobiles employ hydrogen fuel and oxygen from the air to produce electricity.

和柴油车不一样，燃料电池车工作时很

表达库
Bank of expressions

► 【从地区角度来看，特别是城市，混合动力车能减少空气中氮氧化物】At a local level, particularly in urban areas, HEV can reduce the amount of oxides of nitrogen in the atmosphere.

► 【1900 年左右，电动车是主要的运输方式】The electric vehicle was a dominant transportation factor around 1900.

► 【没能克服自身缺点】was not able to overcome the shortcomings

► 【从而失去早期竞争优势】lose its early competitive edge

► 【蓄电池是它致命弱点】The electric storage battery was its Achilles' heel.

► 【通过外部电源，比如说墙上插座，进行充电的汽车】can be recharged from any external source of electricity, such as wall sockets

► 【电动汽车可以改善空气质量，减少燃油消耗】Electric vehicles could improve air quality and reduce fuel consumption.

► 【当前电池技术的限制】limitations of current battery technology

► 【基础设施的缺口】gaps in required infrastructure

► 【安全性能不确定】uncertain safety

► 【市场前景不明朗】uncertain market potential

► 【售价过高】high purchase price

► 【电动车项目任重道远】The electric vehicle program has a long way to go.

► 【和柴油车不一样】Unlike diesel-powered cars...

► 【燃料电池车工作时很安静】fuel cell cars run with no noise

核心词
Keywords

1. 插电式混合动力车（plug-in hybrid electric vehicle）

安静，尾气只有水。燃料电池通过电化学反应将氢气燃料和氧气的化学能直接转化成电能。燃料电池最有希望解决未来能源问题。

太阳能经常用来为在太阳系内运转的卫星和宇宙飞船提供能量，一些科学家已经研制出来用太阳能驱动的汽车。太阳能板上的太阳能电池将光能直接转化成电能，这部分电能或储存在电池中或直接用来驱动汽车。但是，太阳能电池车有其缺点，比如，在没有阳光的条件下，汽车要依赖电池能量。尽管阳光是免费的，但是捕捉阳光的太阳能板造价很高。

世界太阳能汽车挑战赛参赛汽车
Solar vehicle, produced by Honda, made to compete in the World Solar Challenge.

To the well-organized mind, death is but the next great adventure.

J. K. Rowling

罗伯特·拉蒂默对十二岁的瘫痪女儿实施安乐死

In 1993, a Canadian wheat farmer, Robert Latimer, ended his 12-year-old daughter's severely compromised life, in what became Canada's most famous case of mercy killing. He killed his daughter Tracy Latimer, who had a severe condition of cerebral palsy, by pumping carbon monoxide into his truck. Latimer was granted full parole, effective December 6th, 2010.

安乐死指的是仁慈地结束一个人的生命，使其免遭不治之症、难忍痛苦或有损尊严的死亡。安乐死对医生提出很多道德问题。

主动安乐死[1]是指医生对病人使用可以致死剂量的药品，无痛地结束病人生命。被动安乐死[2]是指医生停止治疗，比如说，医生停止使用呼吸机。自愿安乐死[3]是指一个人主动要求死亡。非自愿安乐死[4]是指结束一个人的生命，但是他已经神志不清无法作出明智的死亡请求。

表达库
Bank of expressions

► 【仁慈地结束一个人的生命】mercifully end a person's life
► 【使其免遭不治之症、难忍痛苦或有损尊严的死亡】in order to release the person from an incurable disease, intolerable suffering, or undignified death
► 【安乐死对医生提出很多道德问题】The issue of euthanasia raises ethical questions for physicians.
► 【医生对病人使用可以致死剂量的药品】doctors administer a lethal dose of medication to a patient
► 【无痛地结束病人生命】painlessly put him or her to death
► 【停止治疗】discontinue common treatment
► 【医生停止使用呼吸机】doctors refrain from using an artificial respirator
► 【一个人主动要求死亡】a person voluntarily asks to die
► 【结束一个人的生命】ending the life of a person
► 【但是他已经神志不清无法作出明智的死亡请求】but he or she is not mentally competent to make an informed request to die, such as a comatose patient

核心词
Keywords

1. 主动安乐死（active euthanasia）
2. 被动安乐死（passive euthanasia）
3. 自愿安乐死（voluntary euthanasia）
4. 非自愿安乐死（nonvoluntary euthanasia）

安乐死支持者所持的理由包括：

- 安乐死合法化有助于减轻不治之症患者的痛苦
- 个体有自由和权利选择死亡
- 安乐死可以减轻家庭的医疗费用负担

安乐死反对者所持的理由包括：

- 安乐死贬低了生命价值
- 医疗工作者的职责是治病救人
- 安乐死被处理不当或被利用的可能性很大
- 家人出于对财产的贪欲结束病人的生命
- 自私的家人不想照顾年迈的病人

I will give no deadly medicine to anyone if asked, nor suggest any such counsel; and in like manner I will not give to a woman an abortive remedy.

The Hippocratic Oath

表达库
Bank of expressions

▶【安乐死合法化有助于减轻不治之症患者的痛苦】legalizing euthanasia would help alleviate suffering of terminally ill patient
▶【个体有自由和权利选择死亡】an individual should have the liberty and freedom to choose death
▶【减轻家庭的医疗费用负担】relieve the economic burden of health care cost
▶【贬低生命价值】devalues human life
▶【医疗工作者的职责是治病救人】medical professionals' purpose is healing people and saving lives
▶【安乐死被处理不当或被利用的可能性很大】there is a greater possibility of euthanasia being mishandled and manipulated
▶【家人出于对财产的贪欲结束病人的生命】family members might want to terminate patents' lives out of greed for inheritance money
▶【自私的家人不想照顾年迈的病人】selfish relatives don't want to look after sick elderly people

笔记
Notes

Everything in the world is about sex except sex. Sex is about power.

Oscar Wilde

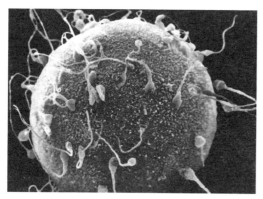

当精子遇见卵子
When sperms meet an egg

从生理学角度来讲，性是人类繁殖的方式。女性的卵子和男性的精子，各包含 23 条染色体，结合形成受精胚胎。在这些染色体中，母亲贡献的 X 染色体和父亲贡献的 X 或 Y 染色体，决定孩子的性别。第二条来自父亲的 X 染色体产生雌性胚胎，来自父亲的 Y 染色体产生雄性胚胎。

一些身体特征将男性和女性区别开来。从一出生，两性就有不同的第一性征。青春期开始于身体分泌某些特定荷尔蒙。身体从青春期开始产生剧烈变化，第二性征开始发育。但是，性别可以通过手术改变。

表达库
Bank of expressions

► 【从生理学角度来讲】From a biological point of view...
► 【性是人类繁殖的方式】sex is the way humans reproduce
► 【女性的卵子和男性的精子，各包含 23 条染色体，结合形成受精胚胎】A female ovum and a male sperm, each containing 23 chromosomes, combine to form a fertilized embryo.
► 【在这些染色体中，母亲贡献的 X 染色体和父亲贡献的 X 或 Y 染色体，决定孩子的性别】To one of these pairs of chromosomes, which determines the child's sex, the mother contributes an X chromosome and the father contributes either an X or a Y.
► 【第二条来自父亲的 X 染色体产生雌性胚胎】A second X from the father produces a female embryo.
► 【来自父亲的 Y 染色体产生雄性胚胎】A Y from the father produces a male embryo.
► 【一些身体特征将男性和女性区别开来】Some differences in the body set males and females apart.
► 【从一出生，两性就有不同的第一性征】Right from birth, the two sexes have different primary sex characteristics.
► 【青春期开始于身体分泌某些特定荷尔蒙】Puberty begins when your body starts to produce more of certain hormones.
► 【身体从青春期开始产生剧烈变化】Puberty is a big step towards having rapid changes...
► 【第二性征开始发育】the secondary sex characteristics are developed
► 【性别可以通过手术改变】Sex can be surgically changed.

变性就是从一种性别变成另一种。变性手术伴随荷尔蒙治疗可以改变个人性征。

异性恋指的是对异性有性吸引。同性恋指的是对同性有性吸引。双性恋指的是对两性都有性吸引。无性恋指的是对任何性别都缺乏性吸引。

很多文化视性为禁忌。即便在今天，很多人也讳莫如深。尽管性可以带来快乐，它也带来混乱、忧虑，有些时候还有恐惧。20世纪，人们对待性和性行为的态度发生了深刻的变化。

城市发展也促进了人们对性的新认识。很多男男女女从乡村移居到迅速发展的城市中。在那里，远离家庭，在工作场合接触新朋

代表美国性解放女性衣着的"摩登女郎"
The "flapper" style symbolized women's increased sexual freedom in the 1920s.

表达库
Bank of expressions

▶【变性就是从一种性别变成另一种】Sex change is a change from one sex to other.

▶【变性手术伴随荷尔蒙治疗可以改变个人性征】Sex-change surgery with accompanying hormonal treatment changes somebody's sex characteristics.

▶【异性恋指的是对异性有性吸引】Heterosexuality means sexual attraction to someone of the other sex.

▶【同性恋指的是对同性有性吸引】Homosexuality means sexual attraction to someone of the same sex.

▶【双性恋指的是对两性都有性吸引】Bisexuality means sexual attraction to people of both sexes.

▶【无性恋指的是对任何性别都缺乏性吸引】Asexuality refers to a lack of sexual attraction to people of either sex.

▶【很多文化视性为禁忌】Many cultures have long treated sex as taboo.

▶【即便在今天，很多人也讳莫如深】Even today, many people avoid talking about it.

▶【尽管性可以带来快乐】Although sex can produce much pleasure…

▶【它也带来混乱、忧虑，有些时候还有恐惧】it causes confusion, anxiety, and sometimes fear as well

▶【20世纪，人们对待性和性行为的态度发生了深刻的变化】Over the course of the 20th century, people witnessed profound changes in sexual attitudes and practices.

▶【很多男男女女从乡村移居到迅速发展的城市中】Many women and men migrate from farms and small towns to rapidly growing cities.

▶【在那里，远离家庭，在工作场合接触新朋友，年轻人拥有相当多的性自由】There, living from their families and meeting new people in the workplace, young people enjoy considerable sexual freedom.

友，年轻人拥有相当多的性自由。在性解放方面，科技扮演着重要角色。避孕药、安全套等让性变得更方便。

性被大众传媒大肆宣传。越来越多的人认为性是生活的一部分，不管他们是否结婚。年轻人中一个有意思的话题是婚前性行为。尽管大众对其态度仍有分歧，婚前性行为还是被年轻人广泛接受。但是，婚外情被广泛谴责。批评者也反对同居和未婚先育这样的趋势。近亲之间的繁殖会无药可救地混乱血亲关系。近亲繁殖增加出生患精神和身体问题后代的概率。

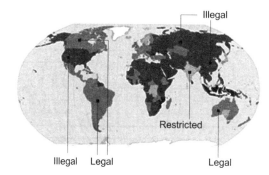

世界各国对卖淫的法律规定
The legal status of prostitution by country

卖淫就是出售性服务。这通常被称作"世界上最古老的职业"，卖淫自有史以来广泛分布。通常是迫于威胁和生计，妇女，甚至是男性，才开始卖淫这一行当。在一些国家，卖淫合法化受到强有力的支持。但是，性工作者中性病的流行，让人们重新关注卖淫这一问题。

性骚扰指的是，发生在工作场合或学校，让人讨厌的涉性的语言或行为。如果一位上司以解雇为名恐吓员工，强迫与其发生性关系，这就算性骚扰。不仅仅是在成年人中，研究表明在儿童和青少年中性骚扰也很普遍。然而，对于一些人，性解放的思潮被谴责为社会道德沦丧。人们提倡回归传统家庭价值，从性自由回归到对性负责。

> *Sex is a part of nature. I go along with nature.*
>
> *We are all born sexual creatures, thank God, but it's a pity so many people despise and crush this natural gift.*

Marilyn Monroe

美国20世纪60年代的嬉皮士
Hippie, 1960s in the US
The Sexual Revolution was a social movement throughout the Western world from the 1960s to the 1980s. The birth control pill (oral contraceptives) arrived on the market in 1960. Within two years, 1.2 million American women were "on the pill".

表达库
Bank of expressions

► 【通常是迫于威胁和生计，妇女，甚至是男性，才开始卖淫这一行当】Women or even men have usually entered prostitution through coercion or under economic stress.

► 【卖淫合法化受到强有力的支持】strong arguments have been made in support of legalizing prostitution

► 【但是，性工作者中性病的流行，让人们重新关注卖淫这一问题】The prevalence of STDs (sexually transmitted diseases) among prostitutes, however, has caused renewed concern about the problem of prostitution.

► 【性骚扰指的是，发生在工作场合或学校，让人讨厌的涉性的语言或行为】Sexual harassment is unwanted verbal or physical behavior of a sexual nature that occurs in the workplace or in an educational setting.

► 【如果一位上司以解雇为名恐吓员工，强迫与其发生性关系，这就算性骚扰】If a supervisor forces an employee to have sex by threatening to fire the employee, that is sexual harassment.

► 【研究表明在儿童和青少年中间性骚扰也很普遍】research indicates that sexual harassment is widespread among children and teenagers

► 【性解放的思潮被谴责为社会道德沦丧】the climate of sexual freedom is criticized by some as evidence of our society's moral decline

► 【人们提倡回归传统家庭价值，从性自由回归到对性负责】There are calls for a return to family values and change from sexual freedom back to sexual responsibility.

All young people, regardless of sexual orientation or identity, deserve a safe and supportive environment in which to achieve their full potential.

Harvey Milk

《断背山》电影海报照片
Brokeback Mountain theatrical release poster
Directed by Ang Lee. It is a film adaptation of the 1997 short story of the same name by Annie Proulx.

性取向[1]有很多种。对异性的性倾向被称为异性恋[2]。对同性的性倾向被称为同性恋[3]。对两性都有性吸引的被称为双性恋[4]。还有一类对其他人缺乏性吸引或对性没有兴趣的人，被称作无性恋[5]。越来越多的迹象表明性取向是天生的。这和人生来就是左撇子或右撇子是一个道理。

从历史角度来看，在每个社会中异性恋都是婚姻和家庭的基础。但是，也不乏其他非主流性取向，这一类人常常被称作为

表达库
Bank of expressions

► 【All young people, regardless of sexual orientation or identity, deserve a safe and supportive environment in which to achieve their full potential】所有的年轻人，不管他们的性倾向和身份如何，都值得拥有安全、友好的环境，来充分发挥其潜能。
► 【对异性的性倾向】sexual orientation toward people of the opposite sex
► 【对同性的性倾向】sexual orientation toward people of the same sex
► 【对两性都有性吸引】sexual attraction to both sexes
► 【对其他人缺乏性吸引】the lack of sexual attraction to others
► 【对性没有兴趣的人】the lack of interest in sex
► 【越来越多的迹象表明性取向是天生的】A growing body of evidence suggests that sexual orientation is innate.
► 【这和人生来就是左撇子或右撇子是一个道理】It is much the same way that people are born right-handed or left-handed.
► 【从历史角度来看，在每个社会中异性恋都是婚姻和家庭的基础】Heterosexuality in every society has historically been the basis of marriage and family
► 【也不乏其他非主流性取向】there are many minority sexual inclinations

核心词
Keywords

1. 性取向（sex orientation）
2. 异性恋（heterosexuality）
3. 同性恋（homosexuality）
4. 双性恋（bisexuality）
5. 无性恋（asexuality 或 nonsexuality）

"酷儿[1]"。"LGBT"是"lesbian""gay""bisexual" "transgender"这4个单词首字母组成的缩略词[2]。

有学者将人分为十种不同的性向：

- 异性恋女性[3]
- 异性恋男性[4]
- 同性恋女性[5]
- 同性恋男性[6]
- 双性恋女性[7]
- 双性恋男性[8]
- 异装癖女性[9]
- 异装癖男性[10]
- 男变女变性者[11]
- 女变男变性者[12]

不同国家文化对同性恋的观念截然不同。在古希腊人中，上流男性认为同性恋是一种最高的关系形式，部分原因是因为他们认为女性智商低。

同性恋恐惧症[13]是指对同性的恐惧、歧视、排斥及憎恨。一些国家中同性性行为被禁止，一些国家却接受同性婚姻。2001年，荷兰成为世界上第一个允许同性结婚的国家。2011年，美国纽约通过了《婚姻平等法案》[14]，允许同性结婚。

里约热内卢同性恋骄傲大游行
Hundreds thousand of people celebrating Gay Pride, Rio de Janeiro, 2007

表达库
Bank of expressions

▶【在古希腊人中，上流男性认为同性恋是一种最高的关系形式，部分原因是因为他们认为女性智商低】Among the ancient Greeks, upper-class men considered homosexuality the highest form of relationship, partly because they looked down on women as intellectually inferior.

▶【同性婚姻】gay marriage 或 same-sex marriage

▶【荷兰成为世界上第一个允许同性结婚的国家】the Netherlands became the first nation in the world to grant same-sex marriages

核心词
Keywords

1. 酷儿（queer）
2. 缩略词（initialism）
3. 异性恋女性（straight woman 或 heterosexual woman）
4. 异性恋男性（straight man 或 heterosexual woman）
5. 同性恋女性（lesbian woman 或 homosexual woman）
6. 同性恋男性（gay man 或 homosexual man）
7. 双性恋女性（bisexual woman）
8. 双性恋男性（bisexual man）
9. 异装癖女性（transvestite woman）
10. 异装癖男性（transvestite man）
11. 男变女变性者（transsexual woman）
12. 女变男变性者（transsexual man）
13. 同性恋恐惧症（homophobia）
14.《婚姻平等法案》（*Marriage Equality Act*）

在很多国家和地区，每年都会举行同性恋骄傲大游行[1]，越来越多的影视作品开始以同性恋为题材，其中影响广泛的影片包括《断背山》[2]和《米尔克》[3]。

核心词
Keywords

1. 骄傲大游行（Gay Pride parade）
2.《断背山》（*Brokeback Mountain*）
3.《米尔克》（*Milk*）

同性权益的里程碑
Milestones in gay rights in history

Ancient Greece	Ancient Greeks recognized same-sex love Alexander the Great had an intimate relationship with his confidante and bodyguard, Hephaestion
Ancient Rome	The Roman emperor Hadrian declared his male lover Antinous a god
Medieval times	Thomas Aquinas argued that sex between two men violated the natural law
Victorian England	Oscar Wilde, married with two children, was involved in a passionate love affair with Lord Alfred Douglas
1989	Denmark was previously the first country in the world to legally recognize same-sex couples through registered partnerships
1993	President Bill Clinton signed into law the bill now known as "Don't Ask, Don't Tell"
1996	President Clinton signed the Defense of Marriage Act
2001	Same-sex marriage ceremonies performed in Ontario, Canada
2004	The Massachusetts Supreme Court made gay marriage legal
2008	California Proposition 8 was passed

哈维·米尔克
Harvey Milk (1930-1978)
American politician and
gay-rights activist

笔记
Notes

I notice that all of the people who support abortion are already born.

Ronald Reagan

堕胎意味着在生产前结束妊娠，导致胎儿死亡。流产[1]是指自然发生的中断怀孕，通常是因为胎儿非正常发育，或者母亲受伤或不适。而人工流产[2]是当今饱受争议的道德问题之一。

支持堕胎的一方称"主张选择[3]"，而反对堕胎一方是"主张生命[4]"。

支持堕胎的人赞同妇女享有生育权利。他们认为胎儿只是潜在的人类，除非可以在母体子宫外生存。胎儿没有法定权利，权利属于怀孕的妇女。支持者的主要观点总结如下：

- 胎儿通过胎盘和脐带与母体相连，不能在母体外生存
- 堕胎是一种安全的医疗措施

It seems to me clear as daylight that abortion would be a crime.

Gandhi

No woman can call herself free until she can choose consciously whether she will or will not be a mother.

Margaret Sanger, an American birth control activist and the founder of the American Birth Control League

表达库
Bank of expressions

- ►【在生产前结束妊娠】termination of a pregnancy before birth
- ►【导致胎儿死亡】resulting in the death of the fetus
- ►【自然发生的中断怀孕】abortions occur naturally
- ►【因为胎儿非正常发育，或者母亲受伤或不适】because a fetus does not develop normally or because the mother has an injury or disorder
- ►【是当今饱受争议的道德问题之一】one of the most widely debated ethical issues of our time
- ►【赞同妇女享有生育权利】favor a woman's reproductive rights
- ►【胎儿只是潜在的人类】the fetus is only a potential human being
- ►【可以在母体子宫外生存】able to survive outside its mother's womb
- ►【胎儿没有法定权利】The fetus has no legal rights.
- ►【权利属于怀孕的妇女】The rights belong to the woman carrying the fetus.
- ►【胎儿通过胎盘和脐带与母体相连】a fetus is attached to a woman's body by the placenta and umbilical cord
- ►【不能在母体外生存】a fetus cannot exist outside a woman's womb
- ►【堕胎是一种安全的医疗措施】abortion is a safe medical procedure

核心词
Keywords

1. 流产（miscarriage）
2. 人工流产（induced abortion）
3. 主张选择（pro-choice）
4. 主张生命（pro-life）

- 对于强暴和乱伦，怀孕给受害者带来精神伤害
- 妇女享有掌控自己身体的权利
- 妇女应该享有生殖权利
- 做一个青少年母亲影响一个人的教育

但是反对者说，从怀孕开始胎儿就是一个人类个体。从卵子和精子结合的一瞬间，胎儿就有法定权利。反对者的主要观点总结如下：

- 堕胎是一种谋杀，贬低了生命的价值
- 堕胎忽略了胎儿的合法权利
- 一个可能有用的人对社会的贡献被抹杀
- 堕胎之后导致各种并发症
- 对于强暴和乱伦，可以采取医疗措施避免怀孕
- 年轻人没有阅历作出成熟的决定
- 堕胎违反医生的誓言

对于堕胎，特蕾莎修女说：

But I feel that the greatest destroyer of peace today is abortion, because it is a war against the child—a direct killing of the innocent child—murder by the mother herself. And if we accept that a mother can kill even her own child, how can we tell other people not to kill one another?

美国圣母大学反堕胎游行
Antiabortion protesters march on the campus of the University of Notre Dame, Indiana, United States, 2009.

▶ 【对于强暴和乱伦，怀孕给受害者带来精神伤害】in the case of rape or incest, pregnancy could cause further psychological harm to the victim

▶ 【妇女享有掌控自己身体的权利】women have the right to control their own bodies

▶ 【妇女应该享有生殖权利】women should have their reproductive choices

▶ 【做一个青少年母亲影响一个人的教育】being a teenage mother could severely affect one's education

▶ 【从怀孕开始胎儿就是一个人类个体】the fetus is a human being from the time of conception

▶ 【从卵子和精子结合的一瞬间】From the moment the egg and sperm unite...

▶ 【胎儿就有法定权利】the fetus has the legal right to life

▶ 【堕胎是一种谋杀】abortion is a form of murder

▶ 【贬低了生命的价值】demeaning the value of human life

▶ 【忽略了胎儿的合法权利】eliminates the legal rights of the unborn child

▶ 【一个可能有用的人对社会的贡献被抹杀】the societal contributions of a potentially valuable human being are wiped out

▶ 【堕胎之后导致各种并发症】an abortion can result in medical complications later in life

▶ 【对于强暴和乱伦，可以采取医疗措施避免怀孕】in the instance of rape and incest, proper medical care can ensure that a woman will not get pregnant

▶ 【年轻人没有阅历作出成熟的决定】young adults might not have the life experience to make mature decisions

▶ 【堕胎违反医生的誓言】abortion is against doctors' Hippocratic Oath

I hate to hear you talk about all women as if they were fine ladies instead of rational creatures. None of us want to be in calm waters all our lives.

Jane Austen

许多文明的大部分历史中，根深蒂固的文化信仰只允许妇女在社会扮演有限的角色。很多人认为妇女的天然角色就是母亲和妻子，这些人认为妇女更适合生儿育女、家庭生活，而不是参加商业或政治这样的公共生活。很多人认为妇女的智力比男性低，这导致多数社会将妇女的教育限定在学习持家技能。

"我们能做到！"海报，设计于第二次世界大战的美国，后用来"女权主义"宣传
"We Can Do It!" is an American wartime propaganda poster produced by J. Howard Miller in 1943 for Westinghouse Electric as an inspirational image to boost worker morale. The "We Can Do It!" image was used to promote feminism and other political issues beginning in the 1980s.

在现代社会，女性的地位已经大为改观，比如：

- 更多的女性参加工作
- 更多的女孩接受教育
- 妇女的平均寿命延长
- 更多女性参与政治

表达库
Bank of expressions

▶ 【None of us want to be in calm waters all our lives.】没有一位女性想平庸地度过一生。

▶ 【许多文明的大部分历史中】Throughout much of the history of many civilizations…

▶ 【根深蒂固的文化信仰只允许妇女在社会扮演有限的角色】deep-seated cultural beliefs allowed women only limited roles in society

▶ 【很多人认为妇女的天然角色就是母亲和妻子】Many people believed that women's natural roles were only as mothers and wives.

▶ 【这些人认为妇女更适合生儿育女、家庭生活】These people considered women to be better suited for childbearing and homemaking…

▶ 【而不是参加商业或政治这样的公共生活】rather than for involvement in the public life of business or politics

▶ 【妇女的智力比男性低】women were intellectually inferior to men

▶ 【导致多数社会将妇女的教育限定在学习持家技能】led most societies to limit women's education to learning domestic skills

▶ 【更多的女孩接受教育】more girls are being educated

▶ 【妇女的平均寿命延长】average life expectancy of women is longer

▶ 【更多女性参与政治】more women are involved in politics

▶ 【立法机构认识到女性权利需要被保护】legislation is recognizing that women's rights need to be protected

- **立法机构认识到女性权利需要被保护**
- **一些国家立法允许女性同性婚姻**

马克思认为社会变革离不开女性的贡献，他说道：

Anyone who knows anything of history knows that great social changes are impossible without feminine upheava. Social progress can be measured exactly by the social position of the fair sex, the ugly ones included.

纵观历史，女性一直在为自己的权利而斗争，尽管道路曲折。启蒙运动[1]发端于17~18世纪，运动的领导者认为每个个体与生俱来平等的自然权利。法国大革命[2]期间，妇女游行至凡尔赛宫要求提供面包。

1792年，英国作家玛丽·沃斯通克拉夫特[3]创作《女权辩护》[4]一书，成为接下来女权主义思潮的催化剂。在书中她认为，和男人一样，女人天生就是理智的，但是女性接受的低劣教育让她们变得愚蠢和多愁善感。《女权辩护》结尾处动情地写道：

Let woman share the rights, and she will emulate the virtues of man; for she must grow more perfect when emancipated, or justify the authority that chains such a weak being to her duty.

1848年，世界上第一个女权大会在纽约塞内卡瀑布召开。会上通过了著名的《感伤宣言与决议》[5]。该文中流传甚广的一句是：

《女权辩护》第一版封面，美国
Title page from the first American edition of
A Vindication of the Rights of Woman

表达库
Bank of expressions

► 【一些国家立法允许女性同性婚姻】some countries legislated to recognize same-sex marriage of lesbian women

► 【great social changes are impossible without feminine upheaval】巨大的社会变革离不开女性动荡

► 【纵观历史，女性一直在为自己的权利而斗争】A snapshot of history shows that women have always struggled for their rights...

► 【道路曲折】the process is not a straight line

► 【运动的领导者认为每个个体与生俱来平等的自然权利】leaders of the Enlightenment argued that every individual was born with equal natural rights

► 【妇女游行至凡尔赛宫要求提供面包】women marched on Versailles to demand bread

► 【成为接下来女权主义思潮的催化剂】became a catalyst for subsequent feminist thinking

► 【和男人一样，女人天生就是理智的】like men, women were naturally rational

► 【但是女性接受的低劣教育让她们变得愚蠢和多愁善感】but inferior education received by women often made them to be silly and emotional

► 【世界上第一个女权大会在纽约塞内卡瀑布召开】the world's first women's rights convention was held in Seneca Falls, New York

核心词
Keywords

1. 启蒙运动（The Age of Enlightenment）
2. 法国大革命（the French Revolution）
3. 玛丽·沃斯通克拉夫特（Mary Wollstonecraft）
4.《女权辩护》（*A Vindication of the Rights of Woman*）
5.《感伤宣言与决议》（*Declaration of Sentiments and Resolutions*）

The history of mankind is a history of repeated injuries and usurpations on the part of man toward woman, having in direct object the establishment of an absolute tyranny over her.

美国著名妇女权利运动领袖索杰纳·特鲁思[1]1851 年在俄亥俄州发表著名演讲《我难道不是一个女人》[2]时说：

If the first woman God ever made was strong enough to turn the world upside down all alone, these women together ought to be able to turn it back, and get it right side up again!

妇女选举权[3]强力主张男女平等的选举及被选举权利。在 1893 年，新西兰成为第一个允许成年妇女投票的国家。苏珊·布朗奈尔·安东尼[4]（以下简称"苏珊"）在 19 世纪美国女权运动中扮演关键角色，她将妇女选举权引入美国。1920 年，美国妇女争得了选举权。

《美国第十九条宪法修正案》
赋予妇女选举权
The 19th Amendment to the United States Constitution was a big step for women's rights in the U.S. This amendment allowed all citizens of any sex to vote. Women suffrage had been fought for many years. This amendment was a great accomplishment for the people who supported women's rights.

表达库
Bank of expressions

► 【The history of mankind is a history of repeated injuries and usurpations on the part of man toward woman】
人类的历史是一部男人对妇女不断伤害与掠夺的历史……

► 【新西兰成为第一个允许成年妇女投票的国家】New Zealand became the first nation to extend the right to vote to all adult women

► 【在 19 世纪美国女权运动中扮演关键角色】played a pivotal role in the 19th century women's rights movement

► 【将妇女选举权引入美国】introduced women's suffrage into the United States

核心词
Keywords

1. 索杰纳·特鲁思（Sojourner Truth）
2.《我难道不是一个女人》（*Ain't I a Woman?*）
3. 妇女选举权（women's suffrage）
4. 苏珊·布朗奈尔·安东尼（Susan Brownnell Anthony）

笔记
Notes

在 1868 年，苏珊发行周刊《革命》[1]，杂志座右铭是"真正的共和国是男人的权利不被增加，而女人的权利不被减少"。在 1873 年，她发表著名演说《论妇女选举权》[2]。

表达库
Bank of expressions

▶ 【真正的共和国是男人的权利不被增加，而女人的权利不被减少】
The true republic—men, their rights and nothing more; women, their rights and nothing less.

核心词
Keywords

1.《革命》（ *The Revolution* ）
2.《论妇女选举权》（ *On Woman's Right to Suffrage* ）
3. 伊丽莎白·凯迪·斯坦顿（Elizabeth Cady Stanton ）

苏珊和伊丽莎白·凯迪·斯坦顿[3]为美国妇女选举权而战
Susan B. Anthony and Elizabeth Cady Stanton were famous American suffragettes who fought to earn U.S. women the right to vote.

笔记
Notes

玛丽·沃斯通克拉夫特
Mary Wollstonecraft
(1759-1797)
English writer and passionate advocate of educational and social equality for women

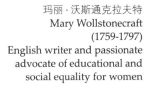

苏珊·布朗奈尔·安东尼
Susan Brownnell Anthony
(1820-1906)
Pioneer crusader for the woman suffrage movement in the United States

I have a dream that one day little black boys and girls will be holding hands with little white boys and girls.

Martin Luther King Jr.

所有人类都可以归为一类——智人[1]。所有人类又可以根据语言、肤色、体态特征细分为不同的人种。种族之间有交流，也有歧视，这类歧视被称作种族歧视[2]。

种族隔离[3]是指在日常生活中将不同种族的人群隔离开来。白人至上主义[4]主张白色人种优越于其他人种。

有关种族歧视，这几个重要事件值得记住：

- 大西洋奴隶贸易[5]
- 犹太人大屠杀[6]
- 美国黑人民权运动[7]
- 南非种族隔离[8]

奴隶制度开始于人类早期历史。《汉谟拉比法典》就有提及奴隶制度，奴隶也频繁出现在《旧约》中。在当时最民主的希腊城邦，奴隶是重要的社会基础。

大西洋奴隶贸易是指在 15~19 世纪至少 1000 万被奴役的非洲人被迫从非洲家园

表达库
Bank of expressions

- 【所有人类都可以归为一类】All human beings belong to one species...
- 【指在日常生活中将不同种族的人群隔离开来】refers to the separation of humans into racial groups in daily life
- 【白色人种优越于其他人种】white people are superior to people of other racial backgrounds
- 【《汉谟拉比法典》就有提及奴隶制度，奴隶也频繁出现在《旧约》中】Slaves are mentioned in the *Code of Hummurabi* and appear frequently in the *Old Testament*.
- 【在当时最民主的希腊城邦，奴隶是重要的社会基础】Slaves were an important foundation of even the most democratic Greek city-states.
- 【在 15~19 世纪至少 1000 万被奴役的非洲人被迫从非洲家园被运送到欧洲或美洲的活动】the forced transportation of at least 10 million enslaved Africans from their homelands in Africa to destinations in Europe and the Americas during the 15th through 19th centuries

核心词
Keywords

1. 智人（Homo sapiens）
2. 种族歧视（racial discrimination）
3. 种族隔离（racial segregation）
4. 白人至上主义（white supremacy）
5. 大西洋奴隶贸易（Atlantic slave trade）
6. 犹太人大屠杀（the Holocaust）
7. 美国黑人民权运动（African-American Civil Rights Movement）
8. 南非种族隔离（Apartheid in South Africa）

被运送到欧洲或美洲的活动。绝大多数的黑奴在农业种植园做苦力。种植园主残忍地让奴隶从早工作到晚。这场黑奴贩卖是当时世界最大的跨洲移民，这对大西洋附近各洲都产生了巨大的影响。

那时，黑色的皮肤和奴隶身份联系在一起，种族主义凸显。在英国社会改革家威廉·威伯福斯[1]领导下，奴隶贸易最终在1807年被禁止；在1833年，大英帝国大部分地区的奴隶都获得自由。

1861年，沙皇亚历山大二[2]世废除俄国农奴制度。尽管严格意义上讲，农奴并非奴隶而是束缚在自己的主人和土地上的农场工人。

在美国直到1862年，亚伯拉罕·林肯[3]总统颁布《解放黑人奴隶宣言》[4]，奴隶制度才被废除。

油画《林肯总统宣读奴隶解放宣言》
Alexander Hay Ritchie print of Francis Bicknell Carpenter's heroic painting of First Reading of the Emancipation Proclamation of President Lincoln. Lincoln's Emancipation Proclamation dramatically changed the meaning of the war by declaring that all persons held as slaves in states still in rebellion were "thenceforward, and forever free".

表达库
Bank of expressions

► 【绝大多数的黑奴在农业种植园做苦力】The vast majority of black slaves worked as laborers on large agricultural plantations.

► 【种植园主残忍地让奴隶从早工作到晚】Planters could make slaves work in inhuman ways, dawn to dusk.

► 【世界最大的跨洲移民】the largest intercontinental migration of people in the world

► 【对大西洋附近各洲都产生了巨大的影响】had enormous consequences for every continent bordering the Atlantic

► 【黑色的皮肤和奴隶身份联系在一起】dark skin alone became associated with slave status

► 【种族主义凸显】racism leapt forward

► 【在英国社会改革家威廉·威伯福斯领导下，奴隶贸易最终在1807年被禁止】Under the leadership of William Wilberforce, a social reformer, the slave trade was banned at last in 1807.

► 【大英帝国大部分地区的奴隶都获得自由】slaves in most parts of the British Empire were also declared free

► 【沙皇亚历山大二世废除俄国农奴制度】Czar Alexander II abolished serfdom in his nation

► 【尽管严格意义上讲，农奴并非奴隶，而是束缚在自己的主人和土地上的农场工人】Though not technically slaves, serfs were peasant farm workers bound to their master and to his land.

核心词
Keywords

1. 威廉·威伯福斯（William Wilberforce）
2. 沙皇亚历山大二世（Czar Alexander II）
3. 亚伯拉罕·林肯（Abraham Lincoln）
4.《解放黑人奴隶宣言》(Emancipation Proclamation)

1896 年，美国通过"普莱西诉弗格森案"[1]，该案标志着"隔离但平等"[2]的种族歧视原则在美国被确立。

1935 年，纳粹德国[3]颁布《纽伦堡法案》[4]，该法案剥夺了犹太人的德国公民权，禁止犹太人和其他德国人通婚。"破窗之夜[5]"，又称"水晶之夜[6]"，标志着纳粹德国对犹太人有组织的屠杀开始。

1942 年，在万湖会议[7]上，惨绝人寰的《最终解决方案》[8]被落实，它是第二次世界大战期间纳粹德国系统屠杀欧洲犹太人的计划。在波兰建立的奥斯维辛集中营[9]见证了纳粹犯下的反人类罪行[10]。

在"人生而平等[11]"理念的感召下，众多仁人志士为民权而战。

马丁·路德·金参与联合抵制蒙哥马利公车运动
Dr. King and Rev. Glen Smiley, a white minister, shared the front seat of a public bus. Sparked by the arrest of Rosa Parks on December 1, 1955, the Montgomery Bus Boycott was a 13-month mass protest that ended with the U.S. Supreme Court ruling that segregation on public buses is unconstitutional.

1955 年，被称为"现代民权运动之母[12]"的罗莎·帕克斯[13]拒绝听从公交车司机的命令将座位让给白人乘客，这一事件引发联合抵制蒙哥马利公车运动[14]。

马丁·路德·金是美国黑人民权运动的灵魂人物，他通过采取"非暴力[15]"和"不服从[16]"的方式推动美国民权进步。

1963 年，他组织了"向华盛顿进军[17]"

表达库
Bank of expressions

▶ 【剥夺了犹太人的德国公民权】deprived Jews of German citizenship
▶ 【禁止犹太人和其他德国人通婚】prohibited marriage between Jews and other Germans
▶ 【第二次世界大战期间纳粹德国系统屠杀欧洲犹太人的计划】Nazi Germany's plan of the systematic genocide of European Jews during World War II
▶ 【拒绝听从公车司机的命令将座位让给白人乘客】refused to obey bus driver's order that she give up her seat to a white passenger

核心词
Keywords

1. "普莱西诉弗格森案"（Plessy v. Ferguson）
2. 隔离但平等（separate but equal）
3. 纳粹德国（Nazi Germany）
4. 《纽伦堡法案》（Nuremberg Laws）
5. 破窗之夜（the Night of Broken Glass）
6. 水晶之夜（Crystal Night）
7. 万湖会议（Wannsee Conference）
8. 《最终解决方案》（Final Solution）
9. 奥斯维辛集中营（Auschwitz Concentration Camp）
10. 反人类罪行（crimes against humanity）
11. 人生而平等（all men are created equal）
12. 现代民权运动之母（the First Lady of Civil Rights）
13. 罗莎·帕克斯（Rosa Parks）
14. 联合抵制蒙哥马利公车运动（Montgomery Bus Boycott）
15. 非暴力（nonviolence）
16. 不服从（disobedience）
17. 向华盛顿进军（March on Washington）

活动，争取非裔美国人的民权和经济权益。并在林肯纪念堂[1]，发表著名演说《我有个梦想》[2]。他领导的非暴力抵制和公民不服从运动收获了《1964 平民权法案》和《1965 年投票权法案》的通过。

《我有个梦想》演讲现场
Martin Luther King's famous *I Have a Dream* speech, delivered at the August 28 1963 March on Washington for Jobs and Freedom

　　1990 年，在纳尔逊·曼德拉[3]和民众努力下，南非解除种族隔离。

亚伯拉罕·林肯
Abraham Lincoln
(1809-1865)
16th president of the United States , who preserved the Union during the American Civil War and brought about the emancipation of the slaves

表达库
Bank of expressions

► 【争取非裔美国人的民权和经济权益】called for civil and economic rights for African Americans
► 【他领导的非暴力抵制和公民不服从运动收获了《1964 年民权法案》和《1965 年投票权法案》的通过】King led a nonviolent campaign of boycotts and civil disobedience that bore fruit in the *Civil Rights Act of 1964* and the *Voting Rights Act of 1965*.

核心词
Keywords

1. 林肯纪念堂（Lincoln Memorial）
2. 《我有个梦想》（*I Have a Dream*）
3. 纳尔逊·曼德拉（Nelson Mandela）

笔记
Notes

罗莎·帕克斯
Rosa Parks (1913-2005)
African American civil
rights activist whose
refusal to relinquish her
seat on a public bus to a
white man precipitated
the 1955-1956
Montgomery Bus Boycott
in Alabama, which is
recognized as the spark
that ignited the U.S. civil
rights movement

小马丁·路德·金
Martin Luther King Jr.
(1929-1968)
Baptist minister and
social activist who led
the civil rights movement
in the United States from
the mid-1950s

纳尔逊·曼德拉
Nelson Mandela
(1918-2013)
Black nationalist and
first black president of
South Africa

Earth provides enough to satisfy every man's needs, but not every man's greed.

Mahatma Gandhi

象征"万物之母"的盖亚（下）将
厄里克托尼俄斯献给雅典娜（右）
Attic red-figure stamnos, 5 century BC. Mother Gaia
presents baby Erichthonios to Athena. Gaia in ancient
Greek mythology represents earth, and the creator
and giver of birth to the earth and the entire universe.

　　地球是个奇迹，生命是个奥秘。我们的
地球仰赖平衡，万物各司其职，任何生物的
生存只能依靠其他生物。今天，我们的生命
仅仅是众多生命组成的锁链中的一环。生命
的力量之源在于联系。万物都联系在一起，
没有任何物种自给自足。这个微妙的、脆弱
的平衡，很容易被打破。

　　地球是目前人类所知的唯一为生命提
供理想生存条件的星球。地球与太阳的距离
正合适，所以不冷不热的温度正适宜生物存

表达库
Bank of expressions

► 【Earth provides enough to satisfy every man's needs, but not every man's greed】地球能够满足每个人的需求，但是不能满足每个人的贪婪。

► 【地球是个奇迹】The earth is a miracle...

► 【生命是个奥秘】the life is a mystery

► 【我们的地球仰赖平衡】Our earth lies on a balance...

► 【万物各司其职】every being has a role to play

► 【生存只能依靠其他生物】exists only through the existence of another being

► 【今天，我们的生命仅仅是众多生命组成的锁链中的一环】Today, our life is just a link of a chain of numerable living beings.

► 【生命的力量之源在于联系】The engine of life is linkage.

► 【万物都联系在一起】Everything is linked.

► 【没有任何物种自给自足】Nothing is self-sufficient.

► 【这个微妙的、脆弱的平衡，很容易被打破】It is a subtle, fragile harmony, which is easily shattered.

► 【地球是目前人类所知的唯一为生命提供理想生存条件的星球】Earth is the only planet that we know of that provides the right conditions for life.

► 【地球与太阳的距离正合适，所以不冷不热的温度正适宜生物存活】Earth is just the right distance from the sun so that temperatures are neither too hot nor too cold for living things to survive.

活。这里有液态水，大气中有氧气，两者对生命都很重要。地球大气和海洋有助于调节温度。地球是数以百万计物种的家园，从最微小的细菌到巨大的蓝鲸。

阿波罗 8 号拍摄的地球
Planet Earth rising above the lunar horizon, an unprecedented view captured in December 1968 from the Apollo 8 spacecraft as its orbit carried it clear of the far side of the moon

人类为什么要珍惜这个星球，或许身为美国航天员及作家的卡尔·萨根[1]在《暗蓝色的点：在太空中想象人类的未来》[2]一书中给出了满意的答案。

Look again at that dot. That's here. That's home. That's us. On it everyone you love, everyone you know, everyone you ever heard of, every human being who ever was, lived out their lives. The aggregate of our joy and suffering, thousands of confident religions, ideologies, and economic doctrines, every hunter and forager, every hero and coward, every creator and destroyer of civilization, every king and peasant, every young couple in love, every mother and father, hopeful child, inventor and explorer, every teacher of morals, every corrupt politician, every "superstar", every "supreme leader", every saint and sinner in the history of our species lived

表达库
Bank of expressions

► 【这里有液态水，大气中有氧气，两者对生命都很重要】There is liquid water, and there is oxygen in the atmosphere—both vital for life.
► 【地球大气和海洋有助于调节温度】Earth's atmosphere and oceans help to control temperatures.
► 【地球是数以百万计物种的家园，从最微小的细菌到巨大的蓝鲸】Earth is home to millions of different living species, from tiny bacteria to giant blue whales.
► 【The aggregate of our joy and suffering】人类快乐和痛苦的集合……
► 【thousands of confident religions, ideologies, and economic doctrines】数以千计的可靠的宗教、意识形态和经济理论

核心词
Keywords

1. 卡尔·萨根（Carl Sagan）
2. 《暗蓝色的点：在太空中想象人类的未来》（Pale Blue Dot: A Vision of the Human Future in Space）

there—on a mote of dust suspended in a sunbeam.

The Earth is a very small stage in a vast cosmic arena. <u>Think of the endless cruelties visited by the inhabitants of one corner of this pixel on the scarcely distinguishable inhabitants of some other corner, how frequent their misunderstandings, how eager they are to kill one another, how fervent their hatreds. Think of the rivers of blood spilled by all those generals and emperors so that, in glory and triumph, they could become the momentary masters of a fraction of a dot. Our posturings, our imagined self-importance, the delusion that we have some privileged position in the universe, are challenged by this point of pale light. Our planet is a lonely speck in the great enveloping cosmic dark. In our obscurity, in all this vastness, there is no hint that help will come from elsewhere to save us from ourselves.</u>

The Earth is the only world known so far to harbor life. There is nowhere else, at least in the near future, to which our species could migrate. Visit, yes. Settle, not yet. Like it or not, for the moment the Earth is where we make our stand. It has been said that <u>astronomy is a humbling and character-building experience</u>. There is perhaps no better demonstration of the folly of human conceits than this distant image of our tiny world. To me, it underscores our responsibility to deal more kindly with one another, and to preserve and cherish the pale blue dot, the only home we've ever known.

表达库
Bank of expressions

► 【on a mote of dust suspended in a sunbeam】在悬浮于阳光中的一粒微尘上

► 【Think of the endless cruelties visited by the inhabitants of one corner of this pixel on the scarcely distinguishable inhabitants of some other corner】想想看，生活在这个微小星球上的一个角落的人给其他地方的几乎没有任何差别的人带来的无尽残暴……

► 【how fervent their hatreds】他们是怎样的苦大仇深

► 【Think of the rivers of blood spilled by all those generals and emperors so that, in glory and triumph, they could become the momentary masters of a fraction of a dot】想想看，所有那些帝王将相造成的血流成河，为的就是他们能光荣胜利地成为这个微小星球一隅的短暂主宰。

► 【Our posturings, our imagined self-importance, the delusion that we have some privileged position in the Universe, are challenged by this point of pale light】这一抹暗光时刻都在挑战人类的做作、自命不凡、和我们在宇宙中享有特权的幻想。

► 【Our planet is a lonely speck in the great enveloping cosmic dark】我们的星球是宇宙的无限黑暗中一粒孤独的尘灰。

► 【In our obscurity, in all this vastness, there is no hint that help will come from elsewhere to save us from ourselves】在我们的卑微中，在这浩瀚的宇宙中，对于任何来自其他地方可以救赎人类自己的帮助，我们找不到一丝线索。

► 【astronomy is a humbling and character-building experience】天文学是让人谦逊和塑造性格的经历

Trees are poems the earth writes upon the sky,

We fell them down and turn them into paper,

That we may record our emptiness.

Kahlil Gibran

在物种的锁链中，树木的地位是至高无上的。树木是完美的、活生生的雕塑。它们是地球上最古老、最高大的生物。树木是生命强大永恒的象征。树木藐视重力，它们面朝天空不断生长。它们朝着太阳不疾不徐地生长，从而获得能量。

一棵存活的树在森林中有着很多不同的功能，比如：

- 光合作用[1]
- 防止土壤侵蚀[2]
- 各种经济价值[3]

树木继承了捕捉阳光的能力。树叶就像是太阳能板，它们汇集太阳的能量，吸收二氧化碳，用光能来制造糖分，并产生氧气。

国家森林面积排名, 2013
List of countries by forest area, 2013

Country	Forested area Source (km²)	Percentage of land area
Russia	7,762,602	45.40%
Brazil	4,776,980	56.10%
Canada	3,101,340	31.06%
United States	3,030,890	30.84%
China	1,821,000	18.21%
Democratic Republic of the Congo	1,819,326	50.00%
Australia	1,470,832	19.00%
Argentina	945,336	34.00%
Indonesia	884,950	46.46%
India	778,424	23.68%
Mexico	710,000	36.50%

通过吸收二氧化碳，树木补充大气，提供新鲜空气。在缓解气候变化方面，森林起着至关重要的作用。树木和森林也会为很多动植物提供栖息地、保护和食物。

树木防止土壤流失。树干树枝抵御强风。在下大雨时，树根有助于巩固土壤。像海绵一样，树根汲取水分，通过树干传导到树枝叶。多余的水分通过树叶释放到空气中。

木材广泛用于建造房屋及其他建筑。很多树木产出各种可以食用的水果和坚果。树干流出的各种树液，可以用来制作枫糖、橡胶和松油等产品。一些树皮可以用作香料。

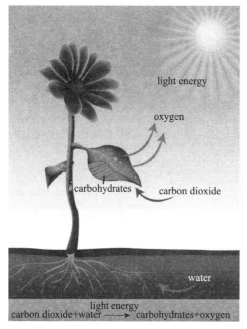

光合作用过程

Photosynthesis, process by which green plants and certain other organisms use the energy of light to convert carbon dioxide and water into the simple sugar glucose. In so doing, photosynthesis provides the basic energy source for virtually all organisms. An extremely important byproduct of photosynthesis is oxygen, on which most organisms depend.

一些树木产出重要的药物，比如说奎宁。

树木最终会死去。倒木分解并逐渐将养分释放到土壤中，让其他植物生长。这是一个漫长的生命循环。

全球的森林面临着被砍伐的威胁，这影响着人类的生计，并威胁大量动植物的生存。美国总统富兰克林·德拉诺·罗斯福[1]曾说：

A nation that destroys its soils destroys itself. Forests are the lungs of our land, purifying the air and giving fresh strength to our people.

最后，让我们一起欣赏一段来自赫尔曼·黑塞[2]赞颂树木的诗句，一起感叹这伟大的生灵。

For me, trees have always been the most penetrating preachers. I revere them when they live in tribes and families, in forests and groves. And even more I revere them when they stand alone. They are like lonely persons. Not like hermits who have stolen away out of some weakness, but like great, solitary men, like Beethoven and Nietzsche. In their highest boughs the world rustles, their roots rest in infinity; but they do not lose themselves there, they struggle with all the force of their lives for one thing only: to fulfill themselves according to their own laws, to build up their own form, to represent themselves. Nothing is holier, nothing is more exemplary than a beautiful, strong tree. When a tree is cut down and reveals its naked death-wound to the sun, one can read its whole history in the luminous, inscribed disk of its trunk: in the rings of its years, its scars, all the struggle, all the suffering, all the sickness, all the happiness and prosperity stand truly written, the narrow years and the luxurious years, the attacks withstood, the storms endured. And every young

表达库
Bank of expressions

▶ 【一些树木出产重要药物，比如说奎宁】Many trees yield important medicines, such as quinine.

▶ 【树木最终会死去】Trees will eventually die.

▶ 【倒木分解并逐渐将养分释放到土壤中】Fallen logs decompose and gradually return their nutrients to the soil...

▶ 【让其他植物生长】allowing other plants to thrive

▶ 【这是一个漫长的生命循环】It is a long cycle of life.

▶ 【全球的森林面临着被砍伐的威胁】Forests around the world are under threat from deforestation...

▶ 【这影响着人类的生计】impacts people's livelihoods

▶ 【并威胁大量动植物的生存】threatens the survival of a wide range of plant and animal species

▶ 【赫尔曼·黑塞】Hermann Hesse, a German-Swiss poet, received the Nobel Prize in Literature in 1946

▶ 【penetrating preachers】最有洞察力的布道者

▶ 【hermits who have stolen away out of some weakness】出于软弱而逃遁的隐士

▶ 【naked death-wound】赤裸裸的致命伤

核心词
Keywords

1. 富兰克林·德拉诺·罗斯福（Franklin Delano Roosevelt）
2. 赫尔曼·黑塞（Hermann Hesse）

farmboy knows that the hardest and noblest wood has the narrowest rings, that high on the mountains and in continuing danger the most indestructible, the strongest, the ideal trees grow.

世界森林砍伐量
Highest deforestation countries in world, 2012

Rank	Country	Forest area cut (in Hectares)
1	Brazil	3, 466, 000
2	Indonesia	1, 447, 800
3	Russian Federation	532, 200
4	Mexico	395, 000
5	Papua New Guinea	250, 200
6	Peru	224, 600
7	United States of America	215, 200
8	Bolivia	135, 200
9	Sudan	117, 807
10	Nigeria	82, 000

笔记
Notes

The beauty, majesty, and timelessness of a primary rainforest are indescribable. It is impossible to capture on film, to describe in words, or to explain to those who have never had the awe-inspiring experience of standing in the heart of a primary rainforest.

Leslie Taylor

在植物界多样性方面，世界哪里也比不上热带雨林。这里给生命提供的环境是如此理想，气候湿润，气温偏暖，而且太阳提供持续的能量。雨林形成几层。最高的植物是突破树冠得到阳光的参天大树。上层是树冠，他们从太阳中搜集能量，形成由树枝树

养牛业是导致巴西亚马逊雨林被砍伐的重要原因之一
In the Amazon, around 17% of the forest has been lost in the last 50 years, mostly due to forest conversion for cattle ranching. Deforestation is a particular concern in tropical rainforests because these forests are home to much of the world's biodiversity.

表达库
Bank of expressions

- 【The beauty, majesty, and timelessness of a primary rainforest are indescribable】原始森林的美丽、雄伟和永恒是难以形容的。
- 【It is impossible to capture on film, to describe in words, or to explain to those who have never had the awe-inspiring experience of standing in the heart of a primary rainforest】站在原始森林深处的那种肃然起敬的感觉，无法用电影捕捉，无法用文字描述，也无法讲给别人听。
- 【在植物界多样性方面，世界哪里也比不上热带雨林】Nowhere is the diversity of the plant kingdom more evident than in the world's tropical rain forests.
- 【这里给生命提供的环境是如此理想】The conditions for life here are so ideal.
- 【气候湿润】The climate is wet…
- 【气温偏暖】the temperature is warm
- 【而且太阳提供持续的能量】and the sun provides constant energy
- 【雨林形成几层】Rain forests grow in several layers.
- 【最高的植物是突破树冠得到阳光的参天大树】The tallest plants are the giant trees that break through the canopy to get the sunlight.
- 【上层是树冠】The overstory is the canopy.
- 【他们从太阳中搜集能量】They gather energy from the sun…
- 【形成由树枝树叶组成的茂密树冠】forming a dense canopy of leaves and branches

叶组成的茂密树冠。在它的下面，林下叶层是一个阳光有限的凉爽地方，但是矮小的树种、蕨类和藤蔓类植物在这里生存。由于几乎没什么光线，所以植物很难在雨林的地面上生长。在这里，腐烂的植物将它们的养分还给土壤。

鸟瞰热带雨林
An aerial view of the rainforest. The Amazon River is flowing through the rainforest.

雨林经过数百万年进化形成现如今如此复杂的生态环境。雨林为人类的生存和福祉贡献了丰富的资源。这些资源包括基本食物、衣物、住房、燃料、调料、工业原材料和药物。作为旅游地，雨林备受重视。

亚马孙雨林被称为"地球之肺"，因为它持续不断地将二氧化碳转化成氧气。世界上超过 1/5 的氧气来自亚马孙雨林。

The mountains, the forest, and the sea, render men savage; they develop the fierce, but yet do not destroy the human.

Victor Hugo

热带雨林内在动态是一个复杂而脆弱的系统。其中的一切都是相互依赖的，影响一部分可以导致未知的破坏，甚至雨林整体的破坏。

被破坏的雨林
Smoldering remains of a plot of deforested land in the Amazon rainforest of Brazil. Annually, it is estimated that net global deforestation accounts for about 2 gigatons of carbon emissions to the atmosphere.

20 世纪 50 年代，地球陆地表面的 15% 被雨林覆盖着。而如今，世界上超过一半的雨林已经消失殆尽，成为大火和链锯下的牺牲品。而且，破坏的速度在加剧。超过 1/5 的亚马逊雨林已经消失。

大量砍伐雨林带来很多严重后果：

- 空气和水污染 [1]
- 土壤侵蚀
- 疟疾的流行 [2]
- 二氧化碳向空气中的释放
- 印第安土著部落的被驱逐
- 动植物灭绝导致的生物多样性消失

雨林越少意味着会有更多的雨、更少可供呼吸的氧气，以及来自全球变暖的更严重威胁。

表达库
Bank of expressions

▶ 【热带雨林内在动态是一个复杂而脆弱的系统】The inner dynamics of a tropical rainforest is an intricate and fragile system.
▶ 【其中的一切都是相互依赖的】Everything is interdependent.
▶ 【影响一部分可以导致未知的破坏，甚至雨林整体的破坏】Upsetting one part can lead to unknown damage or even destruction of the whole.
▶ 【20 世纪 50 年代，地球陆地表面的 15% 被雨林覆盖着】In 1950, about 15 percent of the earth's land surface was covered by rainforest.
▶ 【世界上超过一半的雨林已经消失殆尽】more than half of the world's tropical rainforests has already gone up in smoke
▶ 【成为大火和链锯下的牺牲品】have fallen to be victim to fire and the chain saw
▶ 【破坏的速度在加剧】the rate of destruction is still accelerating
▶ 【超过 1/5 的亚马孙雨林已经消失】More than 20 percent of the Amazon rainforest is already gone.
▶ 【二氧化碳向空气中的释放】the release of carbon dioxide into the atmosphere
▶ 【印第安土著部落的被驱逐】the eviction of indigenous Indian tribes
▶ 【动植物灭绝导致的生物多样性消失】the loss of biodiversity through extinction of plants and animals
▶ 【雨林越少意味着会有更多的雨、更少可供呼吸的氧气，以及来自全球变暖的更严重威胁】Fewer rainforests mean less rain, less oxygen for us to breathe, and an increased threat from global warming.

核心词
Keywords

1. 空气和水污染（air and water pollution）
2. 疟疾的流行（malaria epidemics）

One hundred and fifty years ago, the monster began; this country had become a place of industry. Factories grew on the landscape like weeds. Trees fell, fields were up-ended, rivers blackened. The sky choked on smoke and ash, and the people did, too, spending their days coughing and itching, their eyes turned forever toward the ground. Villages grew into town, towns into cities. And people began to live on the earth rather than within it.

Patrick Ness

污染是指使用影响人类健康、生活质量或生态系统自然功能的物品污染地球环境。人类活动对自然环境造成各种影响，污染便是其中重要的一种。污染有很多种形式：

- 空气污染[1]
- 水污染[2]
- 土壤污染[3]
- 固体垃圾[4]
- 有害垃圾[5]
- 噪声污染[6]

人类对地球大气的污染从使用火来耕种、取暖和煮饭开始。但是在工业革命期间，空气污染变成一个重要的问题。影响深远的两起空气污染事件是，伦敦烟雾事件[7]和洛杉矶光化学烟雾事件[8]。空气污染还会导致酸雨[9]和臭氧层空洞[10]，二氧化碳排放过量会导致全球变暖[11]。

随着世界人口增长，对淡水的需求也在

表达库
Bank of expressions

- 【Factories grew on the landscape like weeds】工厂像野草一样在大地上出现。
- 【使用影响人类健康、生活质量或生态系统自然功能的物品污染地球环境】contamination of earth's environment with materials that interfere with human health, the quality of life, or the natural functioning of ecosystems
- 【人类对地球大气的污染从使用火来耕种、取暖和煮饭开始】Human contamination of earth's atmosphere has existed since humans first began to use fire for agriculture, heating, and cooking.
- 【但是在工业革命期间，空气污染变成一个重要的问题】During the period of the Industrial Revolution, however, air pollution became a major problem.
- 【随着世界人口增长，对淡水的需求也在不断增加】The demand for fresh water rises continuously as the world's population grows.

核心词
Keywords

1. 空气污染（air pollution）
2. 水污染（water pollution）
3. 土壤污染（soil pollution）
4. 固体垃圾（solid waste）
5. 有害垃圾（hazardous waste）
6. 噪声污染（noise pollution）
7. 伦敦烟雾事件（the Great Smog）
8. 洛杉矶光化学烟雾事件（the L.A. Photochemical Smog）
9. 酸雨（acid rain）
10. 臭氧层空洞（ozone depletion）
11. 全球变暖（global warming）

不断增加。污水、工业废物和农业化学品，如化肥和杀虫剂，是水污染的主要原因。水体富营养化[1]、海上漏油[2]、湿地[3]破坏、珊瑚礁[4]破坏等都对环境产生恶劣影响。

受酸雨影响的植被
Sulfuric acid can impact the increase in acid rain and cloud formation. Acid rain affects the terrestrial and aquatic life of plant, animals and marine creatures. It can also raise health concerns as it affects the respiratory system of the humans.

使用化肥、农药和杀菌剂会破坏诸如细菌、真菌等其他有益微生物。不可持续的耕种方法严重降低土壤质量。土壤肥力下降已经成为影响人类生存重要问题之一。

垃圾填埋场
Landfills are the most common place for garbage to be deposited all over the world. While these areas keep refuse out of sight and out of mind for most people, they produce a number of hazardous effects to people, animals, and the environment. Landfills are unsustainable, costly to operate, aesthetically displeasing, offensively smelly, producing harmful chemicals, and hazardous to environment.

表达库
Bank of expressions

► 【污水、工业废物和农业化学品，如化肥和杀虫剂，是水污染的主要原因】Sewage, industrial wastes, and agricultural chemicals such as fertilizers and pesticides are the main causes of water pollution.

► 【使用化肥、农药和杀菌剂会破坏诸如细菌、真菌等其他有益微生物】Treating the soil with chemical fertilizers, pesticides, and fungicides destroys useful organisms such as bacteria, fungi, and other microorganisms.

► 【不可持续的耕种方法严重降低土壤质量】Unsustainable farming methods have seriously degraded soil quality.

核心词
Keywords

1. 水体富营养化（eutrophication）
2. 海上漏油（oil spill）
3. 湿地（wetland）
4. 珊瑚礁（coral reef）

垃圾填埋[1]是世界范围内最便宜、最常见的固体垃圾处理方法。垃圾填埋场很快就填满，还可能污染空气、土壤和水体。生物可降解的[2]包装物和回收利用[3]是两种可行的减少固体垃圾的办法。

放射性废弃物[4]的储存、运输和保存都会影响环境和人体健康。噪声，特别是在人口密集区域，可能导致听力损伤、压力、高血压、失眠、精力不集中和效率下降。

地球主要环境问题
Major environmental issues that face the planet

Over population of humans	The world's population has tripled in the last 60 years placing stress on every aspect of the environment
Climate change	Human activities are currently affecting the climate
Loss of biodiversity	Humans have destroyed and continue to destroy the habitats of species on a daily basis
Water shortage	Currently, one third of humans have inadequate access to clean, fresh water
Ocean acidification	The oceans absorb as much as 25% of all human carbon dioxide emissions
Electronic and nuclear waste	Millions of electronic products such as computers, laptops, television sets and mobile phones are discarded annually in developed countries
Ozone layer depletion	Increased ultraviolet radiation in the atmosphere
Over fishing	Ocean overfishing is simply the taking of wildlife from the sea at rates too high for fished species to replace themselves
Deforestation	Trees provide habitats for many species in this world
Greenhouse gas emissions	Come from combustion of carbon-based fuels, principally wood, coal, oil, and natural gas
Animal poaching	Poaching is considered to have a detrimental effect on biodiversity The functionality of ecosystems is disturbed

表达库
Bank of expressions

► 【是世界范围内最便宜、最常见的固体垃圾处理方法】is the cheapest and most common disposal method for solid wastes worldwide
► 【垃圾填埋场很快就填满，还可能污染空气、土壤和水体】Landfills quickly become overfilled, and they may contaminate the air, soil, and waters.
► 【在人口密集区域】in densely populated areas
► 【可能导致听力损伤、压力、高血压、失眠、精力不集中和效率下降】can cause hearing loss, stress, high blood pressure, sleep loss, distraction, and lost productivity

核心词
Keywords

1. 垃圾填埋（landfill）
2. 生物可降解的（biodegradable）
3. 回收利用（recycling）
4. 放射性废弃物（radioactive waste）

笔记
Notes

These sprays, dusts, and aerosols are now applied almost universally to farms, gardens, forests, and homes—nonselective chemicals that have the power to kill every insect, the "good" and the "bad", to still the song of birds and the leaping of fish in the streams, to coat the leaves with a deadly film, and to linger on in soil—all this though the intended target may be only a few weeds or insects. Can anyone believe it is possible to lay down such a barrage of poisons on the surface of the earth without making it unfit for all life? They should not be called "insecticides", but "biocides".

Excerpt from *Silent Spring*, Rachel Carson

《寂静的春天》[1] 的作者是美国海洋生物学家[2]蕾切尔·卡逊[3]。这本书深刻地介绍了杀虫剂，尤其是滴滴涕，对野生生物的危害，生动地阐述了滥用杀虫剂如何造成鸟类种群数量下降，甚至灭绝。

这本书发起全世界环境保护运动，推动民间环保运动，推动美国政府成立环境保护局（简称 EPA 或 USEPA，1970 年成立），推

《寂静的春天》第一版封面
First edition cover art of *Silent Spring*

表达库
Bank of expressions

► 【These sprays, dusts, and aerosols are now applied almost universally to farms, gardens, forests, and homes】这些喷雾、粉尘和气溶胶现在被普遍用于农场、花园、森林和家庭中……

► 【still the song of birds and the leaping of fish in the streams, to coat the leaves with a deadly film, and to linger on in soil】让鸟儿不再鸣叫，让溪水中的鱼儿不再跳跃，给树叶披上一层致命的薄膜，并将它们残留在土壤中

► 【杀虫剂】pesticide 或 insecticide

► 【滴滴涕】化学名：双对氯苯基三氯乙烷（dichlorodiphenyltrichloroethane，简称 DDT）

► 【滥用杀虫剂】indiscriminate use of pesticides

► 【鸟类种群数量下降】decline in bird populations

► 【灭绝】be doomed to extinction, be in danger of extinction, become extinct

► 【发起全世界环境保护运动】launched the environmental movement across the world 或 advanced the global environmental movement

► 【推动民间环保运动】inspired a grassroots environmental movement

► 【成立环境保护局】the creation of the U.S. Environmental Protection Agency

核心词
Keywords

1.《寂静的春天》(Silent Spring)
2. 海洋生物学家 (marine biologist)
3. 蕾切尔·卡逊 (Rachel Carson)

动美国各州立法规定禁止生产和使用滴滴
涕。《寂静的春天》这本书在开篇首先描述
"和谐的自然环境"。

*THERE WAS ONCE a town in the heart
of America where all life seemed to live
in harmony with its surroundings. The
town lay in the midst of a checkerboard
of prosperous farms, with fields of grain
and hillsides of orchards where, in spring,
white clouds of bloom drifted above the
green fields. In autumn, oak and maple
and birch set up a blaze of color that
flamed and flickered across a backdrop of
pines. Then foxes barked in the hills and
deer silently crossed the fields, half hidden
in the mists of the fall mornings.*

*Along the roads, laurel, viburnum and
alder, great ferns and wildflowers delighted
the traveler's eye through much of the year.
Even in winter the roadsides were places
of beauty, where countless birds came to
feed on the berries and on the seed heads of
the dried weeds rising above the snow. The
countryside was, in fact, famous for the
abundance and variety of its bird life, and
when the flood of migrants was pouring
through in spring and fall, people traveled
from great distances to observe them.
Others came to fish the streams, which
flowed clear and cold out of the hills and
contained shady pools where trout lay. So
it had been from the days many years ago
when the first settlers raised their houses,
sank their wells, and built their barns.*

而后，笔锋一转，作者对比描写被杀虫
剂破坏的自然环境。

*Then a strange blight crept over the area
and everything began to change. Some
evil spell had settled on the community:
mysterious maladies swept the flocks of
chickens; the cattle and sheep sickened and
died. Everywhere was a shadow of death.
The farmers spoke of much illness among
their families. In the town the doctors had*

become more and more puzzled by new kinds of sickness appearing among their patients. There had been several sudden and unexplained deaths, not only among adults but even among children, who would be stricken suddenly while at play and die within a few hours.

There was a strange stillness. The birds, for example—where had they gone? Many people spoke of them, puzzled and disturbed. The feeding stations in the backyards were deserted. The few birds seen anywhere were moribund; they trembled violently and could not fly. It was a spring without voices. On the mornings that had once throbbed with the dawn chorus of robins, catbirds, doves, jays, wrens, and scores of other bird voices there was now no sound; only silence lay over the fields and woods and marsh.

说到滴滴涕，这种化学品也算是诺贝尔奖评审的败笔。保罗·穆勒[1]，瑞士化学家，因发现滴滴涕的杀虫功效，于 1948 年得到诺贝尔生理学或医学奖。当时有人称滴滴涕、青霉素及原子弹是第二次世界大战期间最伟大的三个发明。由于人类的短视，抗生素滥用的影响已经不容小视。滴滴涕和原子弹，这另外两个打开的潘多拉魔盒，更是给人类带来了灾难性的影响。

蕾切尔·卡逊
Rachel Carson
(1907-1964)
American biologist well known for her writings on environmental pollution and the natural history of the sea

表达库
Bank of expressions

► 【be stricken suddenly】突然患病

► 【The few birds seen anywhere were moribund】随处可见孤零零垂死挣扎的鸟儿……

► 【It was a spring without voices】这是一个没有鸟鸣的春天。

► 【On the mornings that had once throbbed with the dawn chorus of robins, catbirds, doves, jays, wrens, and scores of other bird voices there was now no sound】曾经，拂晓时分，知更鸟、猫声鸟、鸽子、乌鸦、鹪鹩和其他鸟儿的欢歌奏成一曲盛大的合唱；可是那些充满鸟鸣悸动的清晨，现在，已经死一般寂静。

► 【发现滴滴涕的杀虫功效】discovery of insecticidal qualities and use of DDT

► 【原子弹】atomic bomb 或 nuclear weapon

► 【滥用抗生素】antibiotic misuse, antibiotic abuse 或 antibiotic overuse

► 【打开的潘多拉魔盒】open a Pandora's box (to create evil that cannot be undone)

核心词
Keywords

1. 保罗·穆勒（Paul Müller）

大多数的空气污染来自一种人类活动——燃烧化石燃料，比如：

- 天然气[1]
- 煤炭[2]
- 汽油[3]
- 柴油[4]

燃烧化石燃料释放到大气的各种有害化学物质包括：

- 一氧化碳[5]
- 二氧化碳[6]
- 氮氧化物[7]
- 二氧化硫[8]
- 各种微尘[9]

这些有害气体可能导致的各种环境问题，包括全球变暖、臭氧层空洞、酸雨。有两次影响深远的空气污染事件值得大家记住，它们是：

- 伦敦烟雾事件
- 洛杉矶光化学烟雾事件

烟雾，指的是一氧化碳、二氧化硫和其他有机化合物的混合物，来自化石燃料的不完全燃烧。1952 年发生在英国伦敦的毒雾，是一次重大的大气污染事件。虽然伦敦一直被称为雾都，这一次却是致命的毒雾。

1952 年 12 月初，整个伦敦笼罩在浓雾中。几千人因呼吸系统疾病和心血管疾病丧命。这次污染直接推动首批现代环境法规，如《1956 年清洁空气法案》[10] 的制定。

表达库
Bank of expressions

- ▶【大多数的空气污染来自一种人类活动】Most air pollution comes from one human activity...
- ▶【燃烧化石燃料】burning fossil fuels
- ▶【有害化学物质】harmful chemical compounds
- ▶【一氧化碳、二氧化硫和其他有机化合物的混合物】a mixture of carbon monoxide, sulfur dioxide, and other organic compounds
- ▶【来自化石燃料的不完全燃烧】coming from incomplete combustion of fossil fuels
- ▶【毒雾】pea soup fog, black fog 或 killer fog
- ▶【雾都】a land of mists and fogs
- ▶【整个伦敦笼罩在浓雾中】a dense smoke-filled fog shrouded London
- ▶【呼吸系统疾病和心血管疾病】respiratory or cardiovascular problems
- ▶【直接推动首批现代环境法规】directly prompt some of the first major modern environmental legislation

核心词
Keywords

1. 天然气（natural gas）
2. 煤炭（coal）
3. 汽油（gasoline）
4. 柴油（diesel）
5. 一氧化碳（carbon monoxide）
6. 二氧化碳（carbon dioxide）
7. 氮氧化物（nitrogen oxides）
8. 二氧化硫（sulfur dioxide）
9. 各种微尘（particulate）
10.《1956 年清洁空气法案》（*Clean Air Act 1956*）

1952 年伦敦烟雾事件
The Great Smog affected London during December, 1952.

还有一种烟雾被称为光化学烟雾[1]，是由汽车和飞机发动机内燃料的燃烧产生。燃烧时释放的氮氧化物和来自未燃尽燃料的碳氢化合物[2]在阳光照射下结合并将氧气变成臭氧。臭氧可以腐蚀橡胶、侵害植物、刺激肺部。

1943 年洛杉矶光化学烟雾
Photograph of photochemical smog in the Los Angeles area. Photochemical smog, first identified in Los Angeles in 1944, is a serious environmental concern, and it poses a health problem to people living in many metropolitan regions around the world.

1943 年在三面环山、一面临海的洛杉矶，排放到空气中的汽车尾气产生的二氧化氮没有及时散去，在夏季充沛的阳光和高温作用下，导致城市低空形成臭氧富集，造成众多市民眼睛刺激[3]、喉咙刺激[4]、呼吸困难加重及其他呼吸道疾病[5]。

表达库
Bank of expressions

► 【是由汽车和飞机发动机内燃料的燃烧产生】is caused by combustion of fuels in car and airplane engines
► 【未燃尽燃料】unburned fuels
► 【结合并将氧气变成臭氧】combine and turn oxygen into ozone
► 【腐蚀橡胶、侵害植物、刺激肺部】attacks rubber, injures plants, and irritates lungs
► 【排放到空气中的汽车尾气产生的二氧化氮】nitrogen dioxide emitted from vehicles into the air
► 【夏季充沛的阳光和高温】abundance of sunlight and high temperatures during the summer
► 【城市低空形成臭氧富集】high ozone concentrations at lower levels
► 【呼吸困难加重】breathing problems can become aggravated

核心词
Keywords

1. 光化学烟雾（photochemical smog）
2. 碳氢化合物（hydrocarbons）
3. 眼睛刺激（eye irritation）
4. 喉咙刺激（throat irritation）
5. 呼吸道疾病（respiratory problems）

常见空气污染物
Common air pollutants

Carbon monoxide (CO)	Chiefly from the exhaust of internal combustion engines and incomplete combustion of various other fuels
Ground-level ozone (O_3)	Decreases lung function and causes respiratory symptoms, such as coughing and shortness of breath, and also makes asthma and other lung diseases get worse
Lead (Pb)	From combustion of leaded gasoline engines and battery manufacturing Damages the developing nervous system, resulting in IQ loss and impacts on learning, memory, and behavior in children
Nitrogen dioxide (NO_2)	From fuel combustion and wood burning Worsens lung diseases leading to respiratory symptoms
Particulate matter (PM)	Formed through chemical reactions, fuel combustion, field burning, and during road constructions Short- and long-term exposures can worsen heart or lung diseases
Sulfur dioxide (SO_2)	From coal combustion; electric utilities and industrial processes Aggravates asthma and makes breathing difficult

笔记
Notes

In one drop of water are found all the secrets of the oceans.

Kahlil Gibran

我们所有人都是太空人。我们乘坐着一架叫作"地球"的宇宙飞船，绕着太阳永不停息地旅行。这架宇宙飞船拥有得天独厚的生命保障系统。它是如此精巧，可以自我更新。它是如此庞大，可以支撑数以亿计的生命需求。

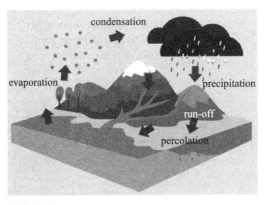

地球水循环
Water circulation on earth

地球水循环是一个持续更新的过程——瀑布[1]、水汽[2]、云、雨、小溪、江河、海洋、冰山[3]——这个循环从来没有被打破。太阳和地球之间合适的距离——既不太远，又不太近——使水得以循环。地球上的水道类似于人体的血管，或树木的枝干。地球水量保持不变，

表达库
Bank of expressions

▶【In one drop of water are found all the secrets of the oceans.】一滴水中蕴藏着大海的博大精深。

▶【我们所有人都是太空人】All of us are astronauts.

▶【我们乘坐着一架叫作"地球"的宇宙飞船，绕着太阳永不停息地旅行】We ride a spaceship called "earth" on its endless journey around the sun.

▶【这架宇宙飞船拥有得天独厚的生命支持系统】This ship of ours is blessed with life-support systems.

▶【如此精巧，可以自我更新】so ingenious that they are self-renewing

▶【如此庞大，可以支撑数以亿计的生命需求】so massive that they can supply the needs of billions

▶【地球水循环是一个持续更新的过程】The earth water cycle is a process of constant renewal...

▶【太阳和地球之间合适的距离】The right distance between the sun and the earth...

▶【使水得以循环】enables the circulation of water

▶【地球上的水道类似于人体的血管】The water channels on earth act like the veins of our body

▶【树木的枝干】branches of a tree

▶【地球水量保持不变】There is always the same quantity of water on earth.

核心词
Keywords

1. 瀑布（waterfall）
2. 水汽（water vapor）
3. 冰山（iceberg）

生生不息的物种得益于这共同的水源。列奥纳多·达·芬奇[1]（以下简称"达·芬奇"）曾说"水是自然的动力"。

Water is the driving force in nature.

美国著名思想家梭罗曾这样赞美湖水：

A lake is the landscape's most beautiful and expressive feature. It is earth's eye; looking into which the beholder measures the depth of his own nature.

地球上超过97%的水是咸水。然而，淡水——我们用来饮用、洗漱、浇灌田地的东西——非常稀缺。水资源匮乏的重要原因包括：

- 水污染
- 低效的农业[2]
- 人口增长[3]

土地干涸，埃及尼罗河附近农田
An Egyptian farmer shows the dryness of the land due to drought in a farm formerly irrigated by the River Nile.

水污染影响地表水、地下水，甚至降水。水污染的主要源头有人类产生的废物、工业垃圾、农药、公路径流。河流、湖泊和含水层要么枯竭，要么污染过重而无法使用。一些污染物可以在生物体内富集。在被严重影响的区域，水污染可以杀死大量的鱼

表达库
Bank of expressions

▶【生生不息的物种得益于这共同的水源】All the succession of species has drunk the same water on earth.

▶【地球上超过97%的水是咸水】More than 97 percent of earth's water is salt water.

▶【然而，淡水——我们用来饮用、洗漱、浇灌田地的东西——非常稀缺】However, freshwater—the stuff we drink, bathe in, irrigate our farm fields with—is incredibly rare.

▶【水污染影响地表水、地下水，甚至降水】Water pollution can affect surface water, groundwater and even rain.

▶【水污染的主要源头有人类产生的废物、工业垃圾、农药、公路径流】The major sources of water pollution are human wastes, industrial wastes, agricultural chemicals, and runoff from roads.

▶【河流、湖泊和含水层要么枯竭，要么污染过重而无法使用】Rivers, lakes and aquifers are drying up or becoming too polluted to use.

▶【一些污染物可以在生物体内富集】Some types of pollutants can build up in the bodies of living things.

▶【在被严重影响的区域】in severely affected areas

▶【水污染可以杀死大量的鱼类、鸟类和其他动物】water pollution can kill large numbers of fish, birds, and other animals

核心词
Keywords

1. 列奥纳多·达·芬奇（Leonardo da Vinci）
2. 低效的农业（inefficient agriculture）
3. 人口增长（population growth）

类、鸟类和其他动物。从被污染水域捕获的鱼类可能是不安全的。长时间接触受污染的水，人们可能患癌症，或者生出有生育缺陷的孩子。

农业生产使用了超过世界上一半的淡水，但是大部分的灌溉用水由于低效的农业设施而被浪费。气候变化改变全球天气模式，导致一些区域干旱缺水，而其他区域洪水泛滥。

在过去的五十年里，全球人口数量增长一倍多。伴随着经济增长和工业化，人口快速增长已经不可逆转地改变了全球水生态系统。水力发电站利用流动水的动能发电。

淡水缺乏原因
Causes of water scarcity

Population expansion	Just 50 years ago, the total number of people on earth has doubled and continues to grow
Urbanization	Cities are growing and expanding more than ever before, which means an increased need to take care of sewage, cleaning, construction and manufacturing
Pollution	Water, air and land pollution together contribute to the reduction of water quality
Vegetation destruction and deforestation	Trees help prevent excessive evaporation or water bodies
The destruction of forests by fire, logging and farming has exposed soil moisture and water bodies to the sun,'s intense heat, leaving them dried out
Climate change	Extreme weather mean more unpredictable floods and droughts

接下来的半个世纪，据预测，水——最重要的自然资源——将取代石油成为触发国际冲突的主要因素。全球超过十亿人缺水。一些中东国家和亚洲、非洲部分地区已经深受水资源匮乏影响。

湿地因其强大的天然净化作用，而被称作"地球之肾"。湿地可以调节河水流量，减缓雨季河水水流，避免洪水，在干旱季节避免旱灾。世界大部分的食物供给仰赖湿地环境。湿地是一些珍稀物种的自然栖息地。湿地又可以调节空气湿度和降水。湿地植物可以消耗大气中的温室气体。湿地是所有人休闲学习的好去处。湿地是天然的污水净

几种常见水污染
Types of water pollution

Nutrients pollution	Some wastewater, fertilizers and sewage which contain high levels of nutrients encourage algae and weed growth in the water Too much algae will also use up all the oxygen in the water
Oxygen depleting	Too much biodegradable matter encourages more microorganism growth, which use up more oxygen in the water
Ground water pollution	When humans apply pesticides and chemicals to soils, they are washed deep into the ground by rain water
Microorganisms	Some pollution caused by microorganisms like viruses, and bacteria
Chemical water pollution	Metals and solvents from industries can pollute water bodies Chemicals are poisonous to many forms of aquatic life
Oil spillage	Oil spills can cause the death of many fish and stick to the feathers of seabirds causing them to lose the ability to fly

表达库
Bank of expressions

- 【接下来的半个世纪】over the next half century
- 【据预测，水——最重要的自然资源——将取代石油成为触发国际冲突的主要因素】it is predicted that water, our most vital natural resource, will replace oil as the prime trigger for international conflicts
- 【全球超过十亿人缺水】More than one billion people worldwide lack access to water.
- 【一些中东国家和亚洲、非洲部分地区已经深受水资源匮乏影响】Some Middle Eastern countries as well as parts of Asia and Africa are already suffering from water shortages.
- 【天然净化】natural filtering processes
- 【被称作"地球之肾"】be dubbed "the kidneys of the earth"
- 【调节河水流量】regulate river volumes
- 【减缓河水雨季流量】slow water flow in the rain season
- 【避免洪水】prevent floods
- 【在干旱季节避免旱灾】prevent droughts in the dry seasons
- 【世界大部分的食物供给仰赖湿地环境】A large portion of the world's food supply depends on wetland.
- 【珍稀物种的自然栖息地】natural habitat for many rare species
- 【调节空气湿度和降水】maintain local levels of humidity and rainfall
- 【消耗大气中的温室气体】remove greenhouse gases from the earth's atmosphere
- 【是所有人休闲学习的好去处】offer tremendous recreation and learning opportunities for people of all ages
- 【湿地是天然的污水净化系统】Wetlands provide natural water filtration.

化系统。当水缓慢地流过湿地，废物沉淀下来。湿地还有助于控制洪水。

世界自然基金会[1]评选出的世界著名湿地包括：巴西的低地湿地[2]、法国的卡玛格湿地[3]、印度尼西亚的瓦素尔国家公园[4]、澳大利亚卡卡杜湿地[5]、印度的喀拉拉邦湿地[6]、赞比亚卡富埃湿地国家公园[7]、美国佛罗里达大沼泽地国家公园[8]和孟加拉国苏达班国家公园[9]等。

湿地经常是填海造地的受害者。据估计，超过 6% 的地表面积被湿地覆盖，这一面积甚至大于整个欧洲面积。自 1990 年，据计算，全世界有一半的湿地被破坏，这是人类活动对地球生态造成的又一重大威胁。

1975 年，18 个缔约国共同签订《湿地公约》，也称《拉姆萨尔公约》[10]。截至 2013 年，《拉姆萨尔公约》总共有 168 个缔约成员。该公约为保护与合理利用湿地及湿地资源的国家行动和国际合作提供框架。

潘塔纳尔湿地，南美洲
The Pantanal is one of the world's largest tropical wetland areas. About 80% of the Pantanal floodplains are submerged during the rainy seasons.

表达库
Bank of expressions

▶【当水缓慢地流过湿地，废物沉淀下来】As water moves slowly through a wetland, waste materials settle out.

▶【湿地还有助于控制洪水】Wetlands also help control floods.

▶【填海造地的受害者】the victim of large draining efforts for real estate development

▶【据估计】It is estimated that...

▶【地表面积被湿地覆盖】the earth's land surface are covered by wetlands

▶【人类活动对地球生态造成的又一重大威胁】another threat to the earth's ecosystems by human activity

▶【《湿地公约》】全称是 Convention of Wetlands of International Importance Especially as Waterfowl Habitats

▶【为保护与合理利用湿地及湿地资源的国家行动和国际合作提供框架】provides a framework for local action and international cooperation in the conservation and rational use of wetlands and wetland resources

核心词
Keywords

1. 世界自然基金会（World Wide Fund for Nature，简称 WWF）
2. 低地湿地（Pantanal）
3. 卡玛格湿地（Camargue）
4. 瓦素尔国家公园（Wasur National Park）
5. 卡卡杜湿地（Kakadu Wetlands）
6. 喀拉拉邦湿地（Kerala backwaters）
7. 卡富埃湿地国家公园（Kafue National Park）
8. 佛罗里达大沼泽地国家公园（Everglades National Park）
9. 苏达班国家公园（Sundarbans）
10. 《拉姆萨尔公约》（Ramsar Convention）

地球上的生命离不开水。如果水中充满有毒化学物质或有害微生物，没有生命可以生存。如果严重，水污染可以杀死大量鱼类、鸟类和其他动物，甚至杀死所有生活在被污染区域的物种。本杰明·富兰克林[1] 曾说：

When the well is dry, we know the worth of water.

关于水污染，1999 年，世界银行发表报告称：

Water is essential for all dimensions of life. Over the past few decades, use of water has increased, and in many places water availability is falling to crisis levels. More than eighty countries, with forty percent of the world's population, are already facing water shortages, while by year 2020 the world's population will double. The costs of water infrastructure have risen dramatically. The quality of water in rivers and underground has deteriorated, due to pollution by waste and contaminants from cities, industry and agriculture. Ecosystems are being destroyed, sometimes permanently. Over one billion people lack safe water, and three billion lack sanitation; eighty percent of infectious diseases are waterborne, killing millions of children each year.

水污染物主要包括：

- 石油产品
- 杀虫剂和除草剂
- 重金属
- 有害废物
- 有机物过量
- 热污染

表达库
Bank of expressions

- ►【地球上的生命离不开水】Life could not exist without water.
- ►【如果水中充满有毒化学物质或有害微生物，没有生命可以生存】Life cannot survive if water is loaded with toxic chemicals or harmful microorganisms.
- ►【如果严重，水污染可以杀死大量鱼类、鸟类和其他动物】If severe, water pollution can kill large numbers of fish, birds, and other animals...
- ►【甚至杀死所有生活在被污染区域的物种】and even kill all members of a species in an affected area
- ►【Water is essential for all dimensions of life】水对于生命所有方面都是不可或缺的。
- ►【water availability is falling to crisis levels】水资源供应量正逼近警戒线
- ►【facing water shortages】面临水资源短缺
- ►【eighty percent of infectious diseases are waterborne80%】传染病通过水传播
- ►【石油产品】petroleum products
- ►【杀虫剂和除草剂】pesticides and herbicides
- ►【重金属】heavy metals
- ►【有害废物】hazardous wastes
- ►【有机物过量】excess organic matter
- ►【热污染】thermal pollution

核心词
Keywords

1. 本杰明·富兰克林（Benjamin Franklin）

■ 感染性微生物

从石油中提炼出的汽油、柴油和其他化合物常用作燃料、润滑剂、塑料生产或其他用途。石油产品主要通过船舶意外溢油、油罐车、输油管道和地下储油桶泄漏等途径进入水体。

当动物食用了被无法降解的化学品污染过的植物，这些化学物质就被吸收进入动物的组织或器官。当其他动物以被污染的动物为食，这些化学物质便通过食物链传递。这个过程被称为生物富集作用。

Up to 90 % of wastewater in developing countries flows untreated into rivers, lakes and highly productive coastal zones, threatening health, food security and access to safe drinking and bathing water.

Source: World Water Development Report 2012

Many industries, some of them known to be heavily polluting (such as leather and chemicals) - are moving from high-income countries to emerging market economies. Despite improvements in some regions, water pollution is on the rise globally.

Source: World Water Assessment Program (WWAP)

重金属，如铅[1]、水银[2]和硒[3]，可以通过工业废水、汽车尾气、矿山等途径排入水体。和杀虫剂一样，重金属也可以在动物体内富集。

表达库
Bank of expressions

▶【感染性微生物】infectious organisms

▶【从石油中提炼出的汽油、柴油和其他化合物常用作燃料、润滑剂、塑料生产或其他用途】Gasoline, diesel, and chemicals derived from oil are used for fuel, lubrication, plastics manufacturing, and many other purposes.

▶【石油产品主要通过船舶意外溢油、油罐车、输油管道和地下储油桶泄漏等途径进入水体】These petroleum products get into water mainly by means of accidental spills from ships, tanker trucks, pipelines, and leaky underground storage tanks.

▶【当动物食用了被无法降解的化学品污染过的植物】When animals consume plants that have been treated with certain nonbiodegradable chemicals...

▶【这些化学物质就被吸收进入动物的组织或器官】these chemicals are absorbed into the tissues or organs of the animals

▶【当其他动物以被污染的动物为食】When other animals feed on these contaminated animals...

▶【这些化学物质便通过食物链传递】the chemicals are passed up the food chain

▶【这个过程被称为生物富集作用】This process is called bioaccumulation.

▶【通过工业废水、汽车尾气、矿山等途径排入水体】get into waters from industry wastes, automobile exhaust and mines

核心词
Keywords

1. 铅（lead）
2. 水银（mercury）
3. 硒（selenium）

化肥和其他促进农田和花园植物生长的养料可能进入水体。这些养分促进水中植物和水藻生长。当植物和水藻死去，微生物将它们分解，并消耗掉溶解于水中的氧气。因此，当植物和水藻过量时，水中氧气含量会变得过低，最终导致水中依赖氧气的动物死亡。水中氧气含量变得过低会导致水中依赖氧气的动物死亡。

历史上有多起影响恶劣的水污染事件，其中包括：

- 水俣病[1]
- 痛痛病[2]

日本水俣病患者
A severe case of Minamata disease
For decades the Chisso Corporation dumped methylmercury into Minamata Bay of Japan, resulting in high levels of mercury in fish caught by bay's residents, leading to miscarriages, congenital Minamata disease, and adult Minamata disease

20世纪50年代，水俣病，一种汞中毒的神经性综合征，发生在日本熊本县水俣市。最后查明，发病原因是当地化肥厂将甲基汞排入工业废水。患者手足麻木，运动失调[3]，麻痹[4]，视觉、听力及言语障碍。重者可能会出现痉挛、昏迷[5]、神经错乱[6]等，这些症状开始后数周便死亡。

几乎同一时期，在日本的富山县，出现了痛痛病，即镉中毒[1]。当地矿山开采向水中排入大量镉，并被水稻吸收，从而进入人体。镉中毒导致骨质疏松症及肾衰竭[2]。病名来自患者由于关节和脊骨极度痛楚而发出的叫喊声。

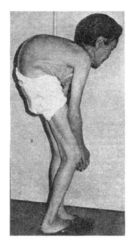

日本痛痛病患者
Itai-itai translated from Japanese is literally "ouch-ouch". It refers to a syndrome that principally consists of a painful skeletal condition resulting from weak and deformed bones. Itai-itai disease was found in the cadmium(Cd) polluted Jinzu River basin in Toyama Prefecture

水污染的影响
Effects of water pollution

Death of aquatic animals	Water pollution kills life that depends on water bodies
Disruption of food-chains	Pollution disrupts the natural food chain Pollutants such as lead and cadmium are accumulated through food chain
Diseases	Human being can get diseases such as hepatitis by eating seafood that has been poisoned Poor drinking water is resulted from contaminated waters.
Destruction of ecosystems	Ecosystems can be severely changed or destroyed by water pollution

表达库
Bank of expressions

▶【骨质疏松症】softening of the bones
▶【病名来自患者由于关节和脊骨极度痛楚而发出的叫喊声】It named for the severe pains caused in the joints and spine.

核心词
Keywords

1. 镉中毒（cadmium poisoning）
2. 肾衰竭（kidney failure）

笔记
Notes

Wilderness is not only a <u>haven for native plants and animals</u> but it is also a refuge from society. It's a place to go to hear the wind and little else, see the stars and the galaxies, smell the pine trees, feel the cold water, touch the sky and the ground at the same time, listen to coyotes, eat the fresh snow, walk across the desert sands, and realize why it's good to go outside of the city and the suburbs.

John Muir

原生态区域可以理解为——地球上没有遭到人类改造的自然生态环境。美国国会 1964 年通过的《荒原法》[1] 中这样定义 "wilderness"：

A wilderness, in contrast with those areas where man and his own works dominate the landscape, is hereby recognized as an area where <u>the earth and its community of life are untrammeled by man</u>, where man himself is a visitor who does not remain.

自然主义者 [2] 梭罗第一个提出 "在荒野中保留一个世界" 的设想。梭罗认为自然是有生命的、有人格的，他这样评价自然：

Nature is full of genius, full of the divinity; so that not a snowflake escapes its fashioning hand.

根据对原生态区域保护目的不同，思想界分为两大流派：保护主义者 [3]，和保护管理主义者 [4]。

表达库
Bank of expressions

► 【 haven for native plants and animals 】天然动植物的天堂
► 【 the earth and its community of life are untrammeled by man 】土地和自然环境不受人类限制

核心词
Keywords

1.《荒原法》(*Wilderness Act*)
2. 自然主义者（ naturalist ）
3. 保护主义者（ preservationist ）
4. 保护管理主义者（ conservationist ）

笔记
Notes

前者认为"为保护环境本身而保护"，这样后代可以享受大自然。他们认为人是自然的一部分，并不是自然的所有者。而保护管理主义者主要对经济感兴趣，他们主张保护环境为将来开发利用。支持原生态区域保护的观点包括：

- 对一些物种的生存很重要
- 保护生物多样性
- 是重要的休闲娱乐去处
- 从事科学实验
- 因为文化、精神、美学等原因被重视

世界著名自然景观
Top 10 amazing natural wonders

Yellowstone National Park	Wyoming, US
The Grand Canyon	Arizona, US
The Great Barrier Reef	Australia
Angel Falls	Venezuela
Aurora Borealis	Northern Hemisphere
The Amazon Rainforest	South America
Milford Sound	New Zealand
Uluru/Ayers Rock,	Australia
Niagara Falls	Canada and US
Mount Qomolangma	Tibet, China

也有反对原生态区域保护的观点。生活在原生态区域的当地人认为，以娱乐为目的保护原生态区域对当地人是自私的、残忍的。况且，开采原材料和自然资源维持了当地经济，保证了当地人的生活标准。原生态区域保护将会破坏当地经济，严重影响当地人的生计。

表达库
Bank of expressions

▶【为保护环境本身而保护】preserve the environment for its own sake
▶【后代可以享受大自然】future generations could enjoy the nature
▶【认为人是自然的一部分，并不是自然的所有者】view human as a part of nature, and not as the owner of it
▶【主要对经济感兴趣】are mainly interested in economics
▶【保护环境为将来开发利用】conserve the environment for future development
▶【对一些物种的生存很重要】important for the survival of certain species
▶【保护生物多样性】protect biodiversity
▶【是重要的休闲娱乐去处】premier outdoor recreation destination
▶【从事科学实验】conduct scientific research
▶【因为文化、精神、美学等原因被重视】deeply valued for cultural, spiritual, and aesthetic reasons
▶【以娱乐为目的保护原生态区域对当地人是自私的、残忍的】preservation of wilderness for recreational purposes is selfish and cruel to the local people
▶【开采原材料和自然资源维持了当地经济】raw materials and natural resources exploitation fueled the local economy
▶【保证了当地人的生活标准】maintained the living standard of local people
▶【原生态区域保护将会破坏当地经济】Wilderness area preservation would destroy local economy...
▶【严重影响当地人的生计】severely affect the livelihoods for the local people

一些发达国家通过利用发展中国家资源，推动自己国家经济发展。生活在发达国家的民众一边消耗着发展中国家大量自然资源，一边却仍然保持着不可持续的生活方式，而且享受着原生态区域带来的美，这更是一种残忍。以人类自我为中心的生活方式只能加速对自然的破坏。人类应该对自然心存敬畏，以自然为中心[1]。爱因斯坦曾说：

Our task must be to...embrace all living creatures and the whole of nature and its beauty.

塔肯荒野，澳大利亚
Tarkine Rainforest in Tasmania, a wonderland of wild rivers, secret waterfalls, giant tree ferns, rare birds

亨利·戴维·梭罗
Henry David Thoreau (1817-1862)
American essayist, poet, and practical philosopher, best known for his book *Walden* and his essay *Civil Disobedience*

表达库
Bank of expressions

► 【一些发达国家通过利用发展中国家资源，推动自己国家经济发展】Developed nations fueled their own economic development by exploiting the natural resources of developing countries.
► 【消耗着发展中国家大量自然资源】Consuming a large amount of natural resources imported from developing countries...
► 【享受着原生态区域带来的美】enjoy the beauty of the wilderness areas
► 【以人类自我为中心的生活方式】human-centered way of life
► 【对自然心存敬畏】respect for nature

核心词
Keywords

1. 以自然为中心（natured-centered）

笔记
Notes

The soil is the great connector of lives, the source and destination of all. It is the healer and restorer and resurrector, by which disease passes into health, age into youth, death into life. Without proper care for it we can have no community, because without proper care for it we can have no life.

Wendell Berry

土壤是地球脆弱的皮肤，维系着地球所有的生命。它包含着数不尽的物种，创造了一个充满生机而又复杂的生态系统，是人类宝贵的资源。对农产品的需求增长促使人们将森林和草原改造成田园和农场。从自然植被到农作物的转变不能稳固土壤。

土壤侵蚀造成的影响已经不仅是失去富饶土地那么简单。土壤侵蚀导致污染增加。沉积在小溪和江河的土壤阻塞水道，导致鱼类和其他物种数量下降。

水土流失的原因有很多：

■ 砍伐森林
■ 过度放牧 [1]
■ 滥用农药 [2]

土地荒漠化降低土壤固碳能力
Soil erosion depletes the amount of carbon the soil is able to store

表达库
Bank of expressions

► 【the source and destination of all 】万物的源头和终点
► 【土壤是地球脆弱的皮肤 】Soil is the earth's fragile skin...
► 【维系着地球所有的生命 】anchors all life on earth
► 【它包含数不尽的物种 】It is comprised of countless species...
► 【创造一个充满生机而又复杂的生态系统 】creates a dynamic and complex ecosystem
► 【是人类宝贵的资源 】is among the most precious resources to humans
► 【对农产品的需求增长促使人们将森林和草原改造成田园和农场 】Increased demand for agriculture commodities generates incentives for people to convert forests and grasslands to farm fields and pastures.
► 【从自然植被到农作物的转变不能稳固土壤 】The transition to crops from natural vegetation often cannot hold onto the soil.
► 【土壤侵蚀造成的影响已经不仅是失去富饶土地那么简单 】The effects of soil erosion go beyond the loss of fertile land.
► 【土壤侵蚀导致污染增加 】It has led to increased pollution.
► 【沉积在小溪和江河的土壤阻塞水道 】Sedimentation in streams and rivers clogs these waterways...
► 【导致鱼类和其他物种数量下降 】causes declines in fish and other species

核心词
Keywords

1. 过度放牧（overgrazing）
2. 滥用农药（abuse of agrochemicals）

土壤中含有大量以有机物形式存在的碳元素，这些有机物为植物生长提供营养，提高土壤肥力，有助于水循环。土壤固碳能力很容易被人类活动削弱。砍伐森林、城市发展[1]、过度放牧等活动很容易明显降低土壤含碳量。土壤碳很容易流失，但是很难恢复。

　　随着人口不断增长，越来越多的土地被开垦用于农业，或被开发作其他用途，这使得土壤退化。没有植被覆盖，土壤侵蚀更容易发生。当土地失去肥沃的土壤，农业生产者便继续清除更多的森林，土壤流失的恶性循环不断继续。

土壤侵蚀的影响
Effects of soil erosion

Loss of arable land	Loss of topsoil and destruction of soil characteristics
Clogged and polluted waterways	Soil eroded from the land, along with pesticides and fertilizers applied to fields, washes into streams and waterways This sedimentation and pollution can damage freshwater and marine habitats
Increased flooding	The converted land is less able to soak up water, making flooding more common

过度放牧使地表植被减少，并通过风

表达库
Bank of expressions

▶【土壤中含有大量以有机物形式存在的碳元素】Soil contains huge quantities of carbon in the form of organic matter...
▶【为植物生长提供营养，提高土壤肥力，有助于水循环】provides nutrients for plant growth and improves soil fertility and facilitates water movement
▶【土壤固碳能力很容易被人类活动削弱】Soil carbon stocks are highly vulnerable to human activities.
▶【土壤碳很容易流失，但是很难恢复】Soil carbon is easily lost but difficult to rebuild.
▶【随着人口不断增长】As the human population has expanded...
▶【越来越多的土地被开垦用于农业】more and more land has been cleared for agriculture
▶【被开发作其他用途】developed for other pursuits
▶【使得土壤退化】degrade the soil
▶【没有植被覆盖，土壤侵蚀更容易发生】Without plant cover, erosion can be more likely to occur.
▶【当土地失去肥沃的土壤】As land loses its fertile soil...
▶【农业生产者便继续清除更多的森林】agricultural producers move on and clear more forest
▶【土壤流失的恶性循环不断继续】the vicious cycle of soil loss continues
▶【过度放牧使地表植被减少】Overgrazing can reduce ground cover...

核心词
Keywords

1. 城市发展（urban development）

和雨使表层土壤和养分流失。杀虫剂和其他农用化学品有助于提高产量。过度使用这些化学品会改变土壤组分，破坏土壤微生物平衡。土壤的健康是农民和所有人最关切的头等大事。我们的生计依赖于脚下这片土地。

土壤侵蚀造成的沟壑，柏哥利亚湖，肯尼亚
Large scale erosion forming a gully system around six meters deep, Lake Bogoria, Kenya
The cause of the erosion is over grazing due to goats and other livestock. On the global basis, the soil degradation is caused primarily by overgrazing (35%), agricultural activities (28%), deforestation (30%), overexploitation of land to produce fuel wood (7%), and industrialization (4%).

笔记
Notes

温室气体在环境中自然存在。温室气体，如二氧化碳，将热量保存在大气层，调节地球气候。温室气体就像是一层毯子。毯子越厚，地球越暖。通过燃烧化石燃料，人类向大气排放了更多二氧化碳。气候变化对物种和人类的生存构成最根本的威胁，其中包括：

- 出现极端天气
- 冰山融化
- 海平面上升
- 影响动植物生存

全球气温上升导致更多极端和不可预测的天气出现。热浪会变得更加频繁。很多地方会出现创纪录的干旱或强降水。飓风和暴风雨可能变得更强烈。

气候变化的影响
Effects of climate change

Extreme weather	Droughts, violent storms and heavy rains will be more frequent
Natural habitats	Distort natural habitats and lives for many plants and animals
Water bodies drying out	Droughts, bush fires and loss of diversity
Ocean acidification	More CO_2 emitted since the Industrial Revolution More CO_2 absorbed by the oceans
Melting glaciers	Polar ice cap is now melting at an alarming rate Rising sea level Causing more floods Drowning low-lying towns and cities

表达库
Bank of expressions

► 【温室气体在环境中自然存在】Greenhouse gases occur naturally in the environment.

► 【温室气体，如二氧化碳，将热量保存在大气层】Greenhouses gases, such as carbon dioxide, trap heat in the atmosphere...

► 【调节地球气候】regulate the earth's climate

► 【温室气体就像是一层毯子】Greenhouse gases act like a blanket.

► 【毯子越厚，地球越暖】The thicker the blanket is, the warmer our planet becomes.

► 【通过燃烧化石燃料】By burning fossil fuels for energy...

► 【人类向大气排放了更多二氧化碳】human has released far more carbon dioxide into the atmosphere

► 【气候变化对物种和人类的生存构成最根本的威胁】Climate change poses a fundamental threat to the species and people's livelihoods.

► 【极端天气】extreme weather pattern

► 【冰山融化】melting of glaciers

► 【海平面上升】sea level rise

► 【全球气温上升导致更多极端和不可预测的天气出现】The increase in global temperature results in more extreme and unpredictable weather.

► 【热浪会变得更加频繁】Heat waves are becoming more frequent.

► 【很多地方会出现创纪录的干旱或强降水】Many places are experiencing record droughts or intense rainfalls.

► 【飓风和暴风雨可能变得更强烈】Hurricanes, violent storms are likely to become more severe.

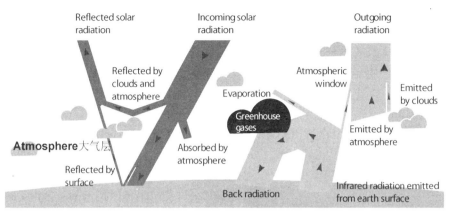

Reflected solar radiation

Incoming solar radiation

Outgoing radiation

Reflected by clouds and atmosphere

Evaporation

Atmospheric window

Emitted by clouds

Greenhouse gases

Atmosphere 大气层

Absorbed by atmosphere

Emitted by atmosphere

Reflected by surface

Back radiation

Infrared radiation emitted from earth surface

温室效应原理

The atmosphere's greenhouse gases (especially water vapor, carbon dioxide, and methane) absorb more infrared radiation, which further warms the earth.

　　冰的融化越来越快。气候变暖已经导致一些区域发生重大变化，其中包括世界范围内的高山冰川、格陵兰岛和南极地区的冰盖，以及北极地区的极地海冰。大规模融冰可能加速全球变暖。世界范围内的冰川融化导致海平面显著上升。海平面上升，海洋变得越来越温暖。海平面上升可能使世界范围内的低洼地带和沿海区域增加被

气候变化影响到海龟筑巢

Climate change has an impact on turtle nesting sites. It alters sand temperatures, which then affects the sex of hatchlings.

表达库
Bank of expressions

▶ 【冰的融化越来越快】Melting of ice is becoming more rapid.

▶ 【气候变暖已经导致一些区域发生重大变化，其中包括世界范围的高山冰川、格陵兰岛和南极地区的冰盖，以及北极地区的极地海冰】Warming temperatures are already causing significant changes to some places, which include mountain glaciers around the world, ice sheets in Greenland and the Antarctic, and polar sea ice in the Arctic.

▶ 【大规模融冰可能加速全球变暖】The large-scale melting of ice may accelerate the pace of global warming.

▶ 【世界范围内的冰川融化导致海平面显著上升】Loss of ice in glaciers worldwide makes a significant contribution to observed sea level rise.

▶ 【海平面上升，海洋变得越来越温暖】Sea levels are rising and oceans are becoming warmer.

▶ 【海平面上升可能使世界范围内的低洼地带和沿海区域增加被淹没的风险】Raising sea levels could bring greater risk of floods to low-lying and coastal regions worldwide.

淹没的风险。海滨城市会变成泽地。低洼地区，如孟加拉国，会被淹没。一些到岛国会消失。随之产生的移民潮会影响民众生活、农业、经济及国家政治稳定。

温室气体排放

Glaciers are melting, sea levels are rising, cloud forests are drying, and wildlife is scrambling to keep pace. It's becoming clear that humans have caused most of the past century's warming by releasing heat-trapping gases, called greenhouse gases, as we power our modern lives.

　　动植物可能很难适应气候变暖影响。科学家发现，春天里一些植物开花更早，一些鸟卵更早孵化。更多持久的严重干旱威胁作物、野生动物和淡水供应。北极熊、海豹、海象等生物依赖海冰生存。

　　世界范围内的科学家已经达成普遍共识，气候变化主要由人类活动导致。燃烧化石燃料，如煤、油和天然气，产生能量，对大气产生巨大影响。世界范围内，森林在以惊人的速度被砍伐，特别是在热带雨林地区。

为防止全球变暖，很多国家致力于减少二氧化碳排放，并且使用可再生能源。减少温室气体排放是控制气候变暖的必要策略。避免二氧化碳进入大气的方法之一是保护及种植树木。减缓森林砍伐速率、种植新树木可以帮助抵消温室气体积累。太阳能、风能和氢燃料电池不排放温室气体。这些能源可以作为化石燃料的替代品。混合动力车使用电能和汽油机或柴油机，比传统汽车释放的二氧化碳更少。

受气候变化影响的动物
Some species at risk caused by climate change

Polar bear	Polar bears are dependent on floating ice to catch prey Sea ice melting endangers the polar bear's habitat and existence
Sea turtle	Sea turtles lay their eggs on Brazilian beaches, many of which are threatened by rising sea levels Nest temperature strongly determines the sex and climate change seriously threatens turtle populations
North Atlantic right whale	Warming waters contain less plankton for whales to feed on
Giant panda	Bamboo, the panda's staple diet, could be affected by the changes caused by global warming

► 【为防止全球变暖，很多国家致力于减少二氧化碳排放，并且使用可再生能源】To prevent global warming, many countries are making efforts to reduce their output of carbon dioxide and use renewable energy sources.

► 【减少温室气体排放是控制气候变暖的必要策略】Reducing emissions of greenhouse gases is a necessary strategy for controlling global warming.

► 【避免二氧化碳进入大气的方法之一是保护及种植树木】One way to keep carbon dioxide emissions from reaching the atmosphere is to preserve and plant more trees.

► 【减缓森林砍伐速率、种植新树木可以帮助抵消温室气体积累】Slowing the rate of deforestation and planting new trees can help counteract the buildup of greenhouse gases.

► 【太阳能、风能和氢燃料电池不排放温室气体】Solar power, wind power, and hydrogen fuel cells emit no greenhouse gases.

► 【这些能源可以作为化石燃料的替代品】These energy sources can be alternatives to fossil fuels.

► 【使用电能和汽油机或柴油机】uses both an electric motor and a gasoline or diesel engine

► 【比传统汽车释放的二氧化碳更少】emits less carbon dioxide than conventional automobiles

The hole in the ozone layer is a kind of skywriting. At first it seemed to spell out our continuing complacency before a witch's brew of deadly perils. But perhaps it really tells of a newfound talent to work together to protect the global environment.

Carl Sagan

臭氧分子由三个氧原子组成。氧气和来自太阳的紫外线作用在地球同温层产生臭氧层。臭氧层就像一面滤镜，吸收太阳光中大部分紫外线，从而避免有害紫外线到达地球，保护地球生物免受其侵害。紫外线中的短波辐射会破坏生命体细胞结构。紫外线辐射可以导致皮肤癌的发生，增加患白内障的风险。它甚至可能削弱人体免疫系统抵抗能力。紫外线辐射也会影响其他生命形式。

臭氧层破坏的后果
Effects of ozone depletion

Human health	Skin cancer Increase in cases of snow-blindness and cataracts Immune system affected
Plants	Plant growth affected Plant nutrients affected Damage to crops
Marine ecosystem	Phytoplankton growth affected Growth of fish, shrimp, crab, and amphibians affected

表达库
Bank of expressions

- 【spell out our continuing complacency】拼写出人类的自豪
- 【witch's brew of deadly perils】女巫酿出的致命危险
- 【臭氧分子由三个氧原子组成】Ozone is a molecule that consists of three oxygen atoms.
- 【氧气和来自太阳的紫外线作用在地球同温层产生臭氧层】Reactions between oxygen and ultraviolet radiation from the sun create a layer of ozone throughout earth's stratosphere.
- 【臭氧层就像一面滤镜】The ozone layer acts as a screen...
- 【吸收太阳光中大部分紫外线】absorbs most of the ultraviolet radiation from the sun
- 【从而避免有害紫外线到达地球】preventing harmful ultraviolet rays from reaching the earth
- 【保护地球生物免受其侵害】protecting life on earth from this biologically damaging form of energy
- 【紫外线中的短波辐射会破坏生命体细胞结构】Short wavelengths of ultraviolet radiation are damaging to the cell structure of living organisms.
- 【紫外线辐射可以导致皮肤癌的发生】Ultraviolet radiation causes skin cancer...
- 【增加患白内障的风险】increases the risk of cataracts
- 【它甚至可能削弱人体免疫系统抵抗能力】It may also weaken the human body's disease-fighting immune system.
- 【紫外线辐射也会影响其他生命形式】Ultraviolet radiation threatens other forms of life as well.

它影响植物光合作用，导致农作物减产。

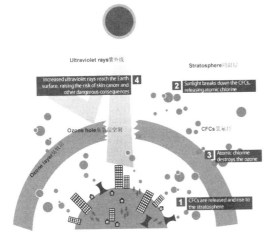

臭氧层破坏及后果
Ozone depleting causes and consequences

20 世纪 80 年代，人们发现臭氧层正在变薄这一事实。南极洲的臭氧层最早遭到破坏。出现在南极洲上空巨大的臭氧空洞不仅威胁南极洲，而且威胁到其他大洲，因为这些地方可能成为南极冰盖融化的受害者。科学家经过研究发现，造成臭氧空洞的罪魁祸首是一系列被称为"氯氟烃[1]"的化合物。氯氟烃被用在生产制造电冰箱、塑料泡沫和一次性餐盒中。为了避免氯氟烃进一步对臭氧层造成破坏，1987 年约 30 个国家签署了《关于消耗臭氧层物质的蒙特利尔议定书》[2]，致力于保护臭氧层不被破坏。

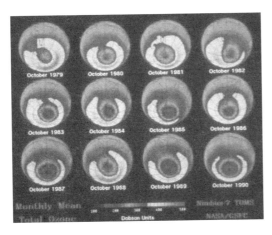

表达库
Bank of expressions

▶【它影响植物光合作用】It may interfere with plant photosynthesis...
▶【导致农作物减产】reduce agricultural production
▶【20 世纪 80 年代，人们发现臭氧层正在变薄这一事实】The fact that the ozone layer was being depleted was discovered in the 1980s.
▶【南极洲的臭氧层最早遭到破坏】Antarctica was an early victim of ozone destruction.
▶【出现在南极洲上空巨大的臭氧空洞不仅威胁南极洲，而且威胁到其他大洲，因为这些地方可能成为南极冰盖融化的受害者】A massive hole in the ozone layer right above Antarctica now threatens not only that continent, but many others because they could be the victims of Antarctica's melting icecaps.
▶【氯氟烃被用在生产制造电冰箱、塑料泡沫和一次性餐盒中】CFCs came to be used in refrigerators, plastic foam, and throwaway food containers.

核心词
Keywords

1.氯氟烃（chlorofluorocarbons，简称为 CFCs）
2.《关于消耗臭氧层物质的蒙特利尔议定书》（*Montreal Protocol on Substances that Deplete the Ozone Layer*）

1979 ~ 1990 年南极上空臭氧层变化
Changes in the size of the ozone hole from October 1979 to October 1990

The worst sin toward our fellow creatures is not to hate them, but to be indifferent to them; that's the essence of humanity.

George Bernard Shaw

每一年，大量的植物和动物从自然中被采摘或被捕捉，而后以食物、宠物、装饰品、皮革、旅游纪念品或药品形式出售。全世界范围狩猎被当做运动和娱乐。尽管很多贸易都是合法的，并不影响野生种群，但让人不安的是其中很大比例是非法的，并且影响到很多濒危物种。

随着人口的增长，人类对野生物的需求也在增加。很多国家的人惯于某种生活方式，他们需要各种海味、皮革、木材、药材或是织物，这助长了对野生物的需求。很多野生动物是非法狩猎主要对象，包括：

- 犀牛（犀牛角）
- 大象（象牙）
- 老虎（虎皮及其他虎产品）

走私虎皮
Smuggling tiger skin
Consumer demand for tiger parts poses the largest threat to tiger survival. Tigers are being hunted to extinction by poachers for their skins, bones, teeth and claws, which are highly valued for their use in traditional Asian medicine.

表达库
Bank of expressions

- ▶【每一年，大量的植物和动物从自然中被采摘或被捕捉】Each year, hundreds of millions of plants and animals are harvested or caught from the wild...
- ▶【而后以食物、宠物、装饰品、皮革、旅游纪念品或药品形式出售】and then are sold as food, pets, ornamental plants, leather, tourist curios, and medicine
- ▶【全世界范围狩猎被当作运动和娱乐】Game animals are hunted for sport and leisure throughout the world.
- ▶【尽管很多贸易都是合法的】While a great deal of this trade is legal...
- ▶【并不影响野生种群】and not harming wild populations
- ▶【但让人不安的是其中很大比例是非法的】a worryingly large proportion is illegal
- ▶【并且影响到很多濒危物种】and threatens the survival of many endangered species
- ▶【随着人口的增长，人类对野生物的需求也在增加】As human populations have grown, so has the demand for wildlife.
- ▶【很多国家的人惯于某种生活方式】People in many countries are accustomed to a lifestyle.
- ▶【他们需要各种海味、皮革、木材、药材或是织物】They expect access to a variety of seafoods, leather goods, timbers, medicinal ingredients and textiles...
- ▶【助长了对野生物的需求】fuels demand for wildlife
- ▶【犀牛角】rhino horn
- ▶【象牙】elephant ivory
- ▶【虎皮】tiger skin
- ▶【虎产品】tiger products

在一些亚洲国家，传说犀牛角可以治疗癌症等疾病，这导致南非大规模非法狩猎。除了人类以外，大象在自然界少有天敌。近二十年，大象种群数量急剧减少，很大程度上由于象牙贸易。为收集它们的条纹皮毛，老虎被大规模猎杀。在很多亚洲国家，虎产品被认为有各种药用价值。爱尔兰作家萧伯纳[1]曾说：

> *When a man wants to murder a tiger he calls it sport; when the tiger wants to murder him he calls it ferocity.*

极端贫困意味着一些人将野生动物视作贸易的对象。腐败、无力的法律、薄弱的司法系统和判罚过轻让有组织犯罪者肆无忌惮地猎杀野生动物。在一些国家，非法狩猎是一项低风险、高回报的行当。

很多发展中国家的居民完全依赖当地可持续供应的野生资源。过度采摘或捕杀野生

濒临灭绝的蓝色金刚鹦鹉
At least 18 species of parrot are endangered or critically endangered at least in part by wildlife trade. Another 40 species are considered vulnerable. Among the most sought-after parrots are the "blue" macaws, prized for their brilliant coloring, large size, intelligence and rarity.

表达库
Bank of expressions

► 【传说犀牛角可以治疗癌症】the legend has that rhino horn can cure cancer
► 【导致南非大规模非法狩猎】has led to massive poaching in South Africa
► 【除了人类以外，大象在自然界少有天敌】Elephants themselves have few natural predators besides man.
► 【很大程度上由于象牙贸易】largely caused by the ivory trade
► 【为收集它们的条纹皮毛】To collect their striped skins...
► 【老虎被大规模猎杀】tigers have been hunted at a large scale
► 【虎产品被认为有各种药用价值】tiger products are believed to have medicinal properties
► 【极端贫困意味着一些人将野生动物视作贸易的对象】Extreme poverty means some people see wildlife as valuable barter for trade.
► 【腐败、无力的法律、薄弱的司法系统和判罚过轻让有组织犯罪者肆无忌惮地猎杀野生动物】Corruption, toothless laws, weak judicial systems and light sentences allow organized criminals to keep plundering wildlife with little regard to consequences.
► 【非法狩猎是一项低风险、高回报的行当】plundering is a low risk business with high returns
► 【很多发展中国家的居民完全依赖当地可持续供应的野生资源】Many people in the developing world depend entirely on the continued availability of local wildlife resources.
► 【过度采摘或捕杀野生动物会影响这些人的生计】Over-harvesting or overexploitation of plants and animals harms these people's livelihoods.

核心词
Keywords

1. 萧伯纳（即"乔治·伯纳德·肖"，George Bernard Shaw）

动物会影响这些人的生计。人类的生存依靠一个正常运作的地球，否则复杂的生命之网就会被打破。非法狩猎和偷运野生动物导致生物多样性大规模、不可挽回的损失。应对非法野生动物贸易的有效方法之一是说服消费者作出明智的选择。进化论[1]的提出者英国博物学家查尔斯·达尔文[2]曾说：

The love for all living creatures is the most noble attribute of man.

非法象牙走私
Illegal trade in the ivory tusks. Ivory is a material used in creating art objects and jewelry where the ivory is carved with designs.

表达库
Bank of expressions

► 【人类的生存依靠一个正常运作的地球】Human life depends on the existence of a functioning planet Earth...
► 【复杂的生命之网就会被打破】the complex web of life would be seriously disturbed
► 【非法狩猎和偷运野生动物导致生物多样性大规模、不可挽回的损失】Illegal wildlife plundering and trafficking leads to massive and irrevocable biodiversity loss.
► 【应对非法野生动物贸易的有效方法之一是说服消费者作出明智的选择】One of the most powerful tools for addressing illegal wildlife trade is persuading consumers to make informed choices.

核心词
Keywords

1. 进化论（Theory of Evolution）
2. 查尔斯·达尔文（Charles Darwin）

笔记
Notes

珊瑚礁
Coral Reefs

Cradle to myriads of species, Millennia to create, Moments to destroy.

珊瑚礁，被称为"海洋中的热带雨林"，珊瑚礁形成了世界上最多样的生态环境，提供复杂而又多样的海洋生物栖息地。珊瑚礁通过吸收海浪能量保护海岸线，没有珊瑚礁的保护很多小岛将不复存在。

珊瑚礁开始于珊瑚虫，当它们在夜晚伸出触角在浮游动物上进食时这些小动物才能被看得最清楚。珊瑚虫吸附于坚硬的表面，分泌出杯状的骨架作为自己的家。成千上万的珊瑚成为珊瑚礁的小丘和峡谷。

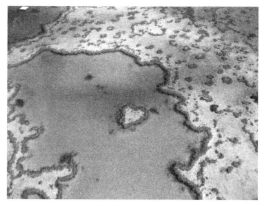

澳大利亚大堡礁
The Great Barrier Reef, off the coast of Queensland, Australia, is the world's largest coral reef

水藻和海草是海洋食物链的基础，它们

表达库
Bank of expressions

▶【Cradle to myriads of species】无数物种的摇篮
▶【Millennia to create】几千年时间创造
▶【Moments to destroy】瞬间就可以破坏
▶【海洋中的热带雨林】rainforests of the sea
▶【珊瑚礁形成了世界上最多样的生态环境】coral reefs form some of the most diverse ecosystems on earth
▶【提供复杂而又多样的海洋生物栖息地】provide complex and varied marine habitats that support a wide range of other organisms
▶【珊瑚礁通过吸收海浪能量保护海岸线】Coral reefs protect shorelines by absorbing wave energy.
▶【没有珊瑚礁的保护很多小岛将不复存在】Many small islands would not exist without their reefs to protect them.
▶【珊瑚礁开始于珊瑚虫】Coral reefs began with single polyps.
▶【只有夜晚才能看清楚的小动物】Small animals best seen, when they stretch out their tentacles to feed on floating plankton at night.
▶【珊瑚虫吸附于坚硬的表面】Polyps attach themselves to hard surface...
▶【分泌出杯状的骨架作为自己的家】excrete a cup-like skeleton for a home
▶【成千上万的珊瑚成为珊瑚礁的小丘和峡谷】Thousands of coral skeletons became the hills and valleys of a reef.
▶【水藻和海草是海洋食物链的基础】Algae and seaweeds lie at the base of the marine food chain.

和珊瑚礁相互依赖。各种动物到珊瑚礁寻找食物和庇护，超过 1/4 的海洋生物以珊瑚礁为家。大量的孔洞为海洋生物提供保护，同时也为捕食性鱼类提供伏击其他鱼类的掩护。

和地球其他生态系统一样，珊瑚礁深受人类活动影响。挖沙和填海造地都对珊瑚礁有害。全球变暖影响下的海洋升温导致珊瑚死亡，过高的温度导致珊瑚白化。美国前总统克林顿对于珊瑚礁破坏曾呼吁公众说：

> *Pollution, overfishing, and overuse have put many of our unique reefs at risk. Their disappearance would destroy the habitat of countless species. It would unravel the web of marine life that holds the potential for new chemicals, new medicines, and unlocking new mysteries.*

尽管珊瑚礁覆盖海洋的一小部分，但它们是海洋的热带雨林，多样、脆弱，而又重要。

表达库
Bank of expressions

► 【各种动物到珊瑚礁寻找食物和庇护】Various animals move into the reef seeking food and shelter...
► 【超过 1/4 的海洋生物以珊瑚礁为家】coral reefs house over twenty-five percent of all marine life
► 【大量的孔洞为海洋生物提供保护】The great mass of holes provide protection for marine animals...
► 【同时也为捕食性鱼类提供伏击其他鱼类的掩护】offer places for predatory fish to ambush other fish
► 【珊瑚礁深受人类活动影响】coral reefs have suffered from human activities
► 【挖沙和填海造地都对珊瑚礁有害】Dredging and filling for land development have hurt reefs.
► 【全球变暖影响下的海洋升温导致珊瑚死亡】Coral die when ocean temperatures rise from global warming...
► 【珊瑚白化】be bleached
► 【destroy the habitat of countless species】破坏无数物种的栖息地
► 【unravel the web of marine life】解密海洋生物的错综复杂
► 【unlocking new mysteries】破解新的奥秘
► 【尽管珊瑚礁覆盖海洋的一小部分】Although coral reefs cover a tiny fraction of the ocean...
► 【但它们是海洋的热带雨林，多样、脆弱，而又重要】they are the rainforest of the sea, diverse, fragile, and vital

上亿人从鱼类中获得蛋白质。全世界范围内，渔业是数以百万计人口的重要生计。持续增加的捕鱼作业和不可持续的捕鱼方法把很多鱼群推向灭绝的边缘。

过度捕鱼是指捕鱼的数量超过种群恢复的数量的情况。很多渔夫意识到需要保护鱼群和海洋环境，但是非法捕鱼仍然大规模存在。

一些正在下降的鱼类包括箭鱼、蓝鳍金枪鱼、红鲷鱼及大西洋鳕鱼。当一些常见的鱼群被捕捞殆尽，渔民开始捕捉其他海产品。

常被食用的海产
Top consumed seafood

Canned Tuna [金枪鱼罐头]
Catfish [鲶鱼]
Clam [蛤蜊]
Cod [鳕鱼]
Crab [螃蟹]
Herring [鲱鱼]
Lobster [龙虾]
Oyster [牡蛎]
Salmon [大马哈鱼]
Sardine [沙丁鱼]
Scallop [扇贝]
Seaweed [海藻]
Shrimp [虾]
Squid [鱿鱼]
Trout [鳟鱼]

表达库
Bank of expressions

► 【上亿人从鱼类中获得蛋白质】Billions of people rely on fish for protein.

► 【全世界范围内，渔业是数以百万计人口的重要生计】Fishing is the principal livelihood for millions of people around the world.

► 【持续增加的捕鱼作业和不可持续的捕鱼方法把很多鱼群推向灭绝的边缘】Increasing fishing efforts as well as unsustainable fishing practices are pushing many fish stocks to the point of collapse.

► 【过度捕鱼是指捕鱼的数量超过种群恢复的数量的情况】Overfishing occurs when more fish are caught than the population can replace through natural reproduction.

► 【很多渔夫意识到需要保护鱼群和海洋环境】Many fishers are aware of the need to safeguard fish populations and the marine environment.

► 【但是非法捕鱼仍然大规模存在】However，pirate fishing still exists in large scales.

► 【一些正在下降的鱼类包括箭鱼、蓝鳍金枪鱼、红鲷鱼及大西洋鳕鱼】Some of the fisheries in decline include swordfish, bluefin tuna, red snapper, and Atlantic cod.

► 【当一些常见的鱼群被捕捞殆尽，渔民开始捕捉其他海产品】Furthermore, as popular fish stocks become depleted, harvesters begin to fish more actively for other seafood.

缺乏监督管理和对捕鱼活动的跟踪，这一点长期困扰渔业。目前的法律规定不足以限制捕鱼保持可持续的水平。

过度捕鱼有很严重的后果。有针对性地捕捉旗鱼、鲨鱼和金枪鱼最终会破坏海洋生态，导致食物链底端的小型海洋动物大量繁殖。

日本捕鲸船
Japan has a long history of whaling. However, it wasn't until 1934 that Japan expanded its whaling to Antarctica.

另外一个重大的挑战是控制副渔获物——无意杀害并不打算捕捞的物种，比如，廉价的鱼、未成熟的鱼或其他海洋哺乳动物。举例说，海豚有时会被捕捉金枪鱼的围网抓住。捕虾的拖网可能抓住海龟并导致其窒息死亡。

被意外捕获的鲨鱼
Shark bycatch. Bycatch refers to the unintended catch of non-target species.

表达库
Bank of expressions

► 【缺乏监督管理和对捕鱼活动的跟踪，这一点长期困扰渔业】A lack of management oversight and traceability of fishing activities has long been a problem in the fishing industry.

► 【目前的法律规定不足以限制捕鱼保持可持续的水平】Current rules and regulations are not strong enough to limit fishing capacity to a sustainable level.

► 【过度捕鱼有很严重的后果】Overfishing has serious consequences.

► 【有针对性地捕捉旗鱼、鲨鱼和金枪鱼最终会破坏海洋生态】Targeted fishing of billfish, sharks and tuna eventually disrupts marine communities...

► 【导致食物链底端的小型海洋动物大量繁殖】causing increased abundance of smaller marine animals at the bottom of the food chain

► 【另外一个重大的挑战是控制副渔获物】Another great challenge is the control of bycatch...

► 【无意杀害并不打算捕捞的物种】the unintentional killing of species not intended to be caught

► 【比如，廉价的鱼、未成熟的鱼或其他海洋哺乳动物】such as low value fish, immature fish, or even other marine mammals

► 【举例说，海豚有时会被捕捉金枪鱼的围网抓住】Dolphins, for example, are sometimes caught in seine nets intended for catching tuna.

► 【捕虾的拖网可能抓住海龟并导致其窒息死亡】Shrimp trawls may catch and drown sea turtles.

Thank God men cannot fly, and lay waste the sky as well as the earth.

Henry David Thoreau

原油和天然气的开采会影响动物的迁徙路线，导致动物栖息地的退化，以及原油泄漏等问题。容易开发的油田已经被开采。现在，石油及天然气的开采已经把触角伸向地球最遥远、最不适宜居住的地方。

尼日利亚海上原油钻井平台
Offshore oil rig, Nigeria

很多国家积极参与到海上石油[1]开采，兴建各种海上石油钻井平台[2]。近年发生的几起事件已经让人们严重忧虑海上原油开采对环境的影响，比如：

■ 阿拉斯加港湾漏油事件
■ 墨西哥湾漏油事件

表达库
Bank of expressions

► 【原油和天然气的开采会影响动物的迁徙路线】Oil and gas exploration causes disruption of migratory pathways...
► 【导致动物栖息地的退化】results in degradation of important animal habitats
► 【容易开发的油田已经被开采】Easily accessible oil has already been developed.
► 【石油及天然气的开采已经把触角伸向地球最遥远、最不适宜居住的地方】oil and gas exploration is probing the earth's most remote and inhospitable places
► 【阿拉斯加港湾漏油事件】Exxon Valdez oil spill
► 【墨西哥湾漏油事件】Gulf of Mexico oil spill

核心词
Keywords

1. 海上石油（offshore drilling）
2. 海上石油钻井平台（offshore platform 或 oil rig）

死在墨西哥湾油污中的海鸟
A dead bird covered in oil from the Deepwater Horizon oil spill in the Gulf of Mexico

发生于 1989 年的阿拉斯加港湾漏油事件被认为是对环境造成重大毁灭性影响的人为事故之一。瓦迪兹号在阿拉斯加州威廉王子湾触礁，导致大量原油泄漏。野生动物深受原油泄漏影响。

发生于 2010 年的墨西哥湾漏油事件导致钻井平台 11 名员工丧命及 17 人受伤，引起当地的海域和海洋生物栖息地大面积破坏，严重影响当地的渔业和旅游业。

几起重大的漏油事件
Some of the world's biggest oil spills

Location	Year	Cause	Amount (millions of gallons)
Persian Gulf	1991	Intentional release by Iraq	240
Gulf of Mexico	1979	Well blowout	140
Trinidad	1979	Ship collision	84.2
Persian Gulf	1983	Blowout	80
Uzbekistan	1992	Blowout	80
South Africa	1983	Tanker fire	78.5
Portsall, France	1978	Ship grounding	68.7
North Atlantic	1988	Tanker rupture	43.1
Libya	1980	Blowout	42
Land's End, Britain	1967	Tanker rupture	38.2
Gulf of Mexico	2010	Blowout	29

导致原油泄漏的原因可能是井喷、管道泄漏或运输事故。原油泄漏对生态系统产生严重的威胁。为便于原油和燃气的开采，需要大规模建设基础设施。道路、石油管道和楼房都会对动物的生存环境、迁徙路径和生物多样性产生负面影响。鲸类和其他海洋哺乳动物在漆黑的深海中使用声音导航、寻找伴侣或者寻找食物。原油和燃气开采带来的噪声会使海洋哺乳动物受伤，带来混乱或者致死。

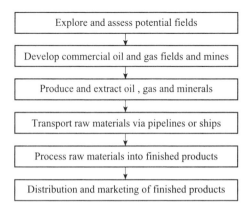

石油生产周期
Petroleum production cycle

笔记
Notes

500 000 BC - 2550 BC

500 000? BC【人类开始使用火】Humans began to control fire for useful purposes between about 500 000 and 400 000 years ago, archaeological evidence suggests.

300 000? BC【人类开始搭建房屋】Humans constructed shelters possibly as early as 300 000 years ago.

200 000? BC【智人出现】Homo sapiens, similar to modern people, emerged between 300 000 and 200 000 years ago in Africa and Asia.

10 000? BC【农业逐渐出现】The transition from hunting and gathering to dependence on food production was gradual, beginning at least 10 000 years ago.

4 400? BC【驯化野马】Domestication of horses provided an important new power of transportation and a new means of conducting warfare.

4500? BC【早期耕犁出现】Early plows were invented to aid agricultural production by turning the soil to bring nutrients closer to the surface.

3500? BC【苏美尔人发明轮子】The Sumerians invented the wheel.

3300? BC【埃及人发明象形文字】Egyptians developed the first known system of writing, which consists of hieroglyphic symbols that represent objects, sounds, and ideas.

3250? BC【纸草发明】Paper made of papyrus reed was first produced in Egypt.

3100? BC【埃及人制造帆船】Egyptians constructed the first sailing ships in order to better navigate upstream on the Nile River.

3000? BC【埃及第一个王朝建立】King Menes founded the first dynasty of Egypt.

2650? BC【古代中国制作丝绸】Ancient Chinese began weaving silk from silkworm cocoons into fabric.

2560 BC【吉萨金字塔始建】Pyramids of Giza begun its construction.

2550? BC【狮身人面像始建】The Great Sphinx was being built.

2550 BC – 500 BC

1772 BC【《汉谟拉比法典》颁布】The *Code of Hammurabi*, a Babylonian law code, was enacted.

1600 BC【商朝建立】The Shang Dynasty was established.

1500? BC【印度教出现】Hinduism emerged as the main religion of India.

1500? BC【铁器时代开始】The Iron Age, in which iron was commonly used for making tools and weapons, started.

1250? BC【摩西领导希伯来人】Moses emerged as Hebrew leader.

800? BC【荷马创作《伊利亚特》和《奥德赛》】Ancient Greek epic poems, *Iliad* and *Odyssey*, were written by Homer.

776 BC【首届奥林匹克运动会】The first Olympic Games, athletic contests for male Greek citizens, were held.

753? BC【罗马建立】Rome was founded.

657 BC【拜占庭建立】Byzantium was founded by Greek colonists from Megara.

594 BC【梭伦改革】Solon's Reform, the Athenian economic system so poor inhabitants of Attica no longer had to go into bondage over debt, started.

585 BC【米利都的泰勒斯预测日食】Greek philosopher Thales of Miletus accurately predicted a solar eclipse in this year.

569 BC【毕达哥拉斯诞生】Pythagoras was born, who combined philosophy and mathematics.

551 BC【孔子诞生】Confucius was born, whose philosophy is centered on respect and tradition.

540 BC【赫拉克利特诞生】Heraclitus, often called dark philosopher or weeping philosopher, was born.

533 BC【乔达摩·悉达多出家修行】Gautama Buddha, born a prince in Nepal, renounced his former life and began a long journey that ultimately results in the founding of Buddhism.

522? BC【大流士一世继任】Cyrus was succeeded by Darius I, the third king of the Persian Achaemenid Empire.

509 BC【罗马共和国建立】The Roman Republic was founded.

508 BC【雅典实行民主制】The powerful Greek city-state of Athens adopted a democratic constitution.

500 BC – AD

500? BC【早期佛教出现】Buddhism developed into one of the world's major religions, as followers spread Buddhist teachings after the Buddha's death.

490 BC【马拉松战役】The complete Greek victory at the Battle of Marathon ended the immediate Persian threat.

469 BC【苏格拉底诞生】Socrates was born, whose methods of questioning in Athens formed the basis for much of later Western philosophy .

438 BC【帕特农神庙建成】The Parthenon, a temple on the Athenian Acropolis, Greece, dedicated to the maiden goddess Athena, was completed.

404 BC【伯罗奔尼撒战争】Defeat in the Peloponnesian War led to the decline of Athens' political power.

400? BC【留基伯提出原子论】Greek philosopher Leucippus proposed the atomic theory of matter, which holds that all matter consists of indivisible particles called atoms.

399 BC【苏格拉底被判刑】Socrates was sentenced to death for allegedly corrupting the minds of youth.

387? BC【柏拉图成立学院】Plato founded his hugely influential Academy in Athens.

370? BC【罗马修建公路】The Romans built their first road.

350? BC【《希波克拉底誓言》被提出】The ancient Greek physician Hippocrates proposed the *Hippocratic Oath*, which sets ethical standards for physicians.

340? BC【第欧根尼创立犬儒主义】Greek philosopher Diogenes of Sinope founded the School of Cynicism.

335? BC【亚里士多德成立学园】Aristotle opened his own school in Athens – the Lyceum.

326 BC【亚历山大大帝称霸】Alexander the Great created one of the largest empires of the ancient world.

300? BC【季蒂昂的芝诺开创斯多葛学派】Zeno of Citium begun to teach the Stoic school of philosophy in Athens.

300 BC【欧几里得创作《几何原本》】Greek mathematician Euclid wrote *Elements*.

259? BC【亚历山大图书馆兴建】Ptolemy I founded the Library of Alexandria, a library and research center in Alexandria, which houses one of the finest literary collections in the world.

280 BC【亚历山大灯塔始建】The construction of the Lighthouse of Alexandria started.

260? BC【阿拉伯数字】Hindus in India developed the Arabic system of number notation.

246? BC【兵马俑始建】The Terracotta Army, which was built to protect the First Qin Emperor in his afterlife, begun its construction.

240? BC【阿基米德计算圆周率】Greek mathematician Archimedes first calculated the value of pi.

240? BC【测量地球周长】Greek scientist and philosopher Eratosthenes measured the earth's circumference.

221 BC【秦始皇统一中国】The First Qin Emperor became the first emperor of a unified China. The Qin Dynasty combined military might with innovations in government to defeat rival states and create a powerful new empire.

220 BC【长城始建】The construction of the Great Wall begun.

202 BC【汉代建立】Han Dynasty, a golden age in Chinese history, was established .

150? BC【《断臂的维纳斯》完成】*Venus de Milo*, carved by Alexandros, was completed.

72 BC【罗马角斗场始建】The construction of Colosseum in Rome started.

51 BC【埃及艳后登基】Cleopatra VII became queen of Egypt when her father, Ptolemy XII, died.

45? BC【儒略历被采用】Julian calendar was adopted.

44 BC【恺撒遇刺】Roman dictator Gaius Julius

Caesar was assassinated, leaving Rome in factional chaos.

***27 BC*【罗马万神殿始建】** The construction of the Pantheon started.

***27 BC*【奥古斯都继位】** Augustus became the first emperor of Rome.

***25? BC*【《拉奥孔和他的儿子们》】** *Laocoon and His Sons* was completed.

AD – 500

***30?*【耶稣离世】** Jesus Christ, founder of Christianity, one of the world's largest religions, died.

***105?*【蔡伦造纸术】** Cai Lun invented the composition for paper along with the papermaking process.

***132*【张衡设计地动仪】** Zhang Heng, a Chinese astronomer, developed the first seismograph.

***170?*【马可·奥勒留创作《沉思录》】** Marcus Aurelius started to write *Meditations*.

***180?*【盖伦总结前人医学经验】** Greek physician Galen summarized medical knowledge of ancient times and influenced medical theory and practice for centuries.

***303*【戴克里先迫害基督徒】** Diocletian began a general persecution of Christians.

***313*【君士坦丁大帝颁布《米兰敕令》】** Constantine I proclaimed religious freedom within the Roman Empire in the *Edict of Milan*.

***324*【君士坦丁大帝击败李锡尼】** Constantine the Great defeated Licinius.

***330?*【君士坦丁大帝建都拜占庭】** Constantine the Great established his new capital at Byzantium.

***395*【罗马分裂】** Crises brought on by both internal and external forces led to the division of the Roman Empire into East and West.

***410*【西哥特人洗劫罗马】** Rome was sacked by Visigoths.

500 – 1000

***529*【《查士丁尼法典》】** *Code of Justinian*, a collection of fundamental works in jurisprudence, issued by order of Justinian I, was issued.

***537*【圣索菲亚大教堂】** The Hagia Sophia Cathedral, which represented the culmination of Byzantine architecture, in Constantinople was completed.

***600?*【伊斯兰教出现】** In Arabia, the Prophet Muhammad founded Islam, one of the major world religions.

***618*【唐朝建立】** Li Yuan declared himself the emperor of a new dynasty, the Tang Dynasty.

***632*【穆罕默德逝世】** Muhammad, the last prophet of God, died.

***642*【阿拉伯人占领埃及】** Arabs conquered Egypt.

***690*【武则天登基】** Empress Wu Zetian deposed her son to become empress and ascended the throne in the Tang Dynasty.

***800*【查理大帝加冕】** Charlemagne crowned the Emperor of the West and became the founder of the Carolingian Dynasty.

***960*【宋朝建立】** Song Dynasty was founded.

1000 – 1500

***1088*【博洛尼亚大学成立】** The University of Bologna was founded.

***1096*【十字远征军出征】** The First Crusade began with a call by Alexius I.

***1099*【十字军占领耶路撒冷】** Christian crusaders captured the holy city of Jerusalem.

***1163*【巴黎圣母院始建】** Work began on Notre-Dame.

***1215*【英王约翰被迫签署《大宪章》】** A group of determined barons forced King John of England to sign the *Magna Carta*.

***1271*【马可·波罗游历中国】** Marco Polo, accompanied by his father, set off for China.

***1274*【托马斯·阿奎那创作《神学大全》】** *Summa Theologica*, the best-known work of Thomas Aquinas, was written, but unfinished.

***1321*【但丁·阿利盖利创作《神曲》】** *Divine Comedy*, an epic poem written by Dante Alighieri, was finished.

***1326*【奥斯曼土耳其帝国成立】** The Ottoman Empire was established.

***1337*【英法百年战争打响】** The Hundred Year's War, a series of conflicts waged from 1337 to 1453 between the Kingdom of England and the Kingdom of France, began.

***1347*【黑死病横扫欧洲】** The Black Death

reached Europe, killing more than a third of the continent's population.

1368【明朝建立】 Zhu Yuanzhang proclaimed the Ming Dynasty and established the capital at Nanjing on the Yangtze River.

1421【明朝迁都】 The Second Ming Emperor moved the capital of China from Nanjing to Beijing.

1429【圣女贞德指挥法军】 Joan of Arc led French troops in a victory over the English during the Hundred Years' War.

1450【欧洲活字印刷术】 The first book printed with movable, or individual, metal type is created by German printer Johannes Gutenberg.

1453【拜占庭帝国陷落】 The Byzantine Empire fell when Ottoman Turks conquered the capital, Constantinople. With the conquest of Constantinople by Mehmed II, the Ottoman state became an empire.

1485【列奥纳多·达·芬奇创作《岩间圣母》】 While serving the duke of Milan as a military advisor, Leonardo da Vinci painted *The Virgin of the Rocks*.

1492【克里斯托弗·哥伦布到达新大陆】 Italian-Spanish sailor Christopher Columbus, funded by Ferdinand V and Isabella I of Spain, made the first of four voyages to the New World.

1492【哥伦布横渡大西洋】 Christopher Columbus crossed the Atlantic and reached the West Indies.

1497【《最后的晚餐》】 At Santa Maria delle Grazie in Milan, Leonardo da Vinci finished *The Last Supper*.

1498【瓦斯科·达·伽马到达印度】 Vasco da Gama, a Portuguese explorer, one of the most successful in the Age of Discovery, reached India.

1500 – 1600

1500【米开朗基罗·博那罗蒂创作《圣母怜子》】 In Rome, Michelangelo Buonarroti carved the *Pietà*.

1504【米开朗基罗创作《大卫》】 *David*, by Michelangelo, was completed.

1506【《蒙娜丽莎》】 Leonardo da Vinci painted the *Mona Lisa*, which he kept with him for the remainder of his life.

1509【美洲贩卖农奴开始】 Spanish settlers enslaved Caribbean native tribes to work on sugar plantations.

1510?【拉斐尔·桑西创作《雅典学院》】 *The School of Athens*, by the Italian Renaissance artist Raphael Sanzio, was completed.

1513【尼可罗·马基亚维利写就《君主论》】 Niccolò Machiavelli wrote *The Prince*.

1514【《西斯廷圣母》】 *Sistine Madonna*, by Raphael, was completed.

1516【托马斯·莫尔创作《乌托邦》】 *Utopia*, by Sir Thomas More, was published .

1517【马丁·路德提出《九十五条论纲》】 Martin Luther nailed his *95 Theses* to the door of Castle Church in Wittenberg, triggering the Reformation.

1519【斐迪南·麦哲伦横渡大西洋】 Portuguese explorer Ferdinand Magellan became the first to cross the Atlantic and the Pacific Oceans in a single journey.

1522【麦哲伦首次环航地球】 One of Ferdinand Magellan's ships completed the global circumnavigation, returning to Seville.

1534【英王亨利八世成立英国国教】 King Henry VIII won parliamentary support to break from the Catholic Church and head the new Church of England.

1541【《最后的审判》】 In Rome, Michelangelo painted *The Last Judgment* on the wall of the Sistine Chapel.

1543【哥白尼提出日心说】 Polish astronomer Nicholas Copernicus revived the long-rejected hypothesis that Earth and the other planets revolve around the Sun.

1589?【伽利略·伽利雷提出自由落体运动定律】 Italian astronomer Galileo Galilei discovered the Law of Falling Bodies.

1600 – 1650

1600【德川家康夺权】 Japanese imperial regent Toyotomi Hideyoshi died, and a crisis arose when Tokugawa Ieyasu led rebel warlords to challenge the rule of Hideyoshi's son.

1600【东印度公司成立】 The English East India Company was granted a Royal Charter.

1600【乔尔丹诺·布鲁诺被烧死在火刑

柱】Renaissance mathematician, astronomer, philosopher, and poet Giordano Bruno was burned at the stake for heresy.

1602【威廉·莎士比亚出版《哈姆雷特》】 *Hamlet*, by William Shakespeare, was published.

1609?【伽利略天文观测】Using a homemade telescope, Italian scientist Galileo discovered the four moons orbiting Jupiter, the rings of Saturn, and the phases of Venus.

1611【《钦定圣经》】 *King James Bible*, an English translation of the Christian Bible by the Church of England, was completed in the reign of King Henry VIII.

1617【彼得·保罗·鲁本斯创作《劫夺留西帕斯的女儿们》】 *Rape of the Daughters of Leucippus* was produced by Peter Paul Rubens.

1618【约翰内斯·开普勒提出行星运动三定律】 German astronomer Johannes Kepler proposed his three laws of planetary motion.

1620【弗朗西斯·培根写就《新工具》】Francis Bacon's *New Organon* was published.

1628【英国议会通过《权利典章》】The English Parliament passed the *Petition of Rights*, which sets out specific liberties of the subject that the king is prohibited from infringing.

1628【威廉·哈维提出血液循环论】English physician William Harvey formally presented his findings about the circulation of blood and how the heart propels it.

1632【伽利略出版《关于托勒密和哥白尼两大世界体系的对话》】Galileo published the *Dialogue Concerning the Two Chief World Systems*.

1633【伽利略被判处终身监禁】The Roman Catholic Church forced Galileo to recant his support of the Copernican system, and placed him under lifelong house arrest.

1636【清朝建立】Qing Dynasty, the last imperial dynasty of China, was founded.

1637【勒内·笛卡儿写就《方法论》】 *Discourse on the Method*, was published by René Descartes.

1642【布莱兹·帕斯卡发明机械计算器】Blaise Pascal invented a mechanical calculator to assist his father, a tax commissioner.

1642【伦勃朗·凡·莱因创作《夜巡》】 *The Night Watch*, by Dutch painter Rembrandt van Rijn, was finished.

1649【查理一世被处死】The execution of King Charles I brought an end to the English Civil War.

1650 – 1700

1651【托马斯·霍布斯出版《利维坦》】 Thomas Hobbes published *Leviathan*.

1653【泰姬陵建成】The Taj Mahal was completed.

1661【欧洲发行纸币】The first European banknotes were issued by Stockholms Banco, a predecessor of the Bank of Sweden.

1665【《戴珍珠耳环的少女》】 *The Girl with the Pearl Earring*, one of Dutch painter Johannes Vermeer's masterworks, was created.

1666【艾萨克·牛顿发明微积分】The English physicist and mathematician Sir Isaac Newton developed calculus independently.

1667【第一例成功输血】The first fully documented human blood transfusion.

1673【安东尼·凡·列文虎克发表显微镜观察到的内容】Antonie van Leeuwenhoek's earliest observations were published.

1677【巴鲁赫·斯宾诺莎写就《伦理学》】 *Ethics, Demonstrated in Geometrical Order*, written by Baruch Spinoza, was published by Spinoza's friends published it after his death.

1684【戈特弗里德·威廉·莱布尼茨提出微积分】German mathematician Gottfried Wilhelm Leibniz published an account of his discovery of calculus.

1687【牛顿写就《自然哲学的数学原理》】English scientist and mathematician Sir Isaac Newton published his seminal work, *Mathematical Principles of Natural Philosophy*, which contained his three laws of motion and the theory of gravitation.

1690【克里斯蒂安·惠更斯提出光的波动理论】 Christiaan Huygens proposed the wave theory.

1690【约翰·洛克写就《人类理解论》】John Locke published *An Essay Concerning Human Understanding*.

1698【第一台蒸汽机】English engineer Thomas Savery builds the "Miner's Friend", the first practical steam engine, which serves as a water pump.

1700 – 1750

1717【伏尔泰被捕入巴士底狱】Voltaire was arrested and exiled to the Bastille for a year.

1721【彼得大帝称帝】Peter I became Emperor of Russia.

1727【约翰·塞巴斯蒂安·巴赫创作《圣马太受难曲》】Johann Sebastian Bach composed the *St. Matthew Passion*.

1735【卡尔·林奈提出生物学分类法】Swedish naturalist Carl Linnaeus introduced a system of naming organisms.

1738【戴维·休谟发表《人性论》】*A Treatise of Human Nature*, written by David Hume, was first published.

1748【孟德斯鸠发表《论法的精神》】*The Spirit of the Laws*, written by Montesquieu was published anonymously.

1750 – 1800

1750【约瑟夫·海顿创作室内乐】Joseph Haydn developed classical chamber music.

1751【德尼·狄德罗出版《百科全书》第一卷】Volume One of Denis Diderot's *Encyclopedia* was published.

1752【本杰明·富兰克林进行风筝实验】Benjamin Franklin conducted his famous experiment with a kite, proving that lightning is an electrical phenomenon.

1762【凯瑟琳大帝夺权】Emperor Peter III of Russia was overthrown by the imperial guard aided by his wife, and was killed. Catherine succeeded him as Empress Catherine II (the Great).

1762【让-雅克·卢梭写就《社会契约论》】Jean-Jacques Rousseau's groundbreaking political work, *The Social Contract*, was published.

1764【珍妮纺纱机】The spinning jenny was invented by James Hargreaves.

1768【库克船长首航】Captain Cook started his first voyage of exploration.

1770【英国宣布拥有澳大利亚东海岸】James Cook claimed the east coast of Australia for Britain

1776【《独立宣言》签署】The *United States Declaration of Independence* was signed.

1776【亚当·斯密写就《国富论》】*The Wealth of Nations*, written by Adam Smith, was first published.

1777【夏尔·库仑提出库仑定律】French physicist Charles Coulomb invented the torsion balance for measuring the force of magnetic and electrical attraction and proposed the Coulomb's Law.

1780【詹姆斯·瓦特改良内燃机】Scottish inventor James Watt began manufacturing a steam engine for industrial use.

1781【伊曼努尔·康德发表《纯粹理性批判》】*The Critique of Pure Reason* by Immanuel Kant, first published.

1783【孟格菲兄弟热气球表演】Montgolfier brothers demonstrated their balloon to Louis XVI and Marie-Antoinette, sending aloft and safely recovering a duck, rooster, and sheep.

1784【《荷拉斯兄弟之誓》】*The Oath of the Horatii*, by Jacques-Louis David, was completed.

1786【《费加罗的婚礼》】The opera the *Marriage of Figaro*, by Wolfgang Amadeus Mozart was first performed.

1789【乔治·华盛顿成为美国首任总统】George Washington was elected as the first president of US.

1789【法国大革命开始】French Revolution, spurred by a growing tax burden, economic hardship among the poor, and a crisis in the French state, started.

1789【杰里米·边沁的《道德与立法原理导论》】Jeremy Bentham published *An Introduction to the Principles of Morals and Legislation*, which developed the theory of utilitarianism.

1789【《人权和公民权宣言》发表】Asserting that "men are born free", *the Declaration of the Rights of Man and of the Citizen* became a preamble to the French Constitution.

1791【沃尔夫冈·莫扎特创作《魔笛》】Wolfgang Amadeus Mozart composed *The Magic Flute*.

1792【黑奴贩卖被禁止】Denmark passed laws to end the international transport and sale of slaves, aimed at ending the trade from Africa.

1792【《女权辩护》】*A Vindication of the Rights of Woman*, written by British feminist Mary Wollstonecraft, was published.

1792【路德维希·凡·贝多芬师从海顿】

Ludwig van Beethoven traveled to Vienna to study with Austrian composer Joseph Haydn and settled in the city.

1793【卢浮宫博物馆对外开放】The Louvre Museum, one of the world's largest museums, the most visited art museum in the world and a historic monument, opened to public.

1793【《马拉之死》】 *The Death of Marat*, by Jacques-Louis David, was completed.

1796【爱德华·詹纳发明天花疫苗】British physician Edward Jenner developed a vaccine against smallpox, a major cause of death in the 18th century.

1800 – 1850

1800【罗伯特·富尔顿发明第一艘潜水艇】 Robert Fulton was commissioned by Napoleon Bonaparte to design the Nautilus, the first practical submarine in history.

1800【伏打电堆】 Alessandro Volta, an Italian scientist, made a significant advance with his voltaic pile, the first true battery.

1803【双缝实验证明光的波动理论】Thomas Young demonstrated the interference of light waves, which helps establish the wave theory of light.

1803【现代原子理论提出】British chemist and physicist John Dalton developed the modern atomic theory upon which modern physical science is founded.

1804【《拿破仑法典》颁布】 *Napoleonic Code*, a French civil code, was established under Napoleon I.

1804【拿破仑·波拿巴称帝】Napoleon Bonaparte was crowned emperor.

1805【《英雄交响曲》首次公演】 *The Symphony No. 3 in E-flat major* op. 55 (*Eroica*), by Ludwig van Beethoven, was first performed.

1811【卢德运动】Luddite Movement started, in which English textile artisans violently protested against the machinery introduced during the Industrial Revolution.

1813【简·奥斯汀《傲慢与偏见》】 *Pride and Prejudice*, authored by Jane Austen, was first published.

1815【滑铁卢战役】Napoleon's forces were defeated at the Battle of Waterloo.

1818【玛丽·雪莱《弗兰肯斯坦》】Mary Shelley published the novel *Frankenstein*.

1818【格奥尔格·威廉·弗里德里希·黑格尔执教柏林大学】German philosopher Georg Wilhelm Friedrich Hegel began teaching philosophy at the University of Berlin.

1818【亚瑟·叔本华《作为意志和表象的世界》】 *The World as Will and Idea*, the central work of the German philosopher Arthur Schopenhauer, was published.

1818【《云海漫游者》创作完成】 *Wanderer above the Sea of Fog*, by the German Romantic artist Caspar David Friedrich, was composed.

1819【蒸汽机轮船首次横渡太平洋】Savannah, the first steam-powered ship crossed the Pacific Ocean.

1819【汉斯·克里斯蒂安·奥斯特发现电磁现象】Danish scientist Hans Christian Oersted discovered electromagnetism when he noticed that an electric current flowing through a wire deflects the pull of a magnetic needle.

1819【《梅杜萨之筏》】 *The Raft of the Medusa*, by the French Romantic painter Théodore Géricault, was finished.

1825【卡尔·高斯发现非欧几里得几何】Mathematicians Carl Friedrich Gauss discovered non-Euclidean geometry.

1826?【第一张照片被拍摄】French inventor Joseph N. Niépce took the first surviving permanent photograph.

1828【弗朗茨·舒伯特逝世】Franz Schubert, a prolific Austrian composer, died.

1829【弗雷德里克·肖邦首场钢琴演奏会】Polish composer and pianist Frédéric Chopin gives his first concerts as a piano virtuoso in Vienna.

1830【《自由引导人民》完成】 *Liberty Leading the People*, by Eugène Delacroix, was completed.

1831【维克多·雨果出版《巴黎圣母院》】 *The Hunchback of Notre-Dame* by Victor Hugo was published.

1831【迈克尔·法拉第发现电磁感应】Michael Faraday discovered electromagnetic induction.

1836【巴黎凯旋门完工】The Arc de Triomphe, which honors those who fought and died for France in the French Revolutionary and the Napoleonic Wars, was completed.

1837【维多利亚女王继位】Alexandrina Victoria became the queen of the United Kingdom of Great Britain and Ireland

1840【第一次鸦片战争开始】The First Opium War was fought between the United Kingdom and the Qing Dynasty of China.

1840【黑便士开始使用】The Penny Black, the world's first adhesive postage stamp, was first issued.

1848【《共产主义宣言》发表】Karl Marx, with German political economist Friedrich Engels, published the *Communist Manifesto*, the central text of modern communism.

1848【首次世界女权大会召开】The world's first women's rights convention was held in Seneca falls, New York.

1849【《论公民不服从》】*Civil Disobedience*, by Henry David Thoreau, was first published.

1850 – 1875

1851【英国伦敦水晶宫落成】The Crystal Palace was completed to house the Great Exhibition of 1851.

1852【《汤姆叔叔的小屋》】*Uncle Tom's Cabin*, by American author Harriet Beecher Stowe, was published, which helped lay the groundwork for the Civil War.

1854【瓦尔登湖】American thinker Henry David Thoreau published *Walden; or, Life in the Woods*.

1855【维多利亚瀑布被发现】David Livingstone discovered the Victorian Falls.

1856【罗伯特·舒曼逝世】Robert Schumann, one of the greatest composers of the Romantic era, died.

1856【第二次鸦片战争】The Second Opium War started and was fought over similar issues as the First Opium War.

1857【拾穗者】*The Gleaners*, by Jean-François Millet, was completed.

1859【查尔斯·达尔文发表《物种起源》】Charles Robert Darwin published *On the Origin of Species*, his complete theory of natural selection.

1859【《论自由》出版】*On Liberty*, a philosophical work by British philosopher John Stuart Mill, was published.

1860【弗洛伦斯·南丁格尔建立护理学校】Florence Nightingale laid the foundation of professional nursing with the establishment of her nursing school at St. Thomas' Hospital in London.

1861【美国内战开始】The American Civil War was started.

1861【《功利主义》出版】John Stuart Mill published *Utilitarianism*.

1863【亚伯拉罕·林肯发表《葛底斯堡演讲》】At a ceremony dedicating a national cemetery on the site of the Battle of Gettysburg, United States president Abraham Lincoln delivered his famous *Gettysburg Address*.

1863【《解放黑人奴隶宣言》发表】*The Emancipation Proclamation* was issued by President Abraham Lincoln.

1865【林肯遇刺】Abraham Lincoln was assassinated.

1865?【格雷戈尔·孟德尔豌豆实验】Using varieties of garden peas, Austrian botanist Gregor Mendel worked out the basic principles of genetics.

1865【路易·巴斯德提出巴氏消毒法】French chemist Louis Pasteur developed pasteurization.

1866【小约翰·施特劳斯《蓝色多瑙河》】Austrian composer Johann Strauss the Younger completed the *Blue Danube*.

1867【混凝土发明获专利】Reinforced concrete was invented by Joseph Monier received a patent.

1867【阿尔弗雷德·诺贝尔获得炸药专利】Swedish chemist Alfred Nobel patented dynamite, an industrial explosive.

1868【明治维新开始】To meet the challenge of European and American imperialism, reformers seized control of Japan in a coup d'état. Meiji Restoration started.

1869【苏伊士运河通航】The Suez Canal, connecting the Mediterranean Sea and the Red Sea, opened to traffic.

1869【列夫·托尔斯泰《战争与和平》】*War and Peace* by the Russian author Leo Tolstoy, first published.

1869【德米特里·门捷列夫提出元素周期表】Russian chemist Dmitri Ivanovich Mendeleev published the first version of the periodic table of elements.

1869【《匈牙利舞曲第五号》】Brahms completed

the *Hungarian Dance No. 5*.

1870【儒勒·凡尔纳《海底两万里》】*Twenty Thousand Leagues Under the Sea*, a classic science fiction novel by French writer Jules Verne, was published.

1871【德国统一】Germany was politically and administratively integrated.

1873【詹姆斯·麦克斯韦提出光的电磁理论】British mathematician and physicist James Maxwell published his electromagnetic theory of light.

1873【《伏尔加河上的纤夫》】*Barge Haulers on the Volga*, by Ilya Repin, was completed.

1873【《印象：日出》】Monet painted *Impression: Sunrise*.

1875【公制度量出现】Seventeen nations adopt the metric system.

1875 – 1900

1876【亚历山大·贝尔发明电话】Using a transmitter and receiver he had constructed, Scottish-American inventor Alexander Graham Bell delivered the first telephone message to his assistant.

1876【尼古拉斯·奥托发明四冲程发动机】Nikolaus August Otto built an internal-combustion engine utilizing the four-stroke cycle.

1876【彼得·柴可夫斯基完成《天鹅湖》】Peter Ilyich Tchaikovsky completed the ballet *Swan Lake*.

1877【托马斯·爱迪生发明留声机】Thomas Edison invented the phonograph.

1879【爱迪生发明灯泡】Thomas Edison invented the first practical incandescent electric light bulb.

1882【三国同盟形成】Under the guidance of German chancellor Prince Otto von Bismarck, Germany, Austria-Hungary, and Italy formed the Triple Alliance.

1885【卡尔·本茨发明汽车】Karl Benz built the world's first practical automobile to be powered by an internal-combustion engine.

1885【巴斯德发明狂犬疫苗】Louis Pasteur saved a boy from rabies.

1885【弗里德里希·尼采《查拉图斯特拉如是说》】Friedrich Nietzsche published *Thus Spake Zarathustra*.

1886【海因里希·赫兹发现无线电波】German physicist Heinrich Hertz discovers radio waves, a form of electromagnetic radiation. traveling at the speed of light.

1886【自由女神像揭幕】The Statue of Liberty was formally dedicated in a ceremony in New York Harbor.

1886【《大碗岛星期日的午后》】*A Sunday Afternoon on the Island of La Grande Jatte*, by Georges Seurat, was completed

1887【自动步枪取得专利】The world's first automatic rifle was patented.

1888【文森特·凡·高创作《向日葵》】*Sunflowers* was completed by Vincent van Gogh.

1888【凡·高割耳】After a violent argument with French painter Paul, Van Gogh cut off his own ear.

1889【埃菲尔铁塔落成】The Eiffel Tower was completed.

1889【凡·高创作《星夜》】Vincent van Gogh painted *Starry Night*.

1889【柴可夫斯基《睡美人》】Peter Ilyich Tchaikovsky completed the ballet *Sleeping Beauty*.

1880【柴可夫斯基完成《1812 序曲》】Tchaikovsky completed the *1812 Overture*.

1890【威廉·詹姆斯《心理学原理》】William James published *The Principles of Psychology*, which establishes psychology as a scientific discipline and sparks a wave of new psychological research.

1890【凡·高自杀】Vincent van Gogh committed suicide soon after completing Crows in the Wheatfields.

1892【柴可夫斯基《胡桃夹子》】Peter Ilyich Tchaikovsky completed the ballet The *Nutcracker*.

1893【安东·德沃夏克创作《自新大陆》】The *Symphony No. 9 in E Minor—From the New World* was composed by Antonín Dvořák.

1893【爱德华·蒙克创作《呐喊》】*The Scream*, by Edvard Munch, was created.

1893【新西兰成年妇女获得投票权】New Zealand became the first nation to extend the right to vote to all adult women.

1895【赫伯特·乔治·威尔斯出版《时间机器》】*The Time Machine*, a science fiction by Herbert Wells, was published.

1895【威廉·伦琴发现 X 射线】Wilhelm Rontgen, a German physicist, discovered X-ray.

1896【安东尼·贝可勒尔发现天然放射性】French physicist Antoine Henri Becquerel discovers natural radioactivity.

1896【"隔离而平等"】 "Plessy v. Ferguson", was passed by Supreme Court of the United States in which upheld the legality of racial segregation.

1896【圣雄甘地开始传授非暴力思想】Mahatma Gandhi began to teach passive resistance as a means of gaining civil rights for Indians in South Africa.

1897【伽利尔摩·马可尼发送第一封无线电报】Guglielmo Marconi sent the first ever wireless communication over open sea.

1897【约翰内斯·勃拉姆斯逝世】Johannes Brahms, a German composer and pianist, died in Vienna.

1898【约瑟夫·汤姆森提出原子模型】Joseph John Thomson advanced the "plum-pudding" theory of atomic structure, holding that negative electrons were like plums embedded in a pudding of positive matter.

1899【西格蒙德·弗洛伊德《梦的解析》】*The Interpretation of Dreams*, written by Sigmund Freud, was published.

1900 – 1925

1902【雕塑《思想者》】*The Thinker*, by Auguste Rodin, was completed.

1903【太平洋海底电缆首次传输信息】First message was sent over Pacific cable.

1903【莱特兄弟试飞成功】At Kitty Hawk, North Carolina, American aviator Orville Wright makes the first successful flight of a piloted, heavier-than-air flying machine.

1904【纽约地铁通车】The first section of the New York Subway system was opened.

1904【约翰·弗莱明发明真空管】John Fleming developed the first vacuum tube.

1905【狭义相对论提出】Albert Einstein published papers on special relativity, Brownian motion, and the photoelectric effect.

1906【芬兰立法赋予妇女选举权】Finland became the first country in Europe to give its woman the right to vote.

1907【《亚维农少女》】Pablo Picasso shocked the art community with *Les demoiselles d'Avignon*.

1908【飞跃英吉利海峡】Louis Bleriot became the first person to fly across the English Channel.

1908【福特 T 型车推出】Model T, the first affordable automobile, was produced by Henry Ford's Ford Motor Company.

1910【居里夫人分离出纯镭】French scientist Marie Curie worked with chemist André Debierne to isolate pure radium.

1911【辛亥革命开始】Chinese Xinhai Revolution started and the Republic of China was established.

1912【泰坦尼克首航灾难】RMS Titanic sank in the North Atlantic Ocean after colliding with an iceberg.

1912?【大陆板块漂移理论提出】German meteorologist Alfred Wegener advocated the theory of continental drift.

1912【痛痛病出现】Itai-itai disease started.

1913【爱迪生发明电影】Thomas Edison produced the first talking motion pictures.

1913【亨利·福特采取流水线生产汽车】Henry Ford began using standardized interchangeable parts and assembly-line techniques in his plant.

1914【德国对法国宣战】Germany declared war against France.

1915【托马斯·摩尔根提出染色体是基因的载体】American geneticist Thomas Hunt Morgan published a paper detailing his theory of linear arrangement of genes on chromosomes.

1916【《童工法》通过】*The Child Labor Law*, the first child labor law, was passed.

1916【广义相对论】Albert Einstein published a paper on general relativity, extending his earlier theory of special relativity.

1916【约翰·杜威《民主与教育》】*Democracy and Education*, written by John Dewey, was published.

1917【十月革命打响】Vladimir Ilich Lenin and Leon Trotsky lead the Bolsheviks in a coup d'état in Russia known as the October Revolution.

1918【流行性感冒】Flu pandemic spread across the world.

1918【伯特兰·罗素入狱】Bertrand Russell was imprisoned for five months as a result of anti-war protests

1919【《凡尔赛和约》签订】*Treaty of Versailles*,

was negotiated during the Paris Peace Conference held in Versailles, thereby officially ending World War I.

1919【欧内斯特·卢瑟福改变化学元素】British physicist Ernest Rutherford bombarded nitrogen gas with alpha particles and obtained atoms of an oxygen isotope and protons.

1920【印度独立运动】Gandhi became the leader of Indian Independence Movement.

1920【《睡莲》】*Water Lilies*, by Claude Monet, was created.

1921【阿尔伯特·爱因斯坦获得诺贝尔物理学奖】Albert Einstein won the Nobel Prize in physics for his work on the photoelectric effect.

1925 – 1950

1925【香奈儿 5 号推出】Coco Chanel launched her first perfume Chanel No. 5.

1926【首次液态火箭试验】American rocket engineer Robert H. Goddard, inventor of the liquid-fueled rocket, conducted the world's first launch from a field near his home in Massachusetts.

1927【石英钟发明】The first quartz clock was built in at Bell Telephone Laboratories.

1928【亚历山大·弗莱明发现青霉素】Scottish bacteriologist Alexander Fleming discovered that Penicillium mold produces a substance that has an antibiotic effect.

1929【哈勃定律提出】American astronomer Edwin Hubble discovered that the farther a galaxy is from Earth, the faster it is receding, known as Hubble's Law.

1929【大萧条席卷世界】The Great Depression, a severe worldwide economic depression, started.

1931【帝国大厦对外开放】The Empire State building in New York, the largest building in the world, opened for the public.

1931【萨尔瓦多·达利创作《记忆的永恒》】*The Persistence of Memory*, by Salvador Dalí, was created.

1931【里约热内卢基督像落成】Christ the Redeemer was completed.

1933【富兰克林·罗斯福就任美国总统】Franklin D. Roosevelt was inaugurated as president of the United States.

1934【长征开始】Mao Zedong set off on Long March, a military retreat undertaken by the Red Army of the Communist Party of China.

1935【《纽伦堡法案》通过】*The Nuremberg Laws* was passed, depriving German Jews of their citizenship and forbidding marriage and sexual relations between Jews and "Aryans".

1936【约翰·凯恩斯创作《就业、利息和货币通论》】*The General Theory of Employment, Interest, and Money*, written by the English economist John Maynard Keynes, was published.

1936【查理·卓别林指导并出演《摩登时代》】*Modern Times*, directed by Charlie Chaplin, was released.

1937【金门大桥完工】Golden Gate Bridge, a suspension bridge spanning the opening of the San Francisco Bay into the Pacific Ocean, was completed.

1937【《格尔尼卡》完成】Pablo Picasso depicted the horrors of the Spanish Civil War in *Guernica*.

1937【华特·迪士尼的电影《白雪公主和七个小矮人》】*Snow White and the Seven Dwarfs*, by Walt Disney, was released to great acclaim, earning a special Academy Award.

1939【阿道夫·希特勒创作《我的奋斗》】Adolf Hitler dictated the first volume of *Mein Kampf (My Struggle)*.

1941【《大西洋宪章》】President Franklin D. Roosevelt and British Prime Minister Winston Churchill drew up the *Atlantic Charter*, which lays the foundation for the United Nations.

1941【日本偷袭珍珠港】Imperial Japanese Navy attacked the United States naval base at Pearl Harbor.

1941【纳粹驱逐犹太人】The Nazis began deporting all the Jews of occupied Europe to the east in order to exterminate them.

1942【斯大林格勒（现称伏尔加格勒）会战】The Battle of Stalingrad, a major and decisive battle of World War II, started.

1942【首座受控核反应堆实验成功】Italian-American physicist Enrico Fermi and his colleagues at the University of Chicago in Illinois initiated a controlled chain-reaction.

1942【曼哈顿计划开始】The Manhattan Project started.

1942【《最终解决方案》全面执行】*The Final Solution* was fully implemented.

1944【诺曼底登陆】The Normandy landings started.

1945【雅尔塔会议】Yalta Conference was held. The Allied leaders Franklin Roosevelt, Winston Churchill and Joseph Stalin met to formulate plans for ending World War II and occupying Germany.

1945【联合国成立】The United Nations was founded.

1945【原子弹试爆成功】The first atomic bomb was detonated in the Trinity test in New Mexico.

1945【广岛、长崎遭核弹打击】The atomic bombings, conducted by the United States, occurred in the cities of Hiroshima and Nagasaki.

1945【约翰·冯·诺依曼提出计算机结构】Hungarian-American mathematician John von Neumann wrote the first paper describing the design of a general-purpose digital electronic computer.

1946【第一台通用电子计算机】Electronic Numerical Integrator And Computer (ENIAC) was completed at the University of Pennsylvania.

1948【特蕾莎修女以自由修女身份行善】Mother Teresa began her ministry, tending to the sick and dying on the streets of Calcutta.

1948【以色列建国】The State of Israel was established.

1949【中华人民共和国成立】The People's Republic of China was officially proclaimed, with Peking as its capital.

1950 – 1975

1950【艾萨克·阿西莫夫创作《我，机器人》】Isaac Asimov published a collection of nine science fiction short stories, *I, Robot*.

1952【小儿麻痹症疫苗出现】A vaccine that prevented polio was developed by Jonas Salk.

1952【第一颗氢弹试爆成功】U.S. detonated the first hydrogen bomb in a test on Enewetak Atoll.

1952【伦敦烟雾事件】Great Smog broke out in London.

1953【DNA 结构确定】American biologist James D. Watson and English geneticist Francis Crick developed a double helix model for the structure of deoxyribonucleic acid (DNA).

1953【奥黛丽·赫本出演《罗马假日》】*Roman Holiday*, a romantic comedy was produced, in which Audrey Hepburn played Princess Anne.

1954【首例肾脏移植手术成功】A team from Harvard Medical School successfully completed the first kidney transplant operation.

1954【波音公司推出 707 客机】Boeing unveiled the "707".

1955【蒙哥马利公共汽车抵制运动】Rosa Parks, a black woman, was arrested after refusing to move to the back of a bus in Montgomery, Alabama. In a direct action against segregation, a boycott of the bus system is quickly organized by Martin Luther King, Jr., and others.

1956【猫王埃尔维斯·普雷斯利发布《心碎旅店》】Elvis Presley released "Heartbreak Hotel".

1956【水俣病出现】Minamata disease was first discovered.

1961【人类首次太空飞行】Yuri Gagarin, Soviet cosmonaut, became the first human to fly in space and made one orbit of the earth.

1962【古巴导弹危机】the Cuban Missile Crisis

1962【小马丁·路德·金发表《我有一个梦想》演说】Martin Luther King, Jr. delivered the speech, *I Have a Dream*, during the March on Washington for Jobs and Freedom.

1962【蕾切尔·卡逊出版《寂静的春天》】*Silent Spring*, by Rachel Carson, was published.

1963【麻疹疫苗】A vaccine against measles was proved.

1963【约翰·肯尼迪遇刺】John F. Kennedy was assassinated.

1964【披头士席卷美国】The Beatles' first public appearance in the United States was watched by an estimated 73 million people.

1964【《荒原法》通过】*The Wilderness Act* was signed into law.

1965【人类首次太空行走】Alexei Leonov became the first person to step out of a spacecraft and walk in space.

1967【切·格瓦拉被杀】Che Guevera was killed in Bolivia.

1968【英特尔公司成立】Intel Corporation was founded by semiconductor pioneers Robert Noyce and Gordon Moore.

1968【男子百米突破 10 秒】Jim Hines was the first man to break the 10-second barrier in the 100m.

1969【尼尔·阿姆斯特朗登月】U.S. astronauts Neil Armstrong became the first people to walk on the Moon.

1972【理查德·尼克松访华】President Nixon arrived in Beijing for a seven-day stay.

1972【奥运会恐怖】Arab terrorists murdered 11 athletes at the Olympic Games.

1973【第一次石油危机】The 1973 Oil Crisis started.

1973【悉尼歌剧院对外开放】Sydney Opera House, one of the great iconic buildings of the 20th century, an image of great beauty and a symbol for a continent, opened.

1974【尼克松宣布辞职】President Richard M. Nixon became the first U.S. president to resign after congressional hearings implicate him and some of his administrative officials in wrongdoing in the Watergate affair.

1975 – 2000

1977【猫王去世】Elvis Presley died at his Memphis home, Graceland.

1978【天花被消灭】The smallpox disease was completely eradicated from the Earth, thanks to a worldwide prevention program, combined with wide distribution of a vaccine.

1978【首例试管婴儿出生】Louise Brown, the first test tube baby, was born.

1979【玛格丽特·撒切尔夫人成为英国首位女性首相】Margaret Thatcher became the first woman to be prime minister of the United Kingdom.

1979【三里岛核电站事故】The Three Mile Island accident, a partial nuclear meltdown, occurred.

1979【第二次石油危机】The 1979 Oil Crisis started.

1980【万维网概念提出】Tim Berners-Lee, a British computer scientist, first proposed the "World Wide Web" project—now known as the World Wide Web.

1984【艾滋病大爆发】AIDS (Acquired Immunodeficiency Syndrome) broke out.

1985【伊朗门事件】the Iran-Contra Affair.

1986【切尔诺贝利核电站事故】Chernobyl disaster, a catastrophic nuclear accident, occurred.

1986【挑战者号航天飞机解体】The U.S. space shuttle Challenger exploded 73 seconds after takeoff. All seven crew members are killed in the explosion.

1988【史蒂芬·霍金出版《时间简史》】*A Brief History of Time*, by British physicist Stephen Hawking, was published.

1989【柏林墙被推倒】tearing down of Berlin Wall

1990【纳尔逊·曼德拉被释放】In response to international pressure, South African President F. W. de Klerk made the anti-apartheid movement legal and released the country's political prisoners, including Nelson Mandela.

1990【哈勃望远镜】The space shuttle Discovery launched the Hubble Telescope.

1990【海湾战争开始】Gulf War, with 34 nations led by the United States, against Iraq in response to Iraq's invasion and annexation of Kuwait started.

1991【昂山素季获诺贝尔和平奖】Aung San Suu Kyi won the Nobel Prize for Peace.

1991【苏联解体】Union of Soviet Socialist Republics (USSR) came to a formal end.

1996【多利羊诞生】Dolly the Sheep, the first mammal cloned, was born.

1997【探路者号登陆火星】The US spacecraft Pathfinder landed on Mars.

1997【《京都议定书》签订】*The Kyoto Protocol* was adopted.

1999【欧元区成立】The Eurozone came into existence.

2000 – Present

2000【同性婚姻立法】Queen Beatrix of the Netherlands signs into law the first same-sex marriage bill in the world.

2001【"9·11"事件】Four groups of terrorists from al-Qaeda, hijacked four aircraft and attacked World Trade Center and Pentagon.

2003【哥伦比亚号航天飞机解体】The space shuttle Columbia broke apart in flames and disintegrated over Texas during reentry into the Earth's atmosphere, killing all seven astronauts aboard.

2010【墨西哥湾漏油事件】The Gulf of Mexico oil spill, the largest accidental marine oil spill in the history of the petroleum industry, occurred.

Abraham Lincoln【亚伯拉罕·林肯】(1809-1865) 16th president of the United States (1861-1865), who preserved the Union during the American Civil War and brought about the emancipation of the slaves

Adam Smith【亚当·斯密】(1723-1790) Scottish social philosopher and political economist, whose *Wealth of Nations* was the first serious attempt to study the nature of capital and the historical development of industry and commerce among European nations

Adolf Hitler【阿道夫·希特勒】(1889-1945) An Austrian-born German politician and the leader of the Nazi Party, chancellor of Germany from 1933 to 1945 and dictator of Nazi Germany from 1934 to 1945

Alan Turing【阿兰·图灵】(1912-1954) British mathematician and logician, who made major contributions to mathematics, cryptanalysis, logic, philosophy, and biology and to the new areas later named computer science, cognitive science, artificial intelligence, and artificial life

Albert Einstein【阿尔伯特·爱因斯坦】(1879-1955) German-born American, generally considered the most influential physicist of the 20th century

Alexander Graham Bell【亚历山大·格拉汉姆·贝尔】(1847-1922) Scottish-born American inventor, scientist, and teacher of the deaf whose foremost accomplishments were the invention of the telephone and the refinement of the phonograph

Alexander the Great【亚历山大大帝】(356-323 BC) King of Macedonia, overthrew the Persian empire, carried Macedonian arms to India, and laid the foundations for the Hellenistic world of territorial kingdoms

Alfred Lothar Wegener【阿尔弗雷德·魏格纳】(1880-1930) German meteorologist and geophysicist who formulated the first complete statement of the continental drift hypothesis

Alfred Nobel【阿尔弗雷德·诺贝尔】(1833-1896) Swedish chemist, engineer, and industrialist, who invented dynamite and other, more powerful explosives, and who also founded the Nobel Prizes

Antoine-Laurent de Lavoisier【安托万-洛朗·德·拉瓦锡】(1743-1794) Prominent French chemist, developed an experimentally based theory of the chemical reactivity of oxygen and coauthored the modern system for naming chemical substances

Antoine Henri Becquerel【安东尼·亨利·贝克勒尔】(1852-1908) French physicist who discovered radioactivity through his investigations of uranium and other substances, shared the Nobel Prize for Physics with Pierre and Marie Curie in 1903

Archimedes【阿基米德】(287-212 BC) The most famous mathematician and inventor of ancient Greece

Aristotle【亚里士多德】(384-322 BC) Ancient Greek philosopher and scientist, one of the greatest intellectual figures of Western history

Arthur Schopenhauer【亚瑟·叔本华】(1788-1860) German philosopher, often called the "philosopher of pessimism," who was primarily important as the exponent of a metaphysical doctrine of the will in immediate reaction against Hegelian idealism

Audrey Hepburn【奥黛丽·赫本】(1929-1993) Slender, stylish motion picture actress known for her radiant beauty, her ability to project an air of sophistication tempered by a charming innocence, and her tireless efforts to aid needy children

Auguste Rodin【奥古斯特·罗丹】(1840-1917) French sculptor, considered by some critics to be the greatest portraitist in the history of sculpture

Augustus【奥古斯都】(63-14 BC) Founder of the Roman Empire and its first Emperor, ruling from 27BC until his death in 14AD

Aung San Suu Kyi【昂山素季】(1945-) Politician and opposition leader of Myanmar, winner of the Nobel Prize for Peace in 1991

Baruch Spinoza【巴鲁赫·斯宾诺莎】(1632-1677) Dutch Jewish philosopher, one of the foremost exponents of 17th-century Rationalism and one of the early and seminal figures of the Enlightenment

Benjamin Franklin【本杰明·富兰克林】(1706-1790) American printer and publisher, author, inventor and scientist, and diplomat, one of the foremost of the Founding Fathers

Bertrand Russell【伯特兰·罗素】(1872-1970) British philosopher, logician, and social reformer, founding figure in the analytic movement in Anglo-American philosophy, and recipient of the Nobel Prize for Literature in 1950

Bill Clinton【比尔·克林顿】(1946-) 42nd president of the United States , who oversaw the country's longest peacetime economic expansion

Blaise Pascal【布莱兹·帕斯卡】(1623-1662) French mathematician, physicist, religious philosopher, laid the foundation for the modern theory of probabilities, formulated the Pascal's law of pressure

Carl Friedrich Gauss【卡尔·弗里德里希·高斯】(1777-1855) German mathematician, generally regarded as one of the greatest mathematicians of all time

Catherine the Great【凯瑟琳大帝】(1729-1796) German-born empress of Russia, led her country into full participation in the political and cultural life of Europe

Charlemagne【查理大帝】(742-814) The founder of the Carolingian Empire, expanded the Frankish kingdom

Charles Augustin de Coulomb【夏尔·奥古斯丁·德·库仑】(1736-1806) French physicist best known for the formulation of Coulomb's law

Charles Darwin【查尔斯·达尔文】(1809-1882) English naturalist whose theory of evolution by natural selection became the foundation of modern evolutionary studies

Charles de Gaulle【夏尔·戴高乐】(1890-1970) French soldier, writer, statesman, and architect of French Fifth Republic

Charles Sanders Peirce【查尔斯·桑德·皮尔斯】(1839-1914) American scientist, logician, and philosopher who is noted for his work on the logic of relations and on pragmatism as a method of research

Charlie Chaplin【查理·卓别林】(1889-1977) British comedian, producer, writer, director, and composer who is widely regarded as the greatest comic artist of the screen and one of the most important figures in motion-picture history

Che Guevara【切·格瓦拉】(1928-1967) Theoretician and tactician of guerrilla warfare, prominent communist figure in the Cuban Revolution

Christiaan Huygens【克里斯蒂安·惠更斯】(1629-1695) Dutch mathematician, astronomer, and physicist, who founded the wave theory of light, discovered the true shape of the rings of

Saturn, and made original contributions to the science of dynamics

Christopher Columbus【克里斯托弗·哥伦布】(1451-1506) Master navigator and opened the way for European exploration, exploitation, and colonization of the Americas, and long been called the "discoverer" of the New World

Claude Monet【克劳德·莫奈】(1840-1926) French painter who was the initiator, leader, and unswerving advocate of the Impressionist style

Coco Chanel【可可·香奈儿】(1883-1971) French fashion designer who ruled over Parisian haute couture for almost six decades

Confucius【孔子】(551-479 BC) China's most famous teacher, philosopher, and political theorist, whose ideas have influenced the civilization of East Asia

Constantine the Great【君士坦丁大帝】(272-337) The first Roman emperor to profess Christianity

David Hume【戴维·休谟】(1711-1776) Scottish philosopher, historian, economist, and essayist, known especially for his philosophical empiricism and skepticism

Diogenes of Sinope【第欧根尼】(412?-323 BC) Greek philosopher, generally considered the founder of Cynicism

Dmitri Ivanovich Mendeleev【德米特里·伊万诺维奇·门捷列夫】(1834-1907) Russian chemist who developed the periodic classification of the elements

Edvard Munch【爱德华·蒙克】(1863-1944) Norwegian painter and printmaker whose intensely evocative treatment of psychological themes built upon some of the main tenets of late 19th-century Symbolism and greatly influenced German Expressionism in the early 20th century

Edward Jenner【爱德华·詹纳】(1749-1823) English surgeon and discoverer of vaccination for smallpox

Edwin Powell Hubble【爱德文·鲍威尔·哈勃】(1889-1953) American astronomer, generally regarded as the leading observational cosmologist of the 20th century

Elizabeth I【伊丽莎白一世】(1533-1603) Queen of England (1558-1603) during a period, often called the Elizabethan Age, when England asserted itself vigorously as a major European power in politics, commerce, and the arts

Elisha Graves Otis【伊莱沙·格雷夫斯·奥的斯】(1811-1861) American inventor of the safety elevator

Elvis Presley【埃尔维斯·普雷斯利】(1935-1977) American popular singer widely known as the "King of Rock and Roll" and one of rock music's dominant performers from the mid-1950s until his death

Empress Wu Zetian【武则天】(624-705) Rose from concubin to become empress of China during the Tang Dynasty. During her reign, Tang rule was consolidated, and the empire was unified

Epicurus【伊壁鸠鲁】(341-270 BC) Greek philosopher, author of an ethical philosophy of simple pleasure, friendship, and retirement

Ernest Rutherford【欧内斯特·卢瑟福】(1871-1937) New Zealand-born British physicist considered the greatest experimentalist since Michael Faraday

Ferdinand Magellan【费迪南德·麦哲伦】(1480-1521) Portuguese navigator and explorer who sailed under the flags of both Portugal and Spain, though killed in the Philippines, one of his ships continued westward to Spain, accomplishing the first circumnavigation of the earth

Florence Nightingale【弗洛伦斯·南丁格尔】(1820-1910) A celebrated English social reformer and statistician, and the founder of modern nursing

Francis Bacon【弗朗西斯·培根】(1561-1626) English philosopher, statesman, scientist, jurist, and author, philosophical advocate and practitioner of the scientific method during the scientific revolution

Franklin D. Roosevelt【富兰克林·罗斯

福】(1882-1945) 32nd president of the United States, elected to the office four times, led the US through the Great Depression and World War Ⅱ

Franz Schubert【弗朗茨·舒伯特】(1797-1828) Austrian composer who bridged the worlds of Classical and Romantic music

Frédéric Chopin【弗里德里克·肖邦】(1810-1849) Polish French composer and pianist of the Romantic period, best known for his solo pieces for piano and his piano concertos

Friedrich Nietzsche【弗里德里希·尼采】(1844-1900) German classical scholar, philosopher, and critic of culture, who became one of the most influential of all modern thinkers

Galen【盖伦】(129-200) Greek physician, writer, and philosopher who exercised a dominant influence on medical theory and practice in Europe from the Middle Ages until the mid-17th century

Galileo Galilei【伽利略·伽利雷】(1564-1642) Italian natural philosopher, astronomer, and mathematician who made fundamental contributions to the sciences of motion, astronomy, and strength of materials and to the development of the scientific method

Genghis Khan【成吉思汗】(1162-1227) One of the most famous conquerors of history, who consolidated tribes into a unified Mongolia and then extended his empire across Asia to the Adriatic Sea

Georg Simon Ohm【格奥尔格·西蒙·欧姆】(1789-1854) German physicist who discovered Ohm's law

Georg Wilhelm Friedrich Hegel【格奥尔奥·威廉·弗里德里希·黑格尔】(1770-1831) German philosopher who developed a dialectical scheme that emphasized the progress of history and of ideas from thesis to antithesis and thence to a synthesis

George Berkeley【乔治·贝克莱】(1685-1753) Anglo-Irish Anglican bishop, philosopher, and scientist, best known for his empiricist and idealist philosophy, which held that everything save the

spiritual exists only insofar as it is perceived by the senses

George Washington【乔治·华盛顿】(1732-1799) American general and commander-in-chief of the colonial armies in the American Revolution and subsequently first president of the United States

Giordano Bruno【乔尔丹诺·布鲁诺】(1548-1600) Italian philosopher, astronomer, mathematician, and occultist whose theories anticipated modern science

Gottfried Wilhelm Leibniz【戈特弗里德·威廉·莱布尼茨】(1646-1716) German philosopher, mathematician, and political adviser, important both as a metaphysician and as a logician and distinguished also for his independent invention of the differential and integral calculus

Gregor Mendel【格雷戈尔·孟德尔】(1822-1884) Austrian botanist, teacher, and Augustinian prelate, the first to lay the mathematical foundation of the science of genetics

Guglielmo Marconi【伽利尔摩·马可尼】(1874-1937) Italian physicist and inventor of a successful wireless telegraph

Hans Christian Oersted【汉斯·克里斯蒂安·奥斯特】(1777-1851) Danish physicist and chemist who discovered that electric current in a wire can deflect a magnetized compass needle

Heinrich Hertz【海因里希·赫兹】(1857-1894) German physicist who was the first to broadcast and receive radio waves

Henry David Thoreau【亨利·戴维·梭罗】(1817-1862) American essayist, poet, and practical philosopher, best known for his book *Walden* and his essay *Civil Disobedience*

Henry Ⅷ【亨利八世】(1491-1547) King of England (1509–1547) who presided over the beginnings of the English Renaissance and the English Reformation

Henry Ford【亨利·福特】(1863-1947) American industrialist, revolutionized factory production with his assembly-line methods

Heraclitus【赫拉克利特】(540-480 BC) Greek philosopher remembered for his cosmology, in which fire forms the basic material principle of an orderly universe

Herbert George Wells【赫伯特·乔治·威尔斯】(1866-1946) English novelist, sociologist, and historian best known for such science fiction novels as *The Time Machine* and *The War of the Worlds*

Hippocrates【希波克拉底】(460-370 BC) Ancient Greek physician who lived during Greece's Classical period and is traditionally regarded as the father of medicine

Humphry Davy【汉弗里·戴维】(1778-1829) English chemist who discovered several chemical elements and compounds, invented the miner's safety lamp

Ilya Repin【伊利亚·列宾】(1844-1930) Russian painter of historical subjects known for the power and drama of his works

Immanuel Kant【伊曼努尔·康德】(1724-1804) German philosopher, considered by many the most influential thinker of modern times

Isaac Asimov【艾萨克·阿西莫夫】(1920-1992) Russian-born American, a highly successful and prolific writer of science fiction

Jacques-Louis David【雅克-路易·大卫】(1748-1825) The most celebrated French artist of his day and a principal exponent of the late 18th-century Neoclassical reaction against the Rococo style

James Clerk Maxwell【詹姆斯·克拉克·麦克斯韦】(1831-1879) Scottish physicist best known for his formulation of electromagnetic theory

James Dewey Watson【詹姆斯·杜威·沃森】(1928-) American geneticist and biophysicist who played a crucial role in the discovery of the molecular structure of deoxyribonucleic acid (DNA)

James Hutton【詹姆斯·赫顿】(1726-1797) Scottish geologist, explained the features of the earth's crust by means of natural processes over geologic time

Jean-François Millet【让-弗朗索瓦·米勒】(1814-1875) French painter renowned for his peasant subjects

Jean-Jacques Rousseau【让-雅克·卢梭】(1712-1778) Swiss-born philosopher, writer, and political theorist whose treatises and novels inspired the leaders of the French Revolution and the Romantic generation

Jeremy Bentham【杰里米·边沁】(1748-1832) English philosopher, economist, and theoretical jurist, the earliest and chief expounder of utilitarianism

Joan of Arc【圣女贞德】(1412-1431) National heroine of France, a peasant girl who, believing that she was acting under divine guidance, led the French army in a momentous victory

Johann Sebastian Bach【约翰·塞巴斯蒂安·巴赫】(1685-1750) Composer of the Baroque era, the most celebrated member of a large family of northern German musicians

Johann Strauss the Younger【小约翰·施特劳斯】(1825-1899) "The Waltz King," a composer famous for his Viennese waltzes and operettas

Johannes Brahms【约翰内斯·勃拉姆斯】(1833-1897) German composer and pianist of the Romantic period, the great master of symphonic and sonata style in the second half of the 19th century

Johannes Gutenberg【约翰内斯·古腾堡】(1398-1468) German craftsman and inventor who originated a method of printing from movable type

Johannes Kepler【约翰内斯·开普勒】(1571-1630) German astronomer who discovered three major laws of planetary motion

Johannes Vermeer【约翰内斯·维米尔】(1632-1675) Dutch artist who created paintings that are among the most beloved and revered images in the history of art

John Dalton【约翰·道尔顿】(1766-1844) English meteorologist and chemist, a pioneer in the development of modern atomic theory

John Dewey【约翰·杜威】(1859-1952) American philosopher and educator who was a founder of the philosophical movement known as pragmatism, a pioneer in functional psychology, and a leader of the progressive movement in education in the United States

John F. Kennedy【约翰·肯尼迪】(1917-1963) 35th president of the United States, who faced a number of foreign crises

John Locke【约翰·洛克】(1632-1704) English philosopher whose works lie at the foundation of modern philosophical empiricism and political liberalism

John Logie Baird【约翰·罗杰·贝尔德】(1888-1946) Scottish engineer, the first man to televise pictures of objects in motion

John Maynard Keynes【约翰·梅纳德·凯恩斯】(1883-1946) English economist, journalist, and financier, best known for Keynesian economics on the causes of prolonged unemployment

John Stuart Mill【约翰·斯图尔特·密尔】(1806-1873) English philosopher, political economist and social reformer who had a huge impact on 19th century thought

Joseph Haydn【约瑟夫·海顿】(1732-1809) Austrian composer who was one of the most important figures in the development of the Classical style in music

Joseph John Thomson【约瑟夫·约翰·汤姆森】(1856-1940) English physicist who helped revolutionize the knowledge of atomic structure by his discovery of the electron

Joseph Stalin【约瑟夫·斯大林】(1878-1953) Secretary-general of the Communist Party of the Soviet Union and premier of the Soviet state, who for a quarter of a century dictatorially ruled the Soviet Union and transformed it into a major world power

Jules Verne【儒勒·凡尔纳】(1828-1905) Prolific French author whose writings laid much of the foundation of modern science fiction

Julius Caesar【尤利乌斯·恺撒】(102-44 BC) Celebrated Roman general and statesman, played a critical role in the events that led to the end of the Roman Republic and the creation of the Roman Empire

Karl Benz【卡尔·本茨】(1844-1929) German mechanical engineer, built the world's first practical automobile to be powered by an internal-combustion engine

Karl Marx【卡尔·马克思】(1818-1883) German political philosopher and revolutionary, the most important of all socialist thinkers and the creator of a system of thought called Marxism

Katharine Hepburn【凯瑟琳·赫本】(1907-2003) Indomitable American stage and film actress, known as a spirited performer with a touch of eccentricity

Katsushika Hokusai【葛饰北斋】(1760-1849) Japanese master artist and printmaker of the ukiyo-e

Konstantin Tsiolkovsky【康斯坦丁·齐奥尔科夫斯基】(1857-1935) Russian research scientist in aeronautics and astronautics who pioneered rocket and space research, among the first to work out the theoretical problems of rocket travel in space

Laozi【老子】(flourished 6th century BC) The first philosopher of Chinese Daoism and alleged author of THE TAO TEHKING (Daodejing)

Léon Foucault【莱昂·傅科】(1819-1868) French physicist who introduced and helped develop a technique of measuring the absolute velocity of light with extreme accuracy, provided experimental proof that the earth rotates on its axis

Leonardo da Vinci【列奥纳多·达·芬奇】(1452-1519) Italian painter, draftsman, sculptor, architect, and engineer whose genius, perhaps more than that of any other figure, epitomized the Renaissance humanist ideal

Louis Jacques Mandé Daguerre【路易·雅克·曼德·达盖尔】(1787-1851) French painter and physicist who invented the first practical process of photography, known as the daguerreotype

Louis Pasteur【路易·巴斯德】(1822-1895) French chemist and microbiologist, one of the most important founders of medical microbiology

Ludwig van Beethoven【路德维希·凡·贝多芬】(1770-1827) German composer, the predominant musical figure in the transitional period between the Classical and Romantic eras

Mahatma Gandhi【莫罕达斯·甘地】(1869-1948) Leader of the Indian nationalist movement against British rule, considered to be the father of his country, internationally esteemed for his doctrine of non-violent protest to achieve political and social progress

Marcus Aurelius【马可·奥勒留】(121-180) Roman emperor (161-180), best known for his *Meditations* on Stoic philosophy

Margaret Thatcher【玛格丽特·撒切尔】(1925-2013) British Conservative Party politician and prime minister (1979-1990), Europe's first woman prime minister

Marie Curie【玛丽·居里】(1867-1934) Polish-born French physicist, famous for her work on radioactivity and twice a winner of the Nobel Prize

Marilyn Monroe【玛丽莲·梦露】(1926-1962) American actress who became a major sex symbol, starring in a number of commercially successful motion pictures during the 1950s

Martin Luther【马丁·路德】(1483-1546) German theologian and religious reformer who was the catalyst of the 16th-century Protestant Reformation

Martin Luther King Jr.【小马丁·路德·金】(1929-1968) Baptist minister and social activist who led the civil rights movement in the United States from the mid-1950s until his death by assassination in 1968

Mary Shelley【玛莉·雪莱】(1797-1851) English Romantic novelist best known as the author of *Frankenstein*

Meiji Tennou【明治天皇】(1852-1912) Emperor of Japan from 1867 to 1912, during whose reign Japan was dramatically transformed from a feudal country into one of the great powers of the modern world

Michael Faraday【迈克尔·法拉第】(1791-1867) English physicist and chemist whose many experiments contributed greatly to the understanding of electromagnetism

Michelangelo Buonarroti【米开朗基罗·博那罗蒂】(1475-1564) Italian Renaissance sculptor, painter, architect, and poet who exerted an unparalleled influence on the development of Western art

Montesquieu【孟德斯鸠】(1689-1755) French political philosopher whose major work, *The Spirit of Laws*, was a major contribution to political theory

Montgolfier brothers:【孟戈菲兄弟】*Joseph-Michel Montgolfier* (1740-1810) *Jacques-Étienne Montgolfier* (1745-1799). French brothers who were pioneer developers of the hot-air balloon and who conducted the first untethered flights

Mother Teresa【特蕾莎修女】(1910-1997) Founder of the Order of the Missionaries of Charity, a Roman Catholic congregation of women dedicated to the poor

Napoléon Bonaparte【拿破仑·波拿马】(1769-1821) French general, first consul, and emperor of the French, one of the most celebrated personages in the history of the West

Neil Armstrong【尼尔·阿姆斯特朗】(1930-2012) U.S. astronaut, the first person to set foot on the moon

Nelson Mandela【纳尔逊·曼德拉】(1918-2013) South African politician, first black president of South Africa

Niccolò Machiavelli【尼可罗·马基亚维利】(1469-1527) Italian Renaissance political philosopher and statesman, secretary of the Florentine republic, whose most famous work, *The Prince*, turned his name into a synonym for cunning and duplicity

Nicolaus Copernicus【尼古拉·哥白尼】(1473-1543) Polish astronomer, the first person to formulate a comprehensive heliocentric cosmology which displaced the earth from the center of the universe

Nikolaus August Otto【尼考罗斯·奥古斯特·奥托】(1832-1891) German engineer, developed the four-stroke internal combustion engine

Novalis【诺瓦利斯】(1772-1801) Early German Romantic poet and theorist who greatly influenced later Romantic thought

Otto von Bismarck【奥托·冯·俾斯麦】(1815-1898) Prime minister of Prussia and founder and first chancellor of the German Empire, unified numerous German states into a powerful German Empire

Pablo Picasso【巴勃罗·毕加索】(1881-1973) Spanish expatriate painter, sculptor, printmaker, ceramicist, and stage designer, one of the greatest and most influential artists of the 20th century and the creator of Cubism with Georges Braque

Peter Paul Rubens【彼得·保罗·鲁本斯】(1577-1640) Flemish painter who was the greatest exponent of baroque painting's dynamism, vitality, and sensuous exuberance

Peter the Great【彼得大帝】(1672-1725) Ruled the Tsardom of Russia and later the Russian Empire, expanded the Tsardom into a huge empire that became a major European power

Pierre Curie【皮埃尔·居里】(1859-1906) French physical chemist, cowinner of the Nobel Prize for Physics in 1903

Plato【柏拉图】(427-347 BC) Ancient Greek philosopher, student of Socrates, teacher of Aristotle, and founder of the Academy, best known as the author of philosophical works of unparalleled influence

Protagoras【普罗泰戈拉】(490?-420? BC) Thinker and teacher, the first and most famous of the Greek Sophists

Pyotr Ilyich Tchaikovsky【彼得·伊里奇·柴可夫斯基】(1840-1893) The most popular Russian composer of all time

Pythagoras【毕达哥拉斯】(?580-500 BC) Greek philosopher, mathematician, contributed to the development of mathematics and Western rational philosophy

The First Qin Emperor【秦始皇】(259-210 BC) Emperor of the Qin Dynasty and creator of the first unified Chinese empire

Queen Victoria【维多利亚女王】(1819-1901) Queen of the United Kingdom of Great Britain and Ireland (1837-1901) and empress of India (1876-1901), gave her name to an era, the Victorian age

Rachel Carson【蕾切尔·卡逊】(1907-1964) American biologist, well known for her writings on environmental pollution and the natural history of the sea

Raphael Sanzio【拉斐尔·桑西】(1483-1520) Master painter and architect of the Italian High Renaissance

Rembrandt van Rijn【伦勃朗·凡·莱因】(1606-1669) Dutch painter and printmaker, one of the greatest storytellers in the history of art, is also known as a painter of light and shade and as an artist who favored an uncompromising realism

René Descartes【勒内·笛卡儿】(1596-1650) French mathematician, scientist, and philosopher, often dubbed as the "Father of Modern Philosophy"

Richard Nixon【理查德·尼克松】(1913-1994) 37th president of the United States , faced with almost certain impeachment for his role in the Watergate scandal, became the first American president to resign from office

Robert Fulton【罗伯特·富尔顿】(1765-1815) American inventor, engineer, and artist who brought steamboating from the experimental stage to commercial success

Robert Goddard【罗伯特·戈达德】(1882-1945) American professor and inventor, generally acknowledged to be the father of modern rocketry

Robert Schumann【罗伯特·舒曼】(1810-1856) German Romantic composer renowned particularly for his piano music, songs, and orchestral music

Ronald Reagan【罗纳德·里根】(1911-2004) 40th president of the United States, noted for his conservative Republicanism, and his appealing personal style

Rosa Parks【罗莎·帕克斯】(1913-2005) African American civil rights activist whose refusal to relinquish her seat on a public bus to a white man precipitated the 1955-1956 Montgomery bus boycott in Alabama, which is recognized as the spark that ignited the U.S. civil rights movement

Saladin【萨拉丁】(1138-1193) Muslim sultan of Egypt, Syria, Yemen, and Palestine, and the most famous of Muslim heroes, who recaptured Jerusalem from the Crusaders

Salvador Dali【萨尔瓦多·达利】(1904-1989) Spanish Surrealist painter and printmaker, influential for his explorations of subconscious imagery

Samuel Morse【塞缪尔·莫尔斯】(1791-1872) American painter and inventor who, independent of similar efforts in Europe, developed an electric telegraph and the Morse Code

Sigmund Freud【西格蒙德·弗洛伊德】(1856-1939) Austrian neurologist, founder of psychoanalysis

Simón Bolívar【西蒙·玻利瓦尔】(1783-1830) South American revolutionary, military leader, and politician known as the Liberator for his leading role in the wars of Spanish American Independence

Sir Alexander Fleming【亚历山大·弗莱明】(1881-1955) Scottish bacteriologist best known for his discovery of penicillin

Sir Isaac Newton【艾萨克·牛顿】(1643-1727) English physicist and mathematician, the culminating figure of the scientific revolution of the 17th century

Sir John Ambrose Fleming【约翰·安布罗斯·弗莱明】(1849-1945) English engineer who made numerous contributions to electronics, photometry, electric measurements, and wireless telegraphy

Sir Thomas More【托马斯·莫尔】(1478-1535) English humanist and statesman, chancellor of England (1529-1532), who was beheaded for refusing to accept King Henry VIII as head of the Church of England

Socrates【苏格拉底】(469-399 BC) Greek philosopher whose way of life, character, and thought exerted a profound influence on ancient and modern philosophy

Stephen Hawking【史蒂芬·霍金】(1942-) English theoretical physicist whose theory of exploding black holes drew upon both relativity theory and quantum mechanics

Sun Yat-sen【孙中山】(1866-1925) Influential in overthrowing the Qing Dynasty

Susan Brownnell Anthony【苏珊·布朗奈尔·安东尼】(1820-1906) Pioneer crusader for the woman suffrage movement in the United States

Thales of Miletus【米利都的泰勒斯】(?624-546 BC) Philosopher renowned as one of the legendary Seven Wise Men

Thomas Alva Edison【托马斯·阿尔瓦·爱迪生】(1847-1931) The quintessential American inventor in the era of Yankee ingenuity

Thomas Aquinas【托马斯·阿奎那】(?1225-1274) Italian Dominican theologian, the foremost medieval Scholastic

Thomas Hobbes【托马斯·霍布斯】(1588-1679) English philosopher, scientist, and historian, best known for his political philosophy, especially as articulated in his masterpiece *Leviathan* (1651)

Thomas Hunt Morgan【托马斯·亨特·摩尔根】(1866-1945) American zoologist and geneticist, famous for his experimental research with the fruit fly by which he established the chromosome theory of heredity

Thomas Jefferson【托马斯·杰斐逊】(1743-1826) Draftsman of the *United States Declaration of Independence* and the nation's first Secretary of State, second vice-president

Thomas Robert Malthus【托马斯·罗伯

特·马尔萨斯】(1766-1834) English economist and demographer who is best known for his theory that population growth will always tend to outrun the food supply and that betterment of humankind is impossible without stern limits on reproduction

Thomas Young【托马斯·杨】(1773-1829) English physician and physicist who established the principle of interference of light and thus resurrected the century-old wave theory of light

Tokugawa Ieyasu【德川家康】(1543-1616) The founder and first shogun of the Tokugawa shogunate of Japan

Toyoda Kiichiro【丰田喜一郎】(1894-1952) Japanese entrepreneur, founded Toyota Motor Corporation

Vincent van Gogh【文森特·凡·高】(1853-1890) Dutch painter, generally considered the greatest after Rembrandt, and one of the greatest of the Post-Impressionists

Vladimir Lenin【弗拉基米尔·列宁】(1870-1924) Founder of the Russian Communist Party, inspirer and leader of the Bolshevik Revolution, and the architect, builder, and first head of the Soviet state

Voltaire【伏尔泰】(1694-1778) French Enlightenment writer, historian and philosopher famous for his wit and for his advocacy of civil liberties, including freedom of religion, freedom of expression, free trade and separation of church and state

Walt Disney【华特·迪士尼】(1901-1966) American motion-picture and television producer, famous as a pioneer of animated cartoon films, planned and built Disneyland

Wernher von Braun【沃纳·冯·布劳恩】(1912-1977) German engineer who played a prominent role in all aspects of rocketry and space exploration, first in Germany and after World War II in the United States

Wilhelm Röntgen【威廉·伦琴】(1845-1923) Physicist who was a recipient of the first Nobel Prize for Physics, in 1901, for his discovery of X-rays, which heralded the age of modern physics and revolutionized diagnostic medicine

William Ⅰ【威廉一世】(1028-1087) First Norman king of England (1066-1087), who has been called one of the first modern kings and is generally regarded as one of the outstanding figures in Western European history

William Harvey【威廉·哈维】(1578-1657) English physician who was the first to recognize the full circulation of the blood in the human body

William James【威廉·詹姆斯】(1842-1910) American philosopher and psychologist, who developed the philosophy of pragmatism

Winston Churchill【温斯顿·丘吉尔】(1874-1965) British statesman and author who as prime minister rallied the British people during World War Ⅱ and led his country from the brink of defeat to victory

Wolfgang Amadeus Mozart【沃尔夫冈·阿玛多伊斯·莫扎特】(1756-1791) Austrian composer, widely recognized as one of the greatest composers in the history of Western music

Wright brothers:【莱特兄弟】*Wilbur Wright* (1867-1912), *Orville Wright* (1871-1948). American brothers, inventors, and aviation pioneers who achieved the first powered, sustained, and controlled airplane flight

Yuri Gagarin【尤里·加加林】(1934-1968) Soviet pilot and cosmonaut, the first human to journey into outer space when his Vostok spacecraft completed an orbit of the earth in 1961

Zeno of Citium【季蒂昂的芝诺】(335-263 BC) Greek thinker who founded the Stoic school of philosophy

Zhu Yuanzhang【朱元璋】(1328-1398) Founded the Ming Dynasty that ruled China for nearly 300 years

Buchholz, E. L., Kaeppele S., Hille K., et al. 2007. *Art: A World History*. New York: Abrams.

Buckingham, W. 2011. *Philosophy Book*. London: Dorling Kindersley Ltd.

Curley, R. 2010. *The Britannica Guide to Inventions that Changed the Modern World*. New York: Britannica Educational Publishing.

Duignan, B. 2010. *The 100 Most Influential Philosophers of All Time*. New York: Britannica Educational Publishing.

Dupre, B. 2007. *50 Philosophy Ideas You Really Need to Know*. London: Quercus Publishing Plc.

Encyclopædia Britannica. 2009. *Encyclopædia Britannica 2009 Ultimate Reference Suite*. Chicago: Encyclopædia Britannica, Inc.

Garyling, A. C. 2008. *The Ideas that Made the Modern World (The People, Philosophy and History of the Enlightenment)*. Chicago: Encyclopædia Britannica, Inc.

Gribbin, J. 2008. *The 100 Most Influential Scientists (The Most Important Scientists from Ancient Greece to the Present Day)*. Chicago: Encyclopædia Britannica, Inc.

Kuiper, K. 2010. *The 100 Most Influential Painters & Sculptors*. New York: Britannica Educational Publishing.

Kuiper, K. 2010. *The 100 Most Influential Women of All Time*. New York: Britannica Educational Publishing.

Kuiper, K. 2010. *The Britannica Guide to Theories and Ideas that Changed the Modern World*. New York: Britannica Educational Publishing.

McKenna, A. 2010. *The 100 Most Influential World Leaders of All Time.* New York: Britannica Educational Publishing.

Microsoft Corporation. 2008. *Microsoft® Student 2009*. Redmond, WA: Microsoft Corporation.

Morris, E, L. 1999. *The Scents of Time: Perfume from Ancient Egypt to the 21st Century (Book and Access ed.)*. Metropolitan Museum of Art. New York: Bulfinch Press.

National Geographic. 2005. *National Geographic Visual History of the World*. Washington, DC: National Geographic.

National Geographic. 2009. *The Knowledge Book: Everything You Need to Know to Get by in the 21st Century*. Washington, DC: National Geographic.

National Geographic. 2010. *1000 Events that Shaped the World*. Washington, DC: National Geographic.

Pletcher, K. 2010. *The Britannica Guide to Explorers and Explorations that Changed the Modern World*. New York: Britannica Educational Publishing.

Reichold, K, Graf B. 2003. *Paintings that Changed the World: From Lascaux to Picasso*. New York: Prestel Publishing.

Shane, G. 1999. *It Could Have Happened: How Things Might Have Turned out if History Had a Sense of Humour*. Welland, Ontario: Soleil Publishing Inc.

Shapiro, F. R. & Epstein. J. 2006. *The Yale Book of Quotations*. New Haven: Yale University Press.

Wade-Matthews, M. & Thompson, W. 2010. The Encyclopedia of Music. Wigston: Anness Publishing Ltd.